# TO INDIA WITH LOVE

From New York to Mumbai

© 2009 Assouline Publishing
601 West 26th Street, 18th Floor
New York, NY 10001, USA
www.assouline.com
ISBN: 978 275 940 4216
Color Separation by Luc Alexis Chasleries
Printed in China
All rights reserved. No part of this publication may be reproduced
or transmitted in any form or by any means, electronic or otherwise,
without prior consent of the publisher.

This book is distributed in India by
The Variety Book Depot
Avg Bhawan, M-3, Connaught Circus
New Delhi 110 001
Phone: +91 11 23417175, 23412567 and 23415030
Fax: +91 11 23415335 and 41517201
varietybookdepot@rediffmail.com

PHOTOGRAPHY CREDITS:
Cover: © Camille Dubois, Maharaja of Mysore from the collection of the Hulton Archive/Getty Images. Back cover: © Steve McCurry.
All the images are courtesy their contributors, except the following: pages 4 and 10, © Fredric Roberts, (to see all of Fredric Roberts's images of India, go to www.fredricroberts.com); pages 22-25, Angelica Huston, © Jaclyn Bashoff; page 38, Dennis Freedman, © Andrew Chapman; page 42, Diane Pernet, © Robb Young; page 44, Fareed Zakaria, © Deshakalyan Chowdhury/AFP/Getty Images; pages 45-46, Elizabeth Hurley, © Daniela Federici; pages 52-53, Franca Sozzani, © Christopher Wray-McCann; pages 58-61, Fredric Roberts, © Fredric Roberts, (to see all of Fredric Roberts's images of India, go to www.fredricroberts.com); pages 74-75, James Ivory, typewriter, Ruth Jhabvala, and James Ivory images © MIP, Production Stills; pages 80-81, Karan Johar, © Dharma Productions; pages 82-83, Kenneth Cole, © Andrew Chapman; pages 90-91, Leetu Shivdasani, photograph courtesy Hemant Padalkar/Hindustan Times; page 96, Pier Luigi Loro Piana, © Sebastiano Moschini; page 103, Mickey Drexler, © Andrew Chapman; pages 116-117, Naveen and Shallu Jindal, © Joy Mukhopadhyay (top), © Mayank Prajapati (middle), © Vijay S. Jodha (bottom); pages 118-119, Owen Wilson, © Laura Wilson; page 127, Saif Ali Khan, © Andrew Chapman; pages 132-133, Shobhaa De, © Mitter Bedi; pages 136-137, Silvia Venturini Fendi, © Robb Kendrick/Aurora/Getty Images; pages 142-143, Tory Burch, © Maggie Neilson; page 155, Zubin Mehta, Courtesy the Taj Mahal Palace & Tower, Mumbai.
Every possible effort has been made to identify legal claimants. Any errors and omissions brought to the publisher's attention will be corrected in subsequent editions.

EDITED BY
WARIS AHLUWALIA, TINA BHOJWANI, AND MORTIMER SINGER

# TO INDIA WITH LOVE
## From New York to Mumbai

ASSOULINE

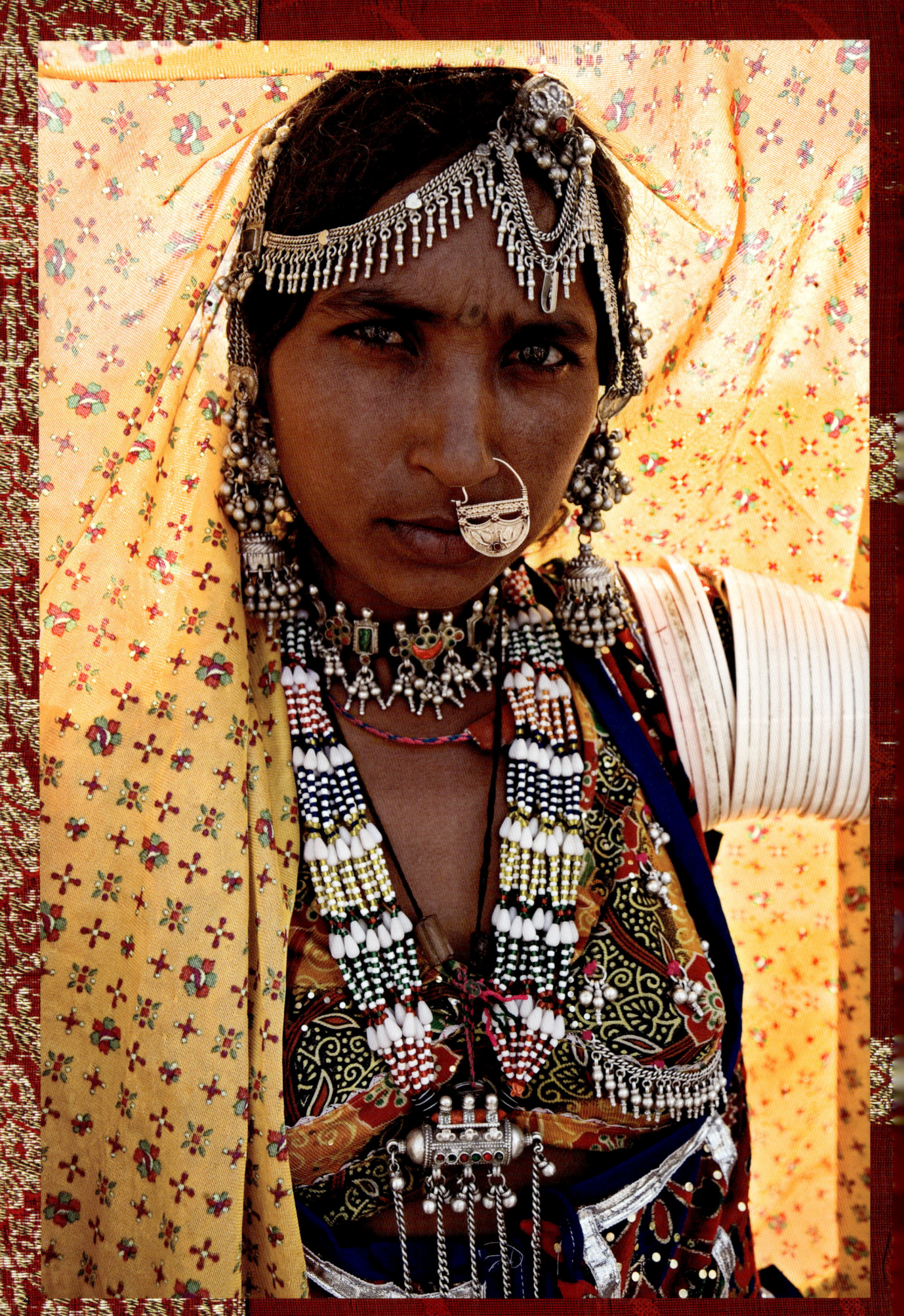

# CONTENTS

Letter from Hardeep S. Puri,
Indian Ambassador to the United Nations     6

Foreword by Raymond N. Bickson,
CEO, Taj Hotels Resorts and Palaces     8

Introduction by Waris Ahluwalia, Tina Bhojwani,
and Mortimer Singer     11

Memoirs of India     12

Index of Contributors     158

About the Taj Public Service Welfare Trust     159

About the Editors     160

Acknowledgments     160

Yellow Dasada Woman. *Photograph by Fredric Roberts.*

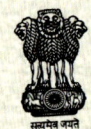

**PERMANENT MISSION OF INDIA
TO THE UNITED NATIONS
235 EAST 43RD STREET
NEW YORK, N.Y. 10017**

This book is a moving tribute to the eternal and indomitable spirit of India and its people—wherever they be—and to the resilience, grace, and humanism of Mumbai and Mumbaikars in the face of tragedy and extreme provocation. It is a cathartic venture by Indians and India-lovers around the world to heal the wounds of the 26/11 terrorist attacks on Mumbai, which evoked the nightmare of the 9/11 attacks in New York. The project stokes the special affinity that has grown stronger with shared experiences, values, and citizenry between New York and Mumbai—great financial and commercial capitals and gateway cities with big hearts.

That "thought has a pair of dauntless wings," as the poet Robert Frost declared, is borne out by each nugget of expression in the book. Each dares to exude confidence that the forces of terror, violence, and divisiveness—national or international—will be overcome. Peace and security, social harmony, economic progress, and most of all, love, will prevail, countless challenges notwithstanding.

Each piece is a loving ode to all that is good and affirmative about India and its microcosm, Mumbai. We catch endearing glimpses of the democratic temperament, generous hospitality, disarming openness, tolerance, and inclusiveness of its people from different walks of life. We are inspired by stories of "can-do" heroism and the positive energy of ordinary folks. We are amazed by the ways differences are accommodated and celebrated. There is admiration for the magical coexistence of traditional culture, customs, and values with high-tech and foreign-infused ones. From the lenses and pens of foreign supporters of India, we get good wishes and encouragement for the modern Indian enterprise. In its universalism, this enterprise seeks to embrace all cultures without losing its authenticity. It works to eradicate poverty, assure a life of dignity to every citizen, and place this nation of a billion people among the ranks of developed countries.

This book, in a way, is a tale of two aspirational cities, a tale that mirrors my personal journey as well. As the son of a refugee from the partition of India, I began my working life in 1973 in Mumbai. That brief contact with the city taught me to take risks and live my dream. It also taught a Punjabi Sikh like me to be open and accepting of myriad "othernesses." So when I fell in love with and married Lakshmi Murdeshwar, a proud daughter of Mumbaikars, living in "exile" in North India, it was destiny. We often visited Mumbai, surrendering ourselves to the stately yet warm hospitality of our beloved Taj hotel. Its quick, phoenixlike reemergence from the flames of 26/11 is an inspiration for us all.

With New York, the other megacity of hope, irrepressible energy, and enterprise, I have a very special connection through my daughter, Himayani. Since 1996, she has been among the multitude of Indians who have audaciously carved out niches for themselves in this city and country of endless possibility, and who have found their life partners here as well. She also lived through the horrors of 9/11.

I have just arrived in New York myself to take up my assignment as India's Permanent Representative to the United Nations. I am convinced that the creative encounters and dialogues between cities of the two largest democracies of the world—India and the United States—will continue to inspire new awakenings globally. They will engender epic struggles against violence, terrorism, and poverty. They will also need to foster what the United Nations calls a world living "in larger freedom," meaning with peace and security, protection of human rights, and development that is economically, socially, and environmentally sustainable. We are so interconnected in our prosperity, security, and humanity that empathy, dialogue, and cooperation among peoples and countries is a small price to pay for this second freedom. This book affirms what Mahatma Gandhi, the architect of our first freedom, said: "Freedom is never dear at any price. It is the breath of life. What would a man not pay for living?"

Hardeep S. Puri
*Indian Ambassador to the United Nations*

# Foreword

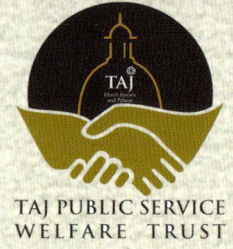

Welcome to Mumbai!

This vibrant, ever-evolving city has been my home since 2003.

I was excited to leave the United States to become part of Mumbai-based Taj Hotels Resorts and Palaces, a rapidly growing company with a hundred-year heritage of warm hospitality, and a commitment to care for local communities and cultural traditions on par with the care offered guests.

As an American born and raised in Hawaii, I had an intimate familiarity with Asian cultures and traditions from an early age. Also, growing up on a small island in the middle of the ocean, I learned that the world is vast, and to respect the diversity of cultures from far-flung places.

But even after seventeen years as a hotel general manager in New York City, I was awed by the scope, the scale, and the sheer energy of India's commercial capital, which greeted me when I arrived to join Taj. And although I had lived through 9/11 in New York, nothing prepared me for the tragic events of 26/11.

Those events could have been a setback for India, for Mumbai, and for my company, whose flagship hotel, the historic 1903 Taj Mahal Palace & Tower, was one of seven targets throughout the city. If it was a setback, it was only momentary.

These attacks cannot and should not be forgotten. But they also should not deter us from moving forward. In fact, they have united us: Undaunted, India will prevail. We have mourned and cried, suffered and sorrowed together. Now we will again do what we do best: care for each other and our visitors.

As I have learned, Indians have indomitable spirits, galvanized by fierce loyalty and faith, tight-knit families, and a persevering nature. Based on the events that have unfolded in the aftermath of the siege, I can say that India has gone beyond surviving to thriving.

I am honored that our hotel is an enduring symbol of Mumbai and India, a bright beacon of hope. Restored as a place of celebration where generations of families will again create cherished memories, it is also now a living monument to our heroic Taj family and extended community.

This inspiring book, lovingly assembled by so many notable talents as an outpouring of solidarity, is another such living monument: a passionate tribute to a city that is truly a place of constant change. That reveres its past while it welcomes the future. That, again and again, shows the world what it can do against all odds. And that daily influences the art, culture, music, fashion, and food in cities around the globe, both large and small.

My kudos and gratitude to Mortimer Singer, Waris Ahluwalia, Tina Bhojwani, and your many contributors for creating this beautiful collection of vivid moments. I hope that these highly personal glimpses touch many hearts and awaken new interest in exploring all that Mumbai and India offer.

Those who come to know India realize that there is no single reflection of India: no one cuisine, no one manner of dress, no one person.

Your visits to India and tales of your travels will inspire others, helping to sustain the many faces of this special place for our children's children and beyond.

I am but one of a billion who stand ready to welcome you to "your" India and to personally thank you for your caring, your kindness, and your thoughtful support.

Namaste,

Raymond N. Bickson

*CEO, Taj Hotels Resorts and Palaces*

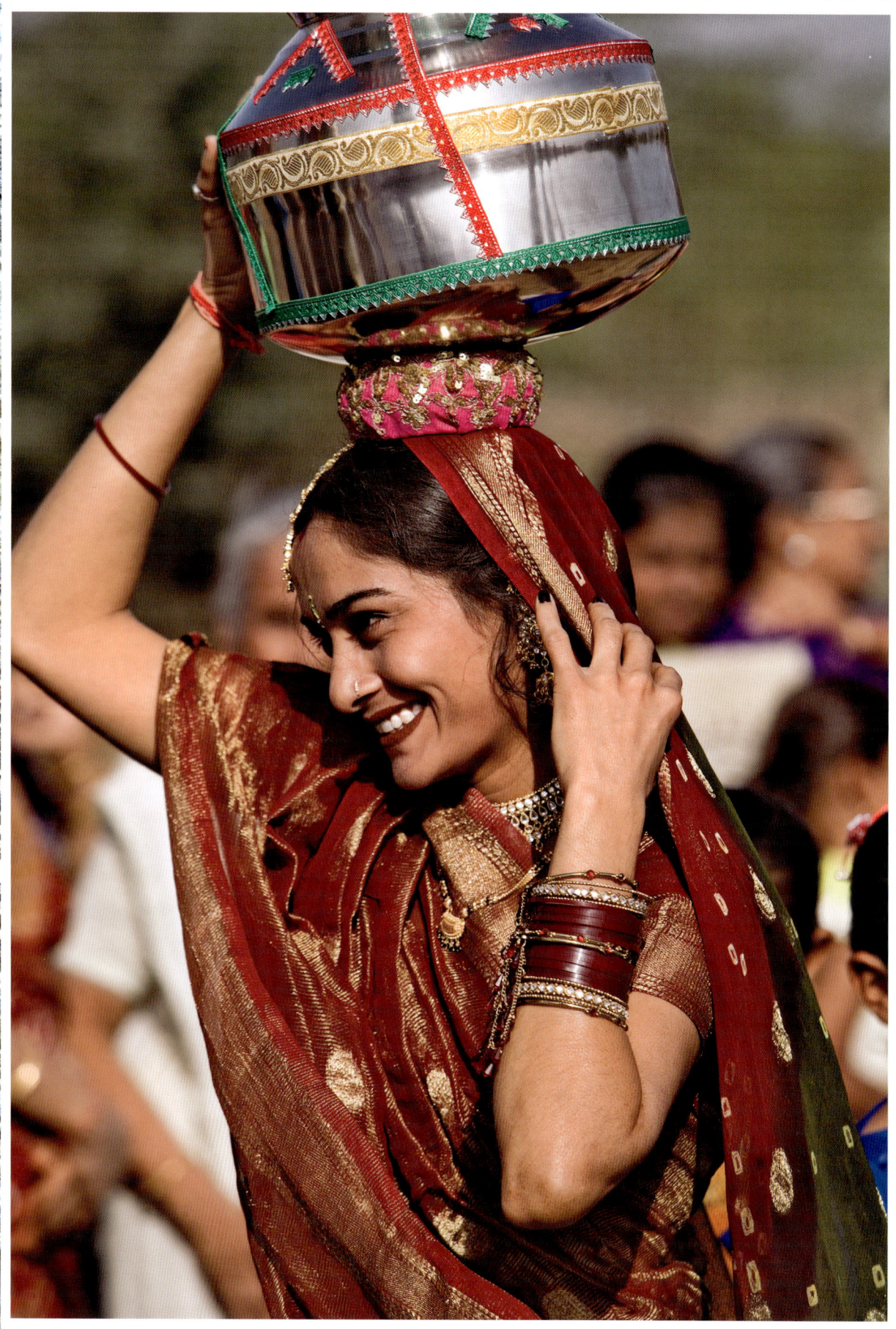

## MUMBAI WE GOT YOUR BACK

Ask any traveler who has been to India, and they'll tell you—it is like no other place in the world. The land and its people jolt every one of your five senses and stay in your heart forever. On November 26, 2008, India felt a very different kind of jolt. Residents and visitors, leaders and institutions were shocked to the core as they witnessed death and destruction aimed at the heart of India, at Mumbai.

As New Yorkers, we know this pain. However, we also know love, the feeling that the whole world is standing beside you, as it did after September 11, 2001. As India and its people suffered, we wanted the citizens of Mumbai to know that, even if we were thousands of miles away, they were in our hearts and in our thoughts. We could think of no clearer way to say this than "We got your back." We founded Mumbai: We Got Your Back to raise spirits, awareness, and funds, leveraging the creative arts to draw attention and travelers to Mumbai and India's beautiful people and places.

*To India With Love* harnesses the immense creative powers of people who are passionate about India. We reached out to friends in film, art, music, fashion, design, and business, and we asked them to share their memories, the stories of their first trips and their everyday lives, and their experiences of the country's beauty, joy, and passion. Their heartfelt tributes highlight solidarity, community, and life's similarities across the globe, and celebrate the differences (and even eccentricities) that make India so singular. Each page urges you to appreciate and to come and visit Mumbai and India, to choose centuries of hope and beauty over momentary chaos.

Our portion of the proceeds from the book will go directly to the Taj Public Service Welfare Trust, about which you'll find more information at the back of the book. We hope you will join us and our esteemed contributors in supporting this cause, and that together we can show the world that the pen (and the camera) are mightier than the sword.

Faithfully yours,
Waris Ahluwalia, Tina Bhojwani, and Mortimer Singer

Jain Beauty. *Photograph by Fredric Roberts.*

# Abu Jani and Sandeep Khosla
*Fashion Designers*

Mumbai: the city that has given birth to four generations of my family. Like every mother's, her love has been unconditional. She has given me the space and freedom to become who I am, yet kept her unrelenting gaze upon me. Mumbai is exacting. She makes you rise but can slap you into shape just when you begin to feel invincible. Her marvelous discipline is maternal; she may strike you, but it is in her warm folds that you will seek refuge. Mumbai is about enterprise, attitude, opportunity, and, ultimately, heart. —*Abu Jani*

Mumbai is the Mecca of the ambitious. An island oasis of opportunity, it embraces all of us who have made our way to it. It mesmerizes with its addictive chaos. Mumbai salutes the different in religion or in gender—everyone is entitled to its bounty. Everyone belongs. Mumbai is a city, but it is also a state of being. Cosmopolitan to the core, Mumbai is the land of the evolved. With its spirit, grace, and resilience, it's the city I call home. —*Sandeep Khosla*

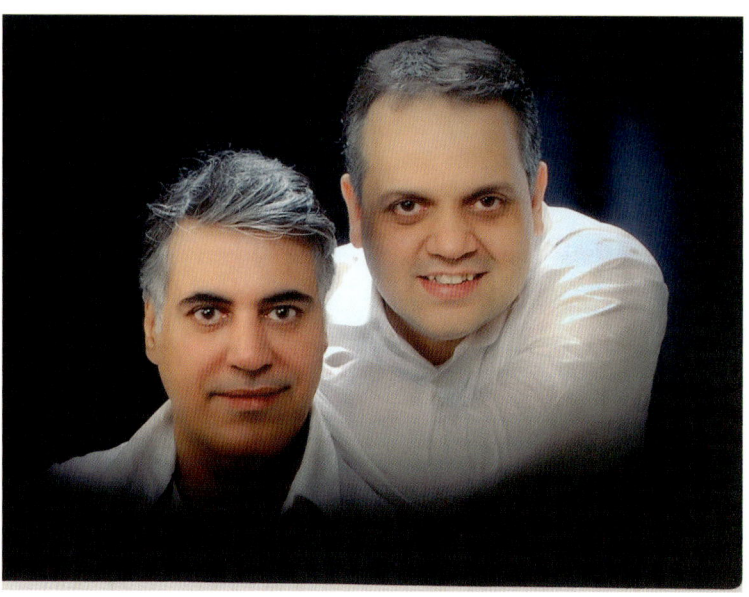

*Abu Jani (left) and Sandeep Khosla*

# Adrien Brody
*Actor*

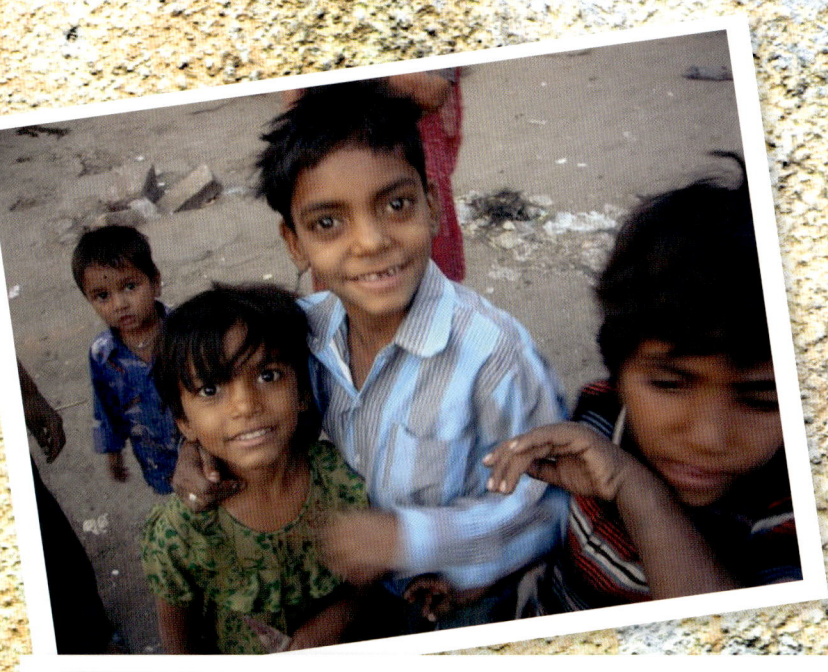

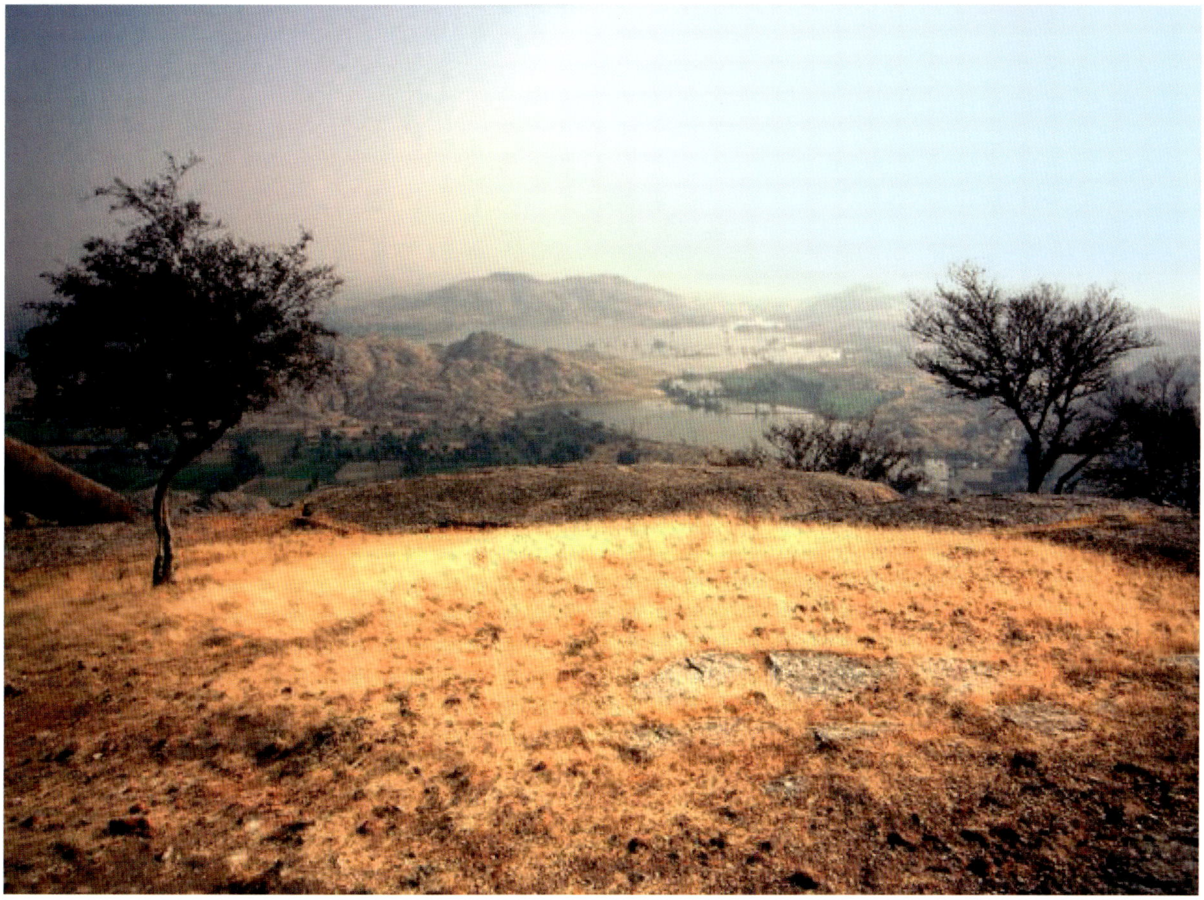

*Narlai, December 2006*

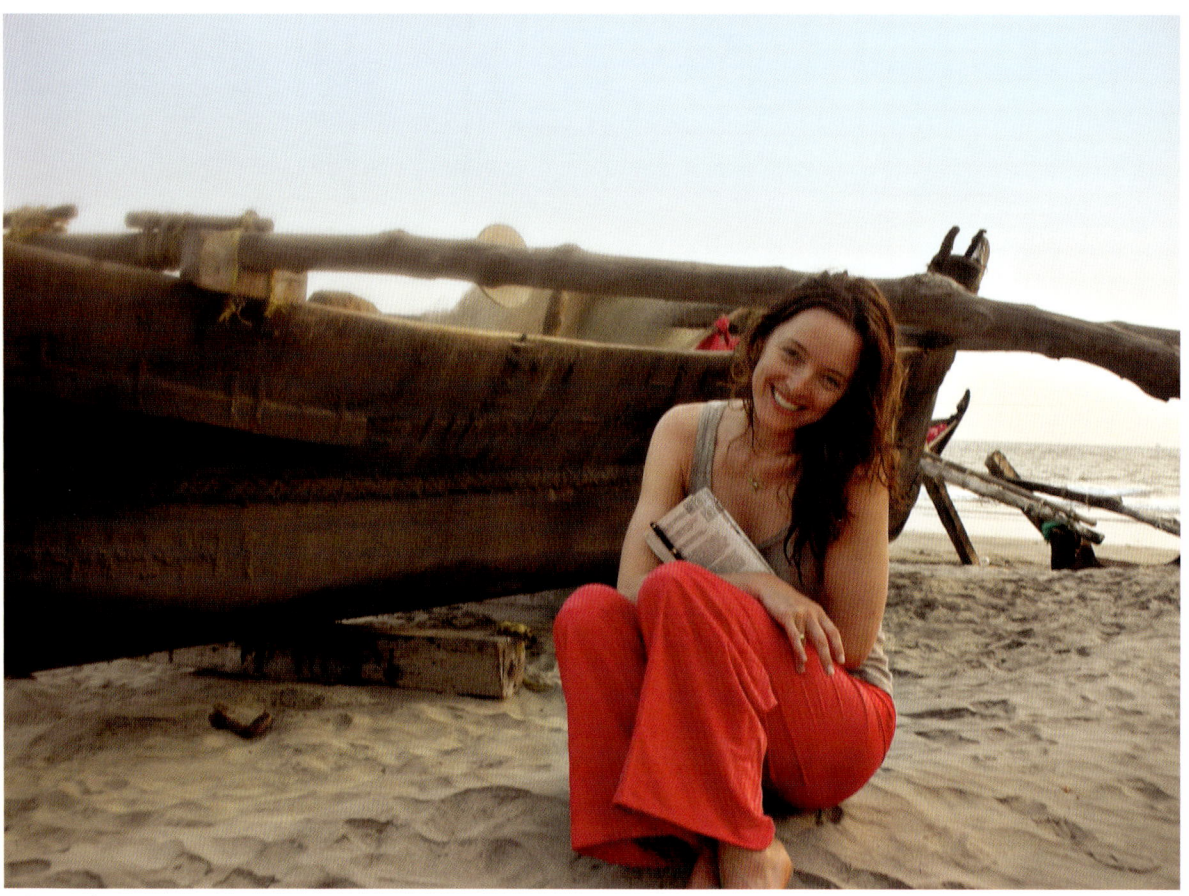

*Goa, February 2007*

# Alice Temperley
*Fashion Designer, Temperley London*

I love India for its variety, and I especially love being in Rajasthan for work. I go at least once a year. The colors of the North, against all the sand and dryness, are so inspiring. I always leave dreaming of buying an old Indian castle and filling it with all the amazing things I collect on my travels. If I can, I try to squeeze in a week on the beaches of Goa.

# Anuradha Mahindra

*Editor and Publisher,* Verve *Magazine*

A simple goodbye turned out to be the final farewell.
That's not the way you imagined life to be.
Everyone's world had changed, but some things on the outside were still the same.
Even under the strong new lights, trauma hangs like a pall, darkening the night.
But in the morning, struggle, determination, and courage bring people back.
From them I want to learn to streak my own daylight with rays of hope.

Yesterday, I lived in oblivion about abrupt endings, I was safe, we were safe,
I had lulled myself, but today I cannot dismiss those deaths as episodes from a nightmare.

I will have to escape from pretenses and confront the loss, and face my own terror
of losing. I have to live to feel the pain. I can no longer deceive myself with my own
conjured-up phantasm of reality. The struggle to fight will first begin from within.

# Anand Mahindra

*Vice Chairman and Managing Director, Mahindra & Mahindra*

The most effective weapon we have against terrorists is to become even more steadfast in our resolve to band together as a community and ensure that no member of the minority cowers in fear of reprisals or discrimination after an attack. We need to erect a wall interlopers cannot penetrate. Behind that wall will be a city that will eject them rapidly and forcefully even if they do manage to stray into it. When every street, every gully, is filled with informers and defenders of the peace, then Mumbai may in fact be held up as a template for battling terrorism. That would be a true victory for people power.

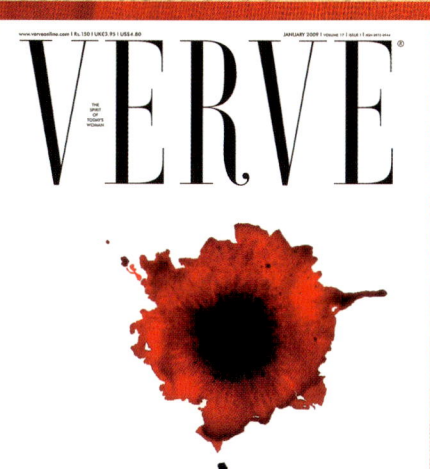

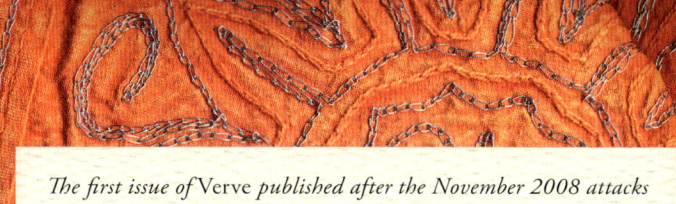

*The first issue of* Verve *published after the November 2008 attacks paid tribute to Mumbai. Instead of a fashionista, the cover showed a flower, a reminder of the promise of tomorrow. In page after page, contributors saluted the city. These are excerpts from that issue.*

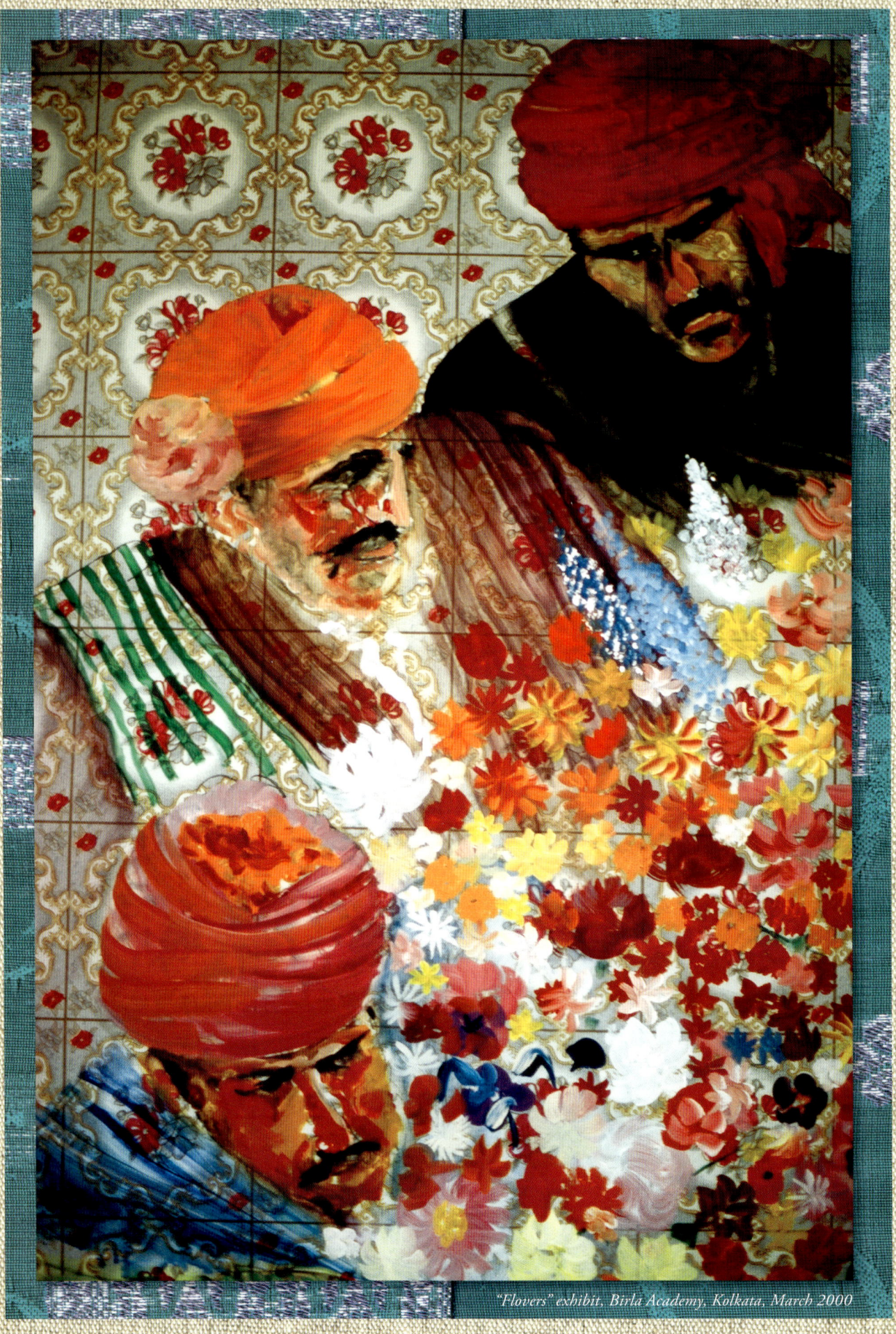

*"Flowers" exhibit, Birla Academy, Kolkata, March 2000*

# Aldo Mondino

*Painter*

❝ *My father, the painter Aldo Mondino, took these pictures during an artist-in-residence program at the Birla Academy in Kolkata in March 2000. His exhibition was called "Flovers," a title that unites the words* flowers *and* lovers. ❞

—Antonio Mondino

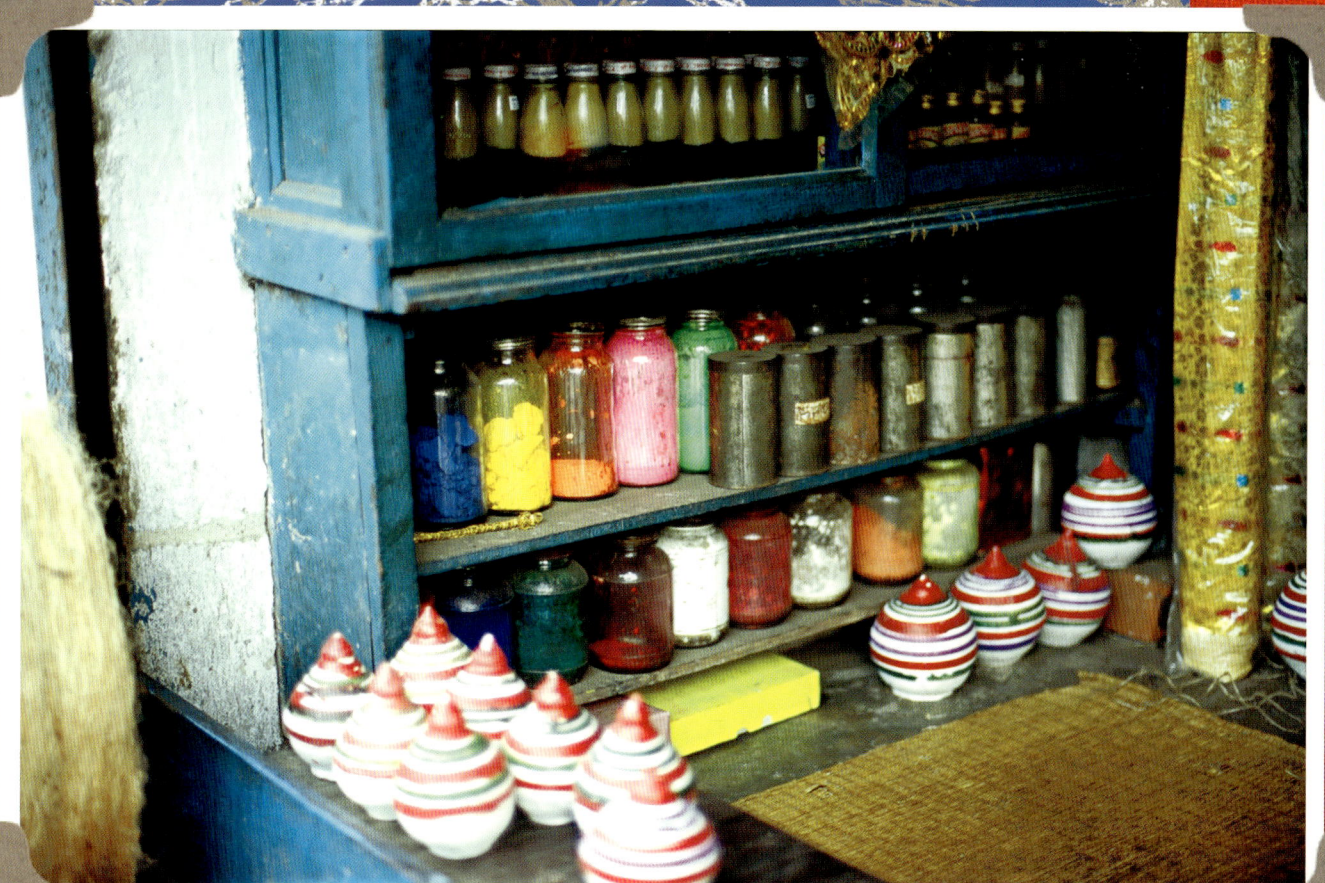

# Alex White

*Fashion Director, W Magazine*

I was twenty-three when I had my first experience of India. I saw as much as I could in the four weeks I was there, drove across the desert in an Ambassador, took a train journey from Udaipur to Kerala, stopped in major cities and desert villages.

The sounds, smells, tastes, colors, people, and pride of India are like nowhere else. Each visit continues to inspire me in a new way.

So far I have been to Ladakh, Jaipur, Jodhpur, Jaisalmer, Udaipur, Chennai, Madurai, Mahabalipuram, Delhi, Mumbai, Gujarat, Kerala, Hampi, Goa, and Varanasi—I would like to go back to all of these places, but next on my list are Calcutta and Pondicherry.

I also have a beautiful reminder at home: My daughter is named India!

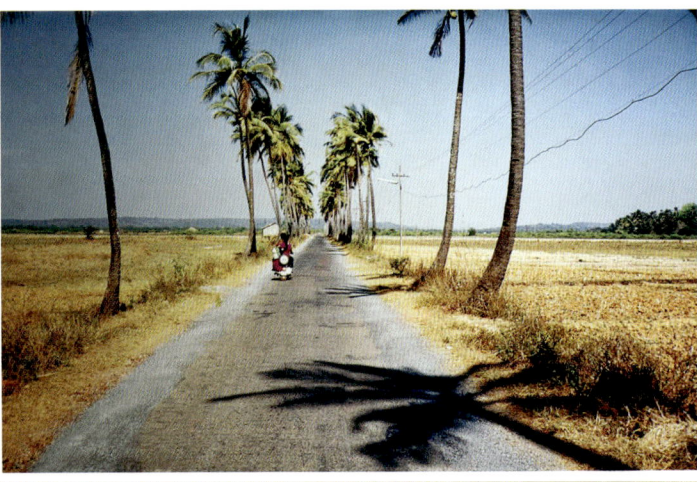

Left: Cruising on an Enfield motorbike through coconut trees on open roads, heading toward the beach—always the perfect ending to a perfect vacation in India. Bottom: This treehouse, right on the beach in Morjim, Goa, is one of my favorite places to stay for a few nights. Center: On my first trip to India, I was struck by, and happy to see, roadblocks for cows. Cows are sacred to India's Hindus, so they are everywhere, and have the right of way. It is always fun to see traffic negotiating with a cow that won't move. Top: One great thing the British left behind in India is the uniform. I have always taken inspiration from uniforms, whether military, police, traffic police, or restaurant staff. These schoolgirls, with their starched white shirts and skirts, matching socks, and perfect braids and ribbons, caught my eye in a temple in Jaisalmer, Rajasthan. Right: Hindu Deity with coconut offering.

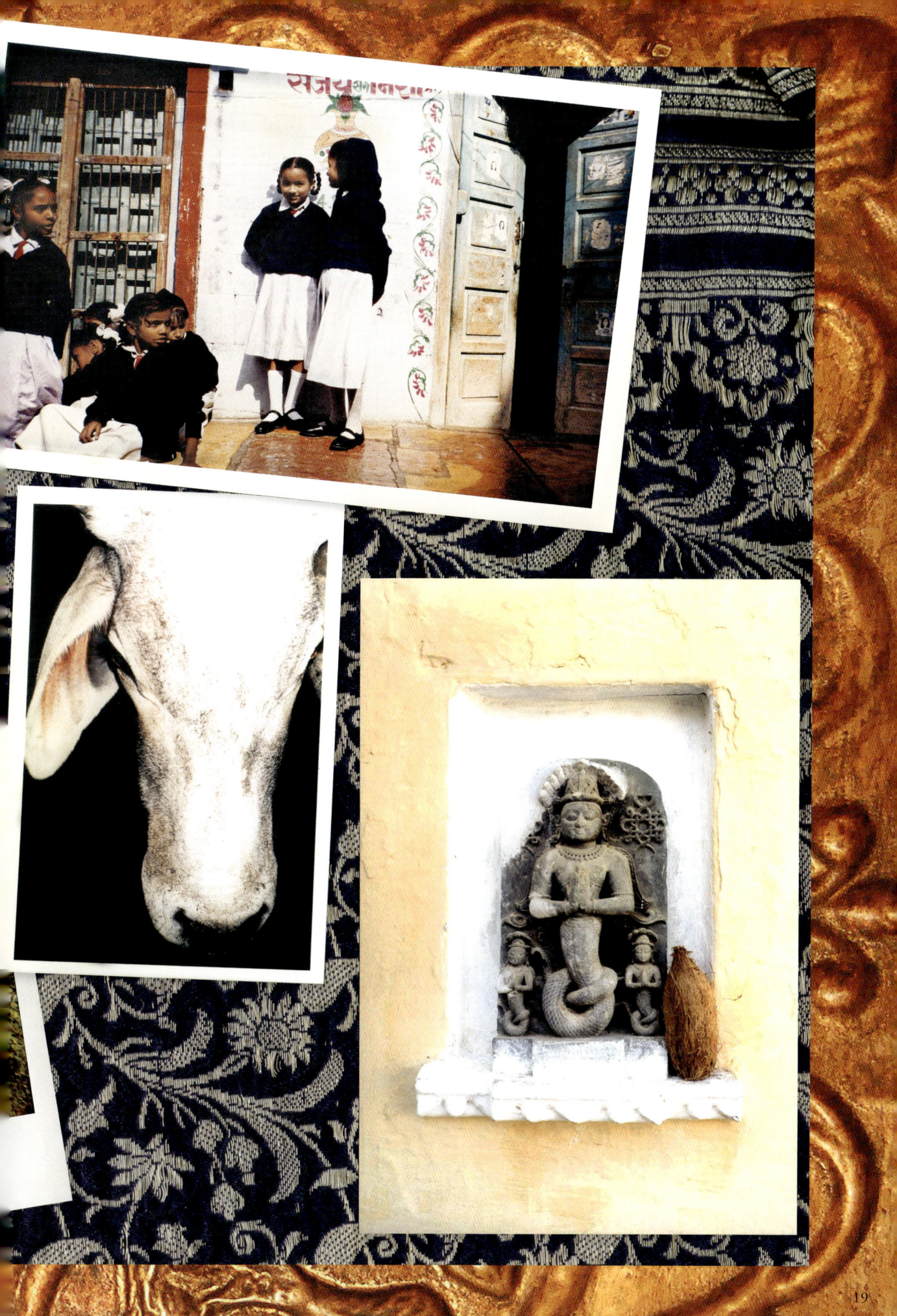

# Anil Kapoor
*Actor and Producer*

The Gateway of India is a special location for me. I don't dwell on superstition, but every film of mine for which I shot at the Gateway has turned out to be a huge hit. It started with *Mr. India*, followed by *Parinda* and *Tezaab*. Besides being my lucky charm, the Gateway is a representation of Mumbai's spirit. This is the place where everyone comes together, no matter their religion, caste, age, or class. This amalgamation of people is true Mumbai to me—where everyone can thrive and survive.

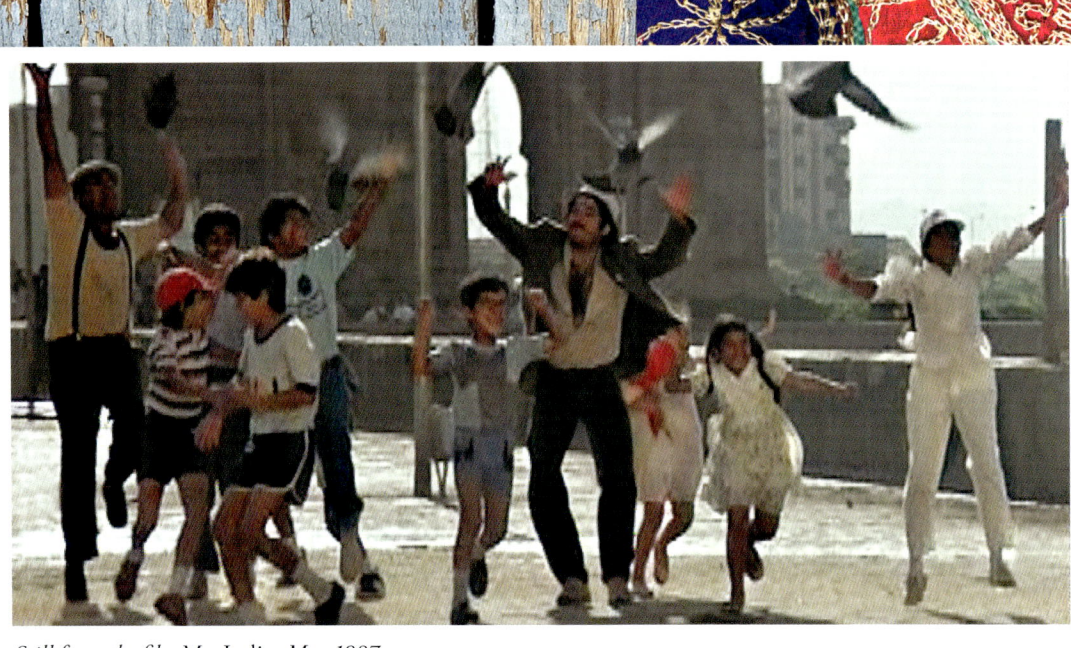

*Still from the film* Mr. India, *May 1987*

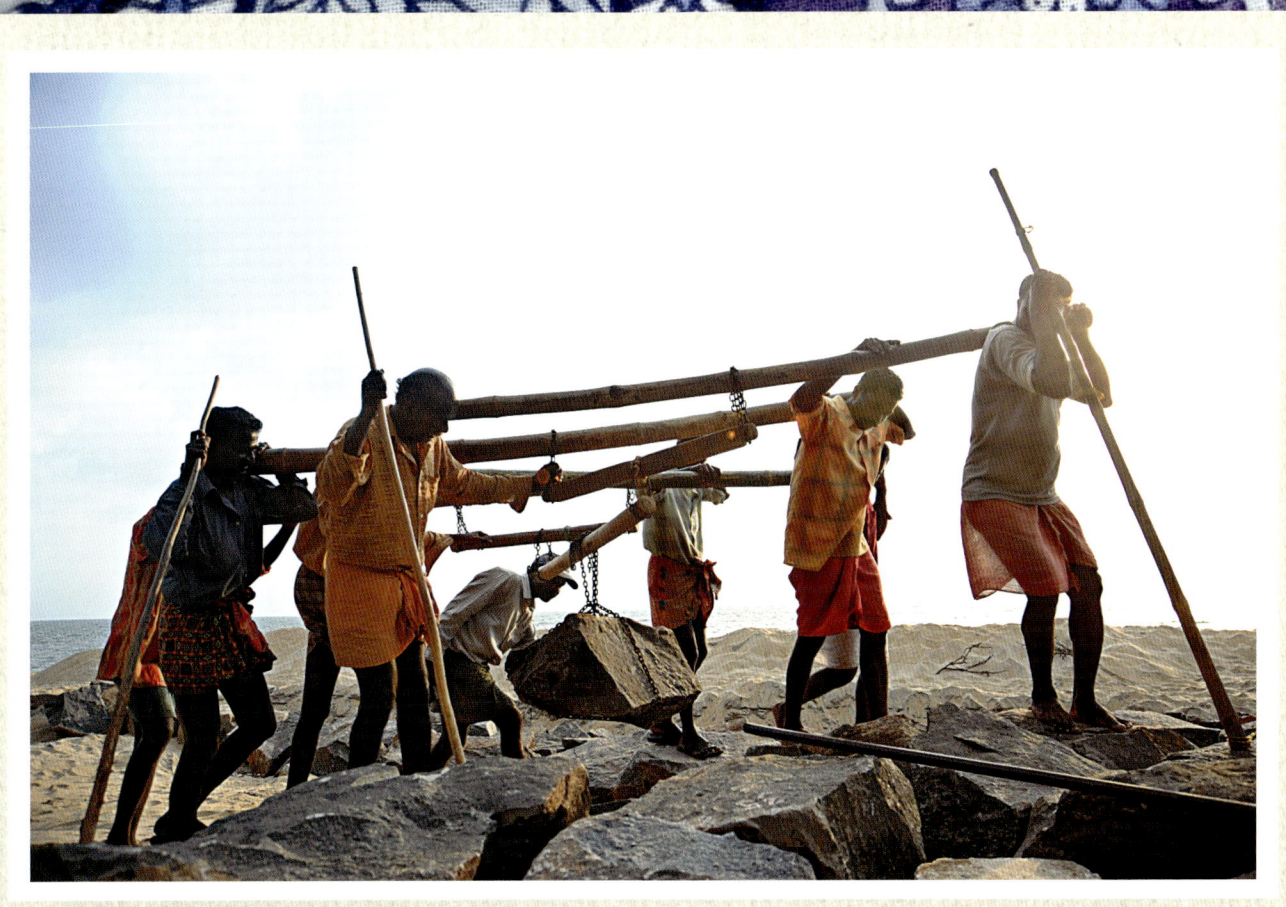

*North of Cherai Beach, Kerala, April 2009*

# Billy Farrell
*Photographer*

“*One thing I love about India is that even if something can't get done, someone will tell you it can be done. Some call this a sense of optimism and some call it India.*”

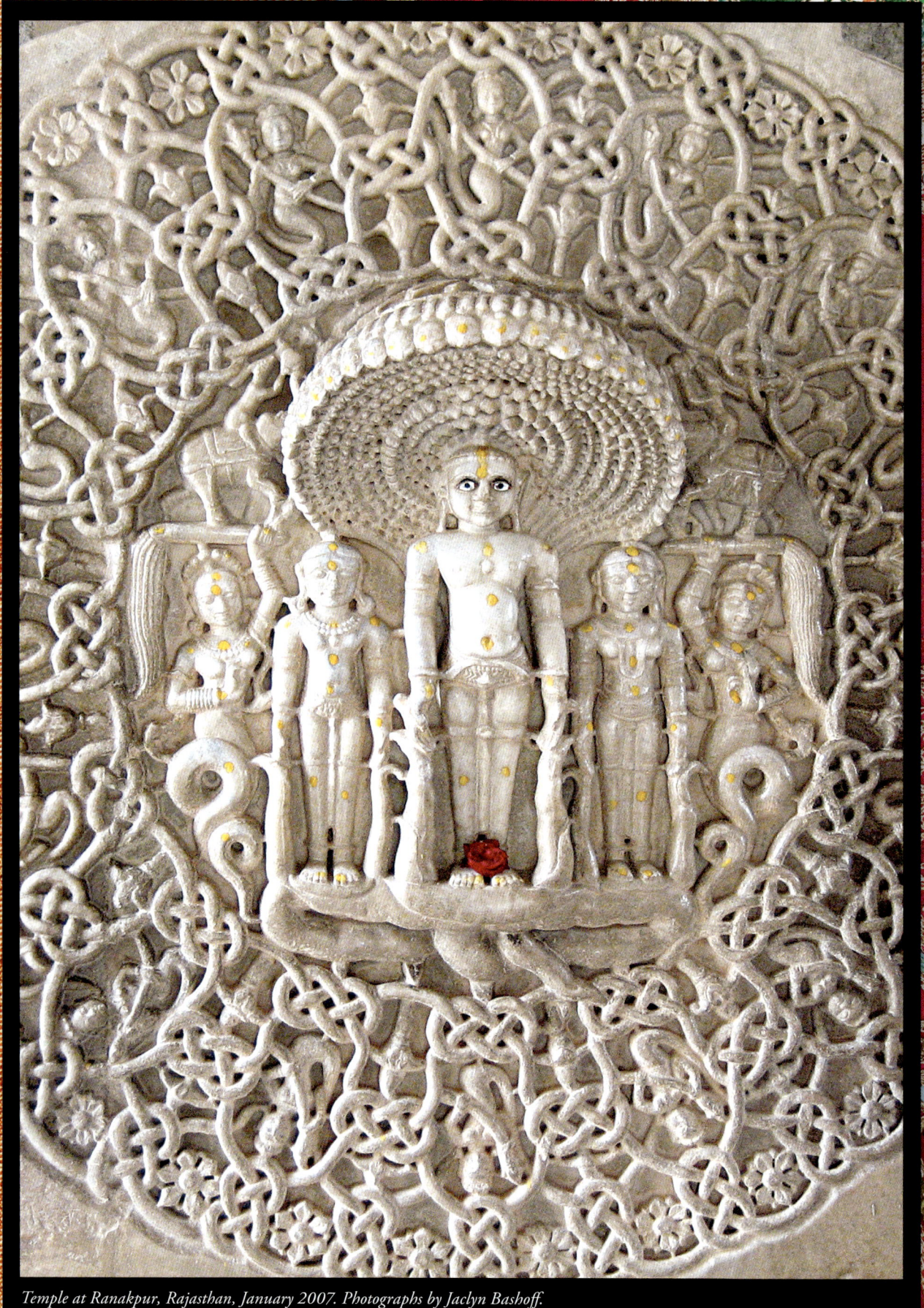
*Temple at Ranakpur, Rajasthan, January 2007. Photographs by Jaclyn Bashoff.*

# Anjelica Huston
*Actor*

India is full of surprises. You never know what lies around the next corner. One evening, we were on our way back from the Jain temple at Ranakpur and we must have seen over two hundred monkeys being fed by a gamekeeper. Some were old grandfather monkeys, some were tiny baby monkeys, but each one held a bright red carrot in their little black hand. It was a perfect picture of democracy.

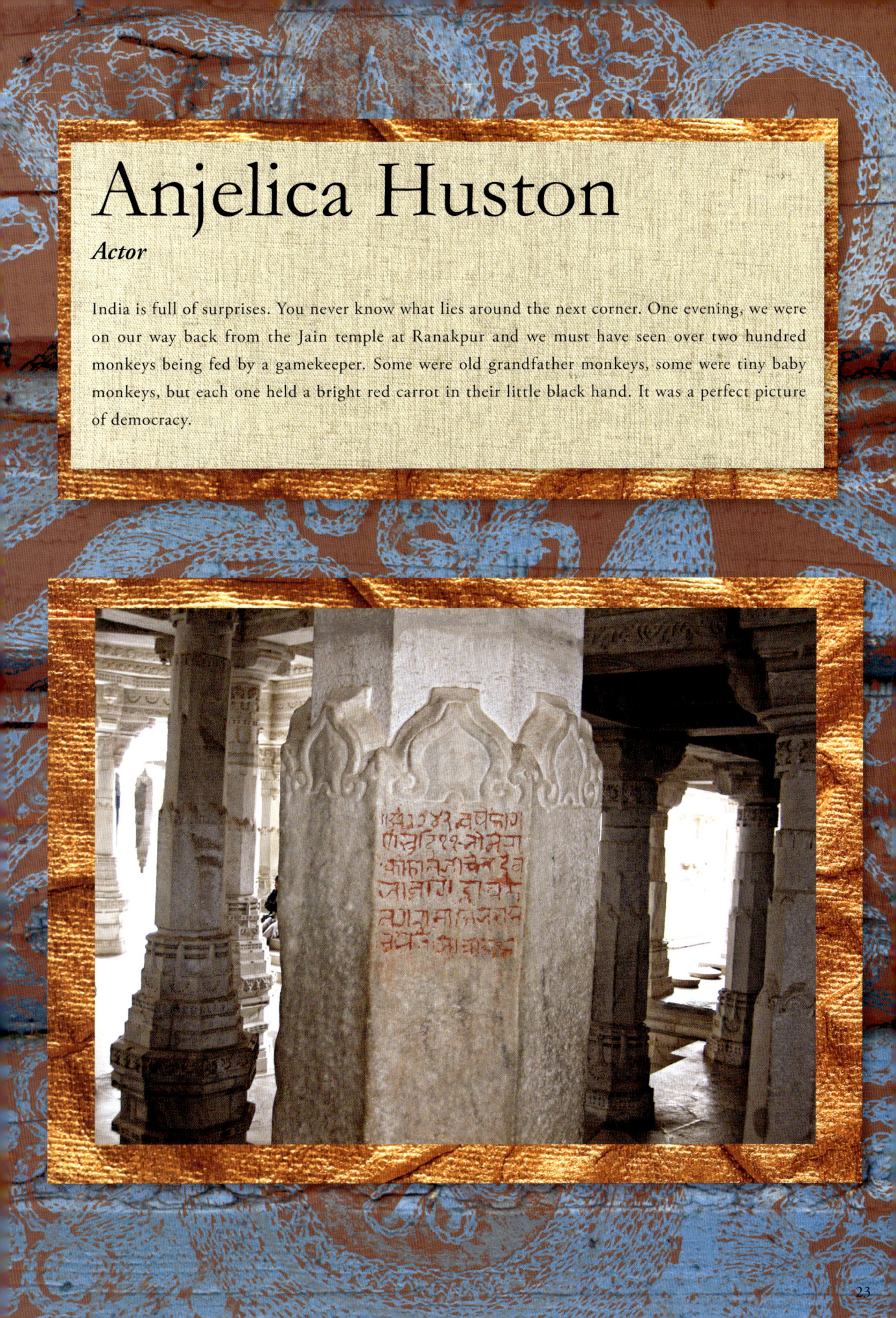

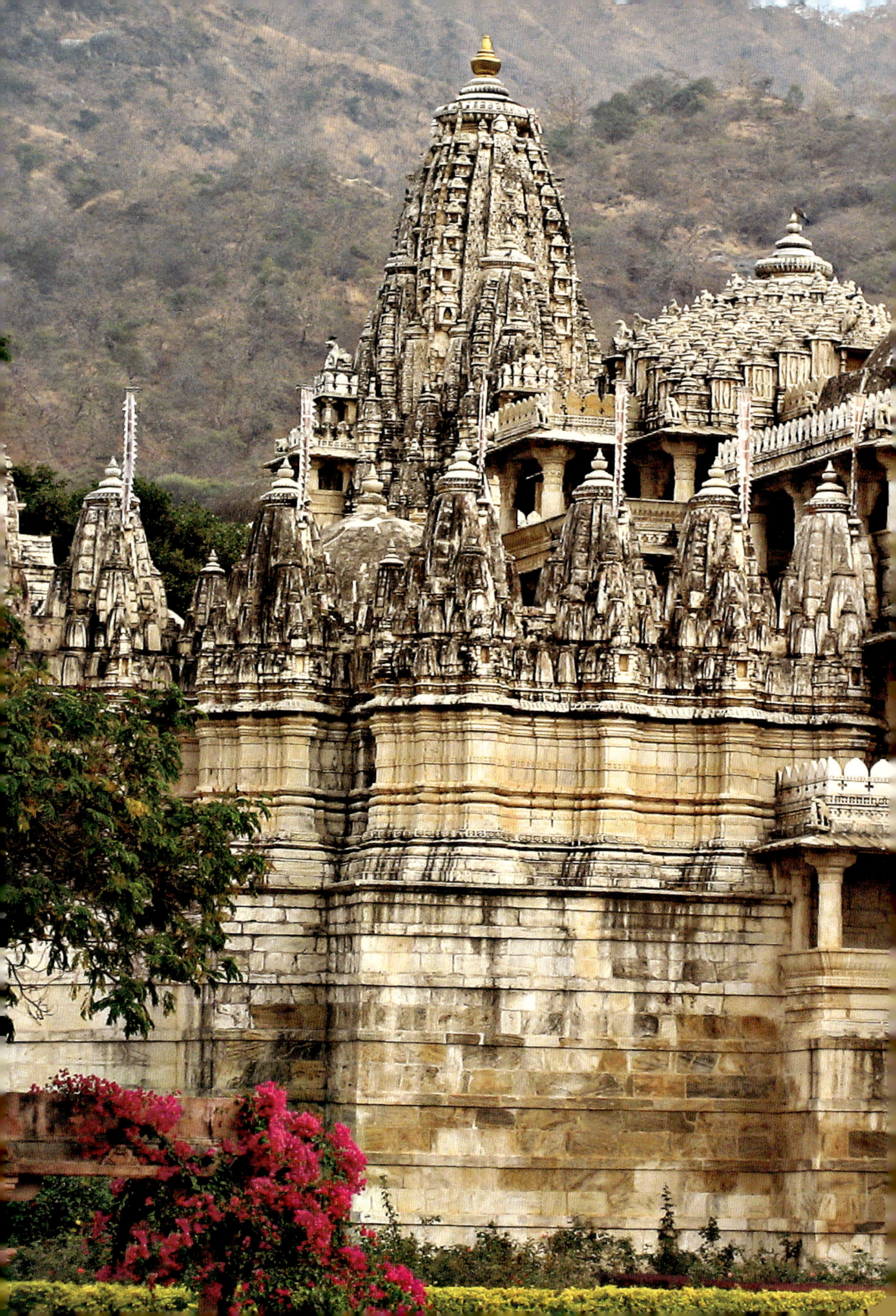

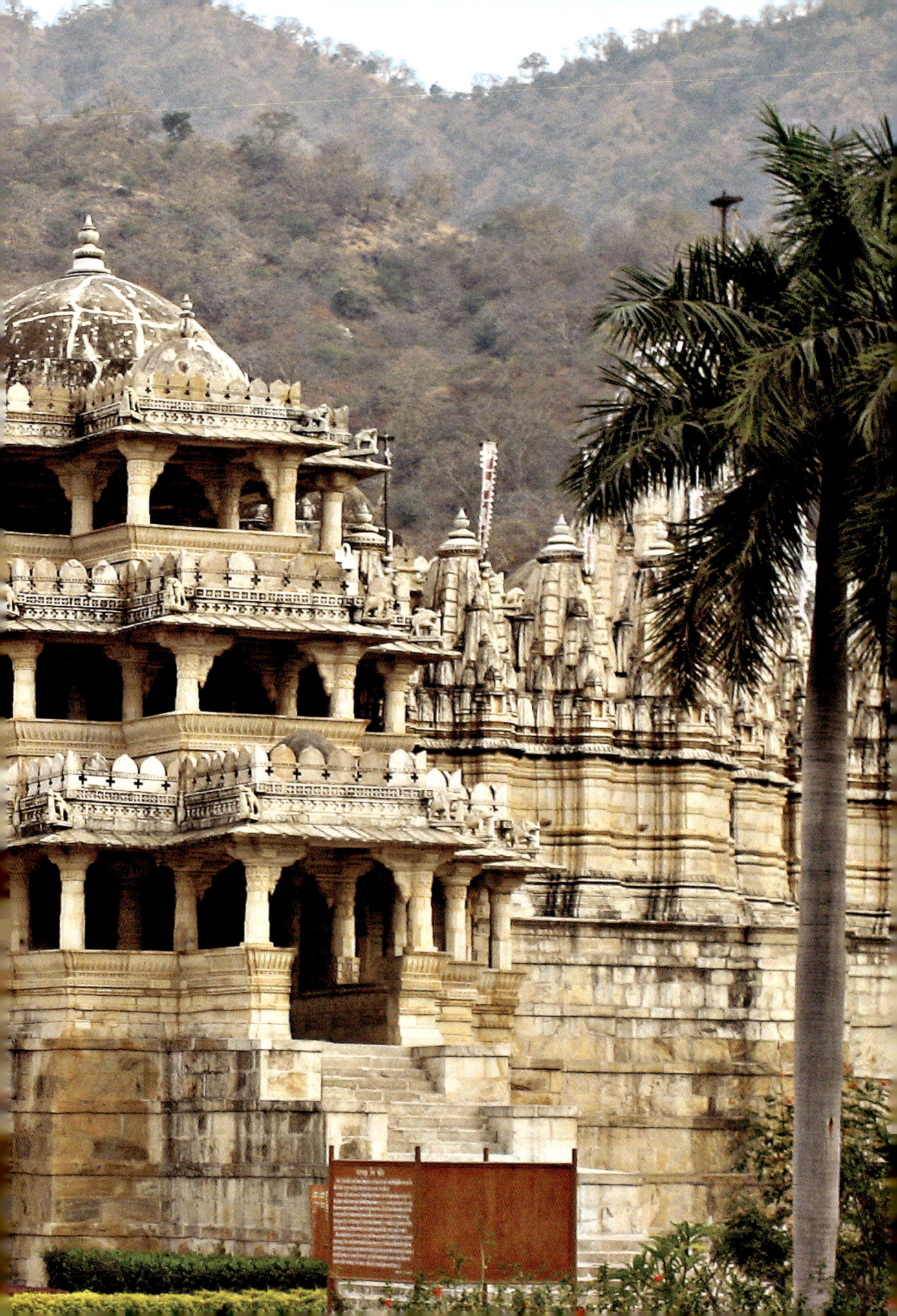

# Anne Slowey

*Fashion News Director,* Elle

I have nothing but gratitude, wonder, and awe for India and its many various cultures and states of mind. My first trip there, in the 1980s, came about by chance. I had never traveled outside of the United States, and I literally had a friend blindfold me while I spun a globe and used my finger to stop it. Wherever it landed, I would go. It landed on India. And there I went.

That trip taught me that the world isn't linear and that color and chaos can coexist without things falling apart. I had never seen such a wellspring of life moving along in all different directions, like a million brilliantly lit blood cells coursing along to a greater destiny. I also learned that one could find happiness without wealth, and though the poverty was devastating, I had never witnessed a civilization so full of joy and hope.

My second trip, just after 9/11, taught me that laughter is the greatest healer. I learned this my first night in Jaisalmer, at a twelfth-century inn across from the Jain temple. My roommate, Aurora, told me I had laughed uncontrollably in my sleep for most of the night. When I woke, I felt I had had a visitation from a laughing deity—I realized that I hadn't laughed or felt so happy in years. I was filled with joy, the kind you have when you squeal with delight as a little child after a carnival ride or doing something naughty but not really bad. We continued to find laughter, whether witnessing a cow watch TV by looking in from the steps of a house, following ladies with water jugs on their heads as they walked to a well in the middle of a desert, or waving aside a battalion of tanks on a two-lane highway as we raced to Jodhpur to catch a flight. Or when I was knocked over by a bull at a sunrise bathing ritual in Jaipur because I foolishly had worn red. This picture of a small barbershop in Jaipur is just one example of how I learned that everything can be experienced with not only joy, but also grace and beauty.

I would like to return to India and hope to spend many years there exploring its vast, wondrous curiosities. It is the one place where I think magic still exists. In India anything can happen. Anything is possible. India cured my doubts. Once you've been there, India never leaves you, wherever you go. You are never the same, and always the better for having made the trek.

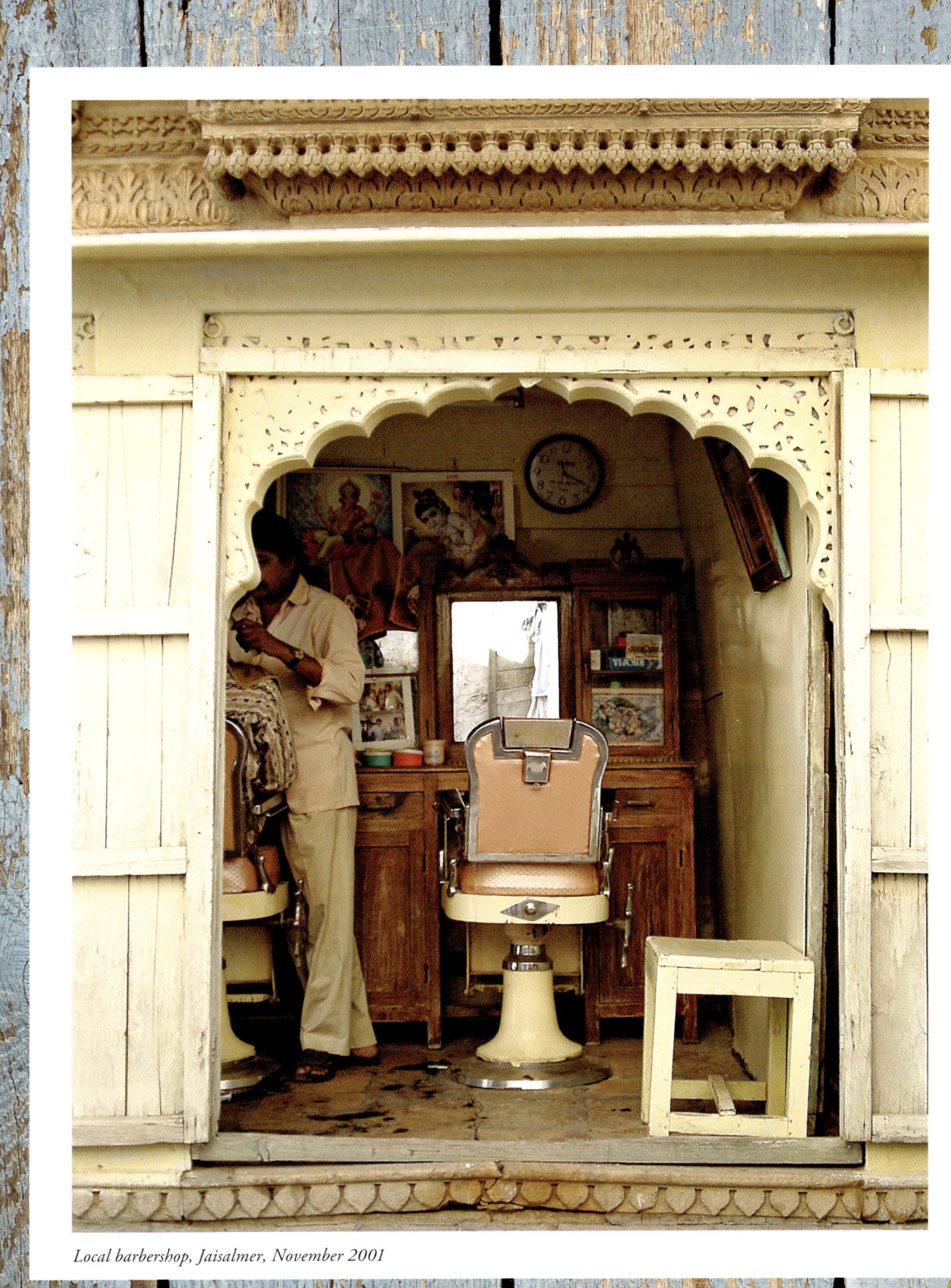

*Local barbershop, Jaisalmer, November 2001*

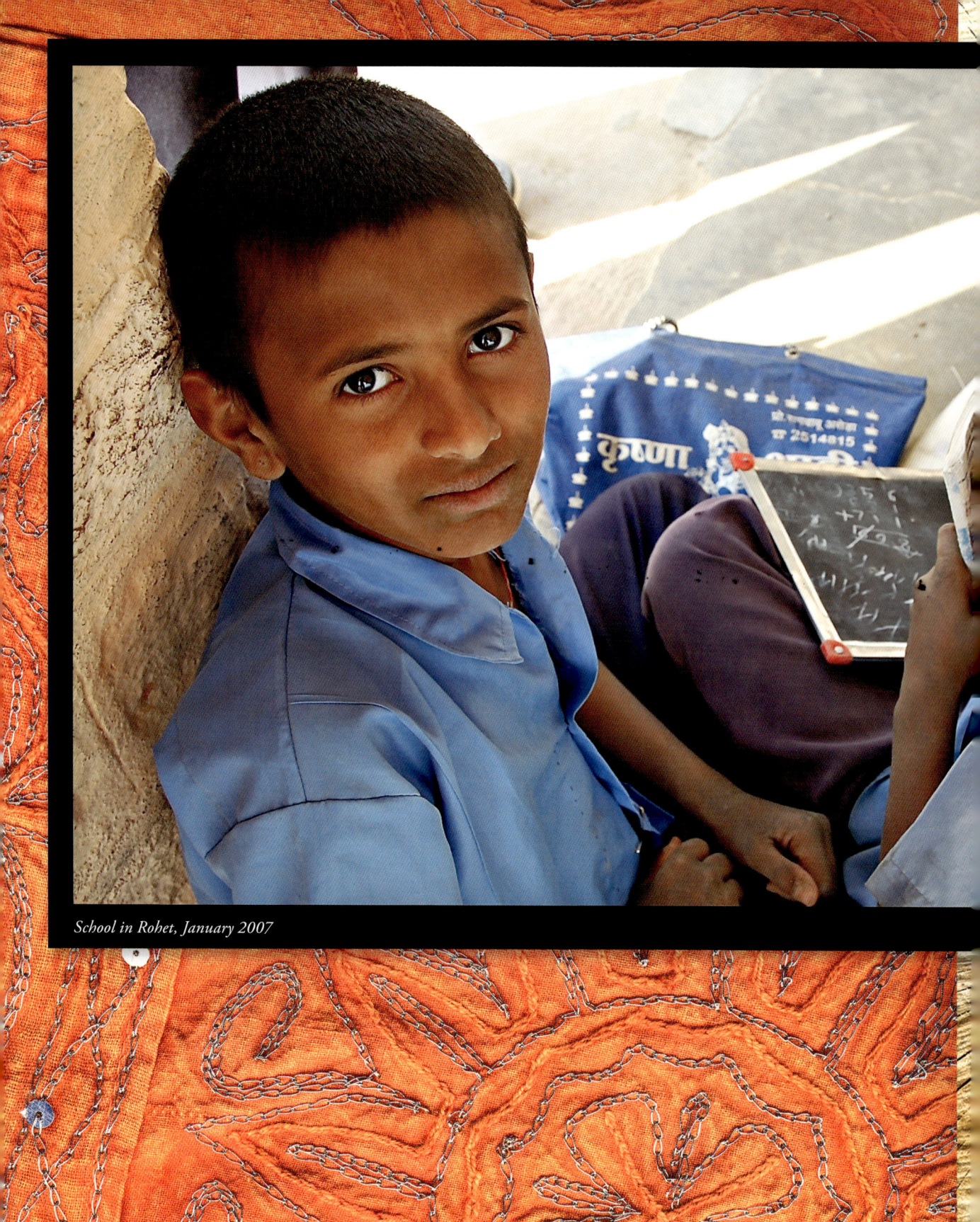
*School in Rohet, January 2007*

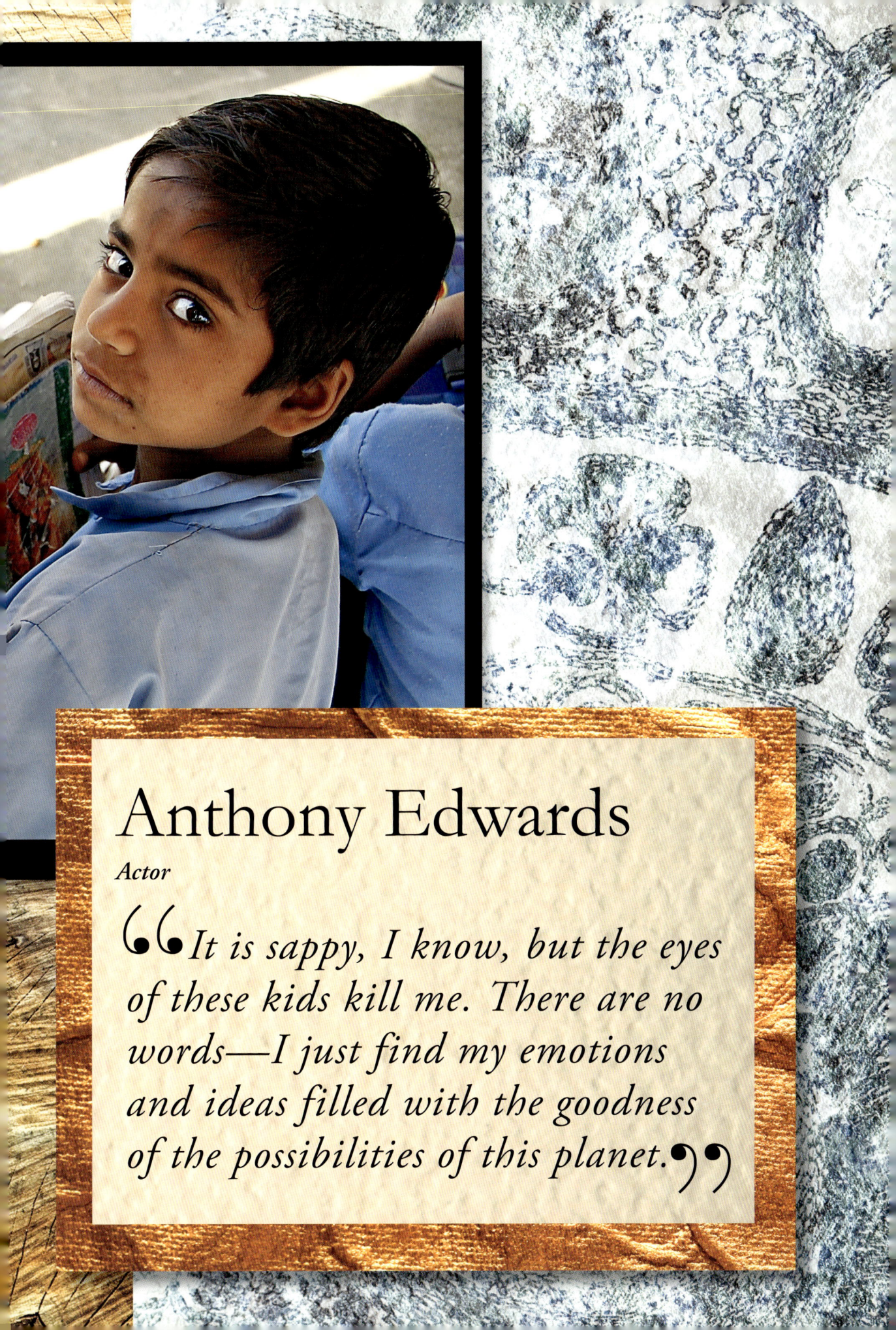

# Anthony Edwards

*Actor*

"*It is sappy, I know, but the eyes of these kids kill me. There are no words—I just find my emotions and ideas filled with the goodness of the possibilities of this planet.*"

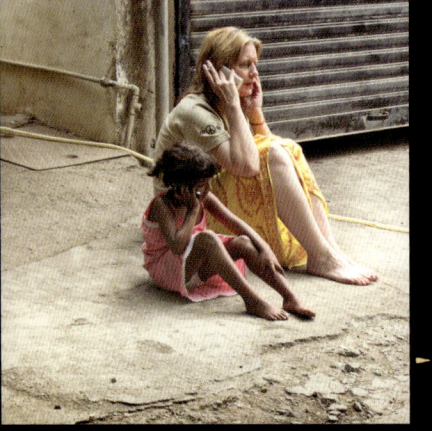
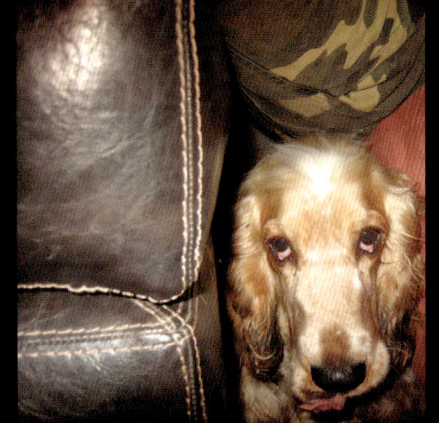
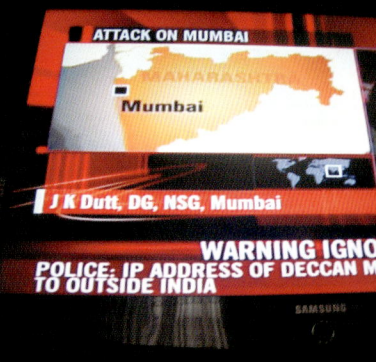
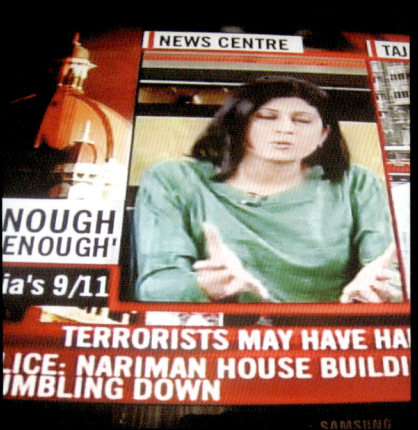
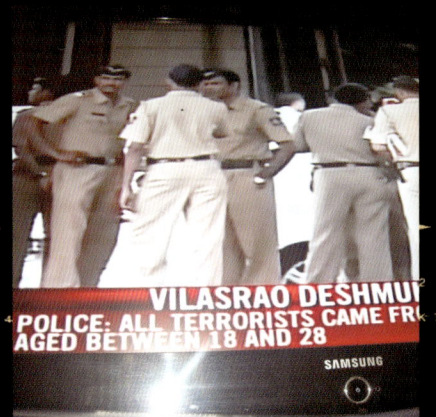
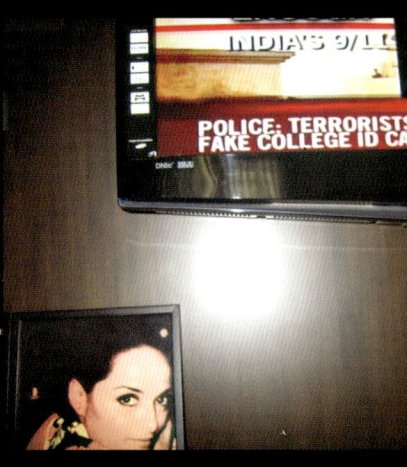
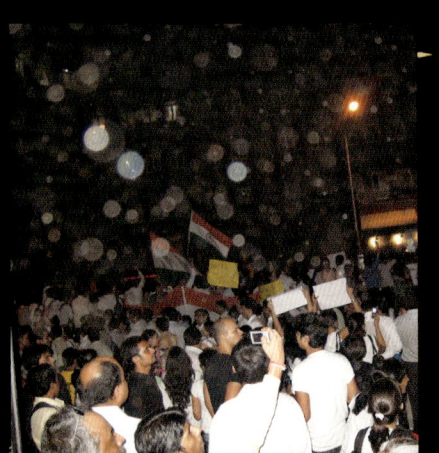
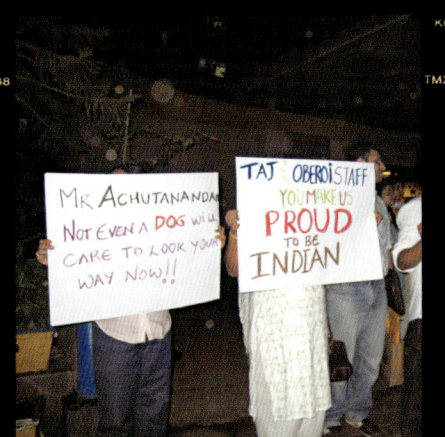
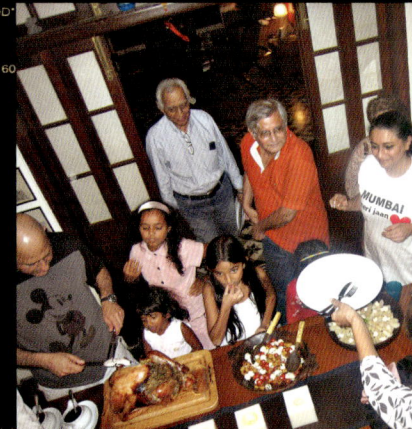

# Bandana Tewari

*Fashion Features Editor,* **Vogue India**

Excerpt from a letter to Waris Ahluwalia, April 13, 2009: *My dearest Waris, these are very rudimentary photos taken by my six-year-old daughter, Mai-rah, on that fateful night. Our lives have changed in Bombay, as I am sure lives have in New York and any other place where terrorist activity is a perennial threat, but this little girl taught me that that life is death; that we know love, because love is nothing but the absence of hate; that we will always be challenged about being good, and always be tempted to be bad; that we are mired in our preconceived notions about what we hold close to our hearts, especially about morality and consciousness. I know this because one day, she picked up a caterpillar with as much gentleness as she would a butterfly, and I shrieked, "Pick up any lil' bug, honey, but a caterpillar is ugly and spiky…" And this mini-Sartre replied promptly, quite stern and sure about what she was saying, "If you don't love the caterpillar, you have no right to love the butterfly. It's metamorphosis, Mama!" Love, Bandana*

My friend Caroline and I were meant to have dinner at the Taj Mahal Hotel on 26/11. I skipped it at the last minute because my husband had fallen ill. But Caroline was caught in the catastrophe, and she went through many, many hours of agony and despair. When she finally escaped, she stayed at my home for a week. Mai-rah tailed Caroline everywhere she went, mimicking her pain and unabashedly, relentlessly asking question after question about how Caroline felt when death was so close. For a six-year-old she asked some hard questions, ones that I wouldn't dare ask. Today, Caroline refers to Mai-rah as her "angel–therapist," her first agent of recovery.

Top left: Mai-rah and Caroline. Top and center: We were transfixed by our TV sets, day in and day out. Mai-rah tried to get a little creative by squeezing a picture of me into the same frame. She also captured the sadness in our dog Rocco's eyes. Bottom left: An antiterrorism rally near the Gateway of India. While the adults went for the rally, the kids huddled together to watch a 3-D Hannah Montana movie. Bottom right: My friends Malini and Rahul Akerkar, the owners of Indigo restaurant, had many turkeys abandoned because Thanksgiving dinner had been sabotaged by the terrorists! They invited friends and family over to help finish off a couple.

# Cynthia Rowley
*Designer and Author*

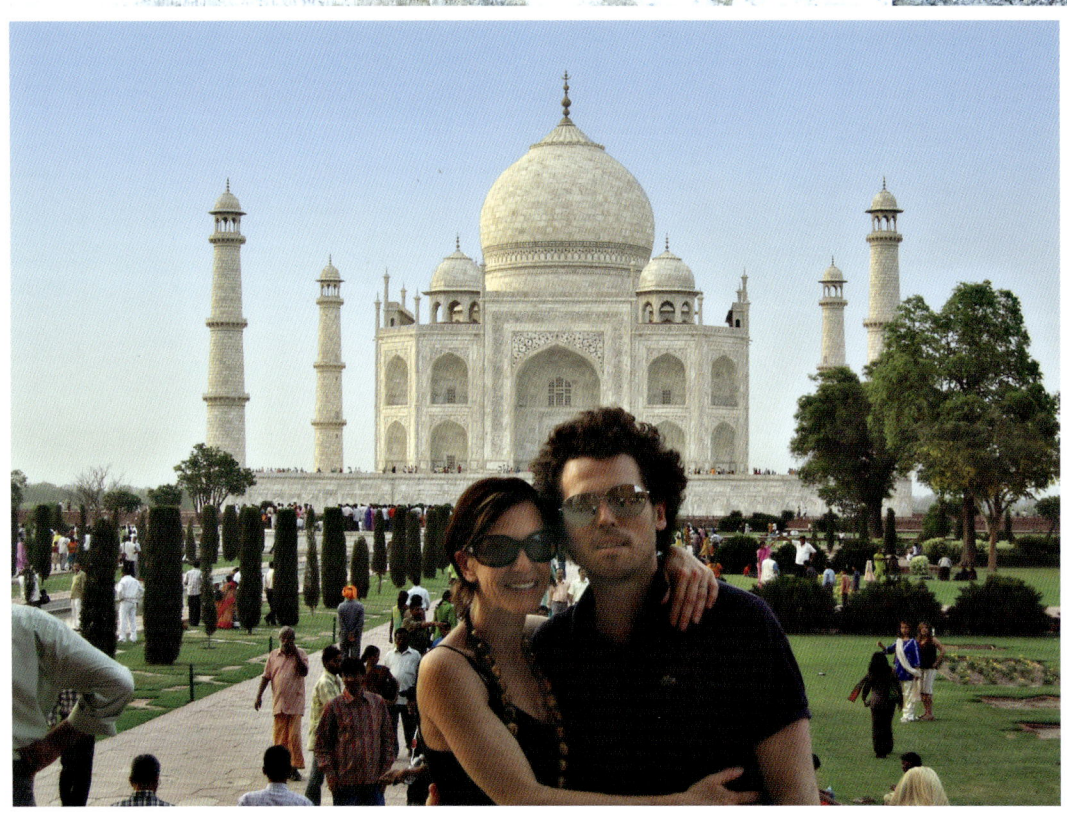

*The most romantic place on earth, the Taj Mahal, Agra, May 2005*

I did not know I was being proposed to. We were sitting on a bench outside the Taj Mahal. It was hot, a hundred-plus degrees, sauna hot.

My boyfriend distracts me by asking for the digital camera, buried in my purse. While I'm searching for it, he says something romantic along the lines of, "Hey, so I have a question for you." I look up and he's down on one knee, ring in hand, the Taj's dome framing his idea. "Will you marry me?" he asks. I answer him with a kiss.

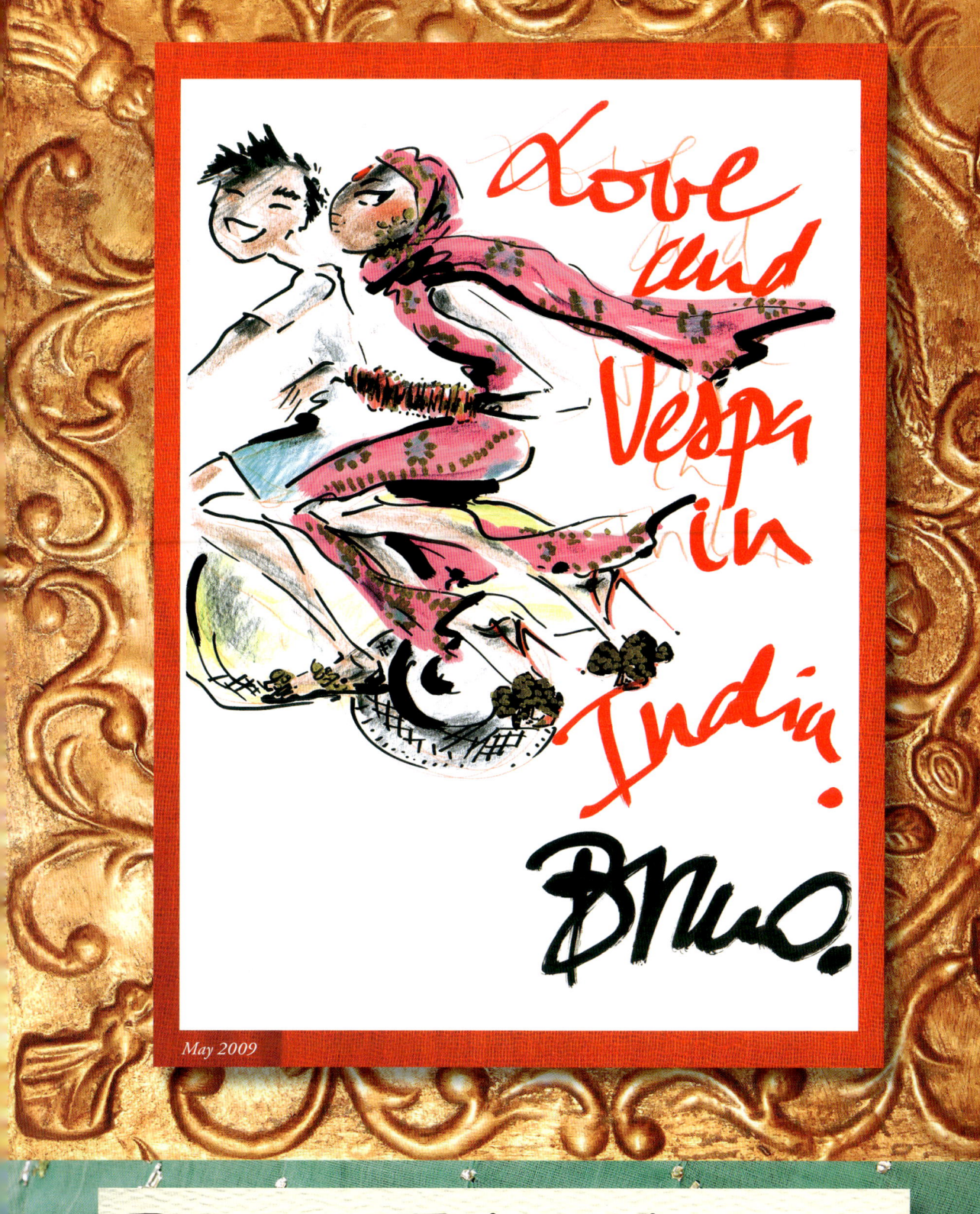

*May 2009*

# Bruno Frisoni

*Footwear Designer*

# Chiara Clemente

*Film Director*

I took my first trip to India when I was in my mother's belly; my first word was in Tamil; my first steps were on the vast beaches of Madras. Cobra temples, painted elephants, a ruby given as a gift by a befriended crow, my first realization of death, my first true love. To this day India remains the place where I feel most at home.

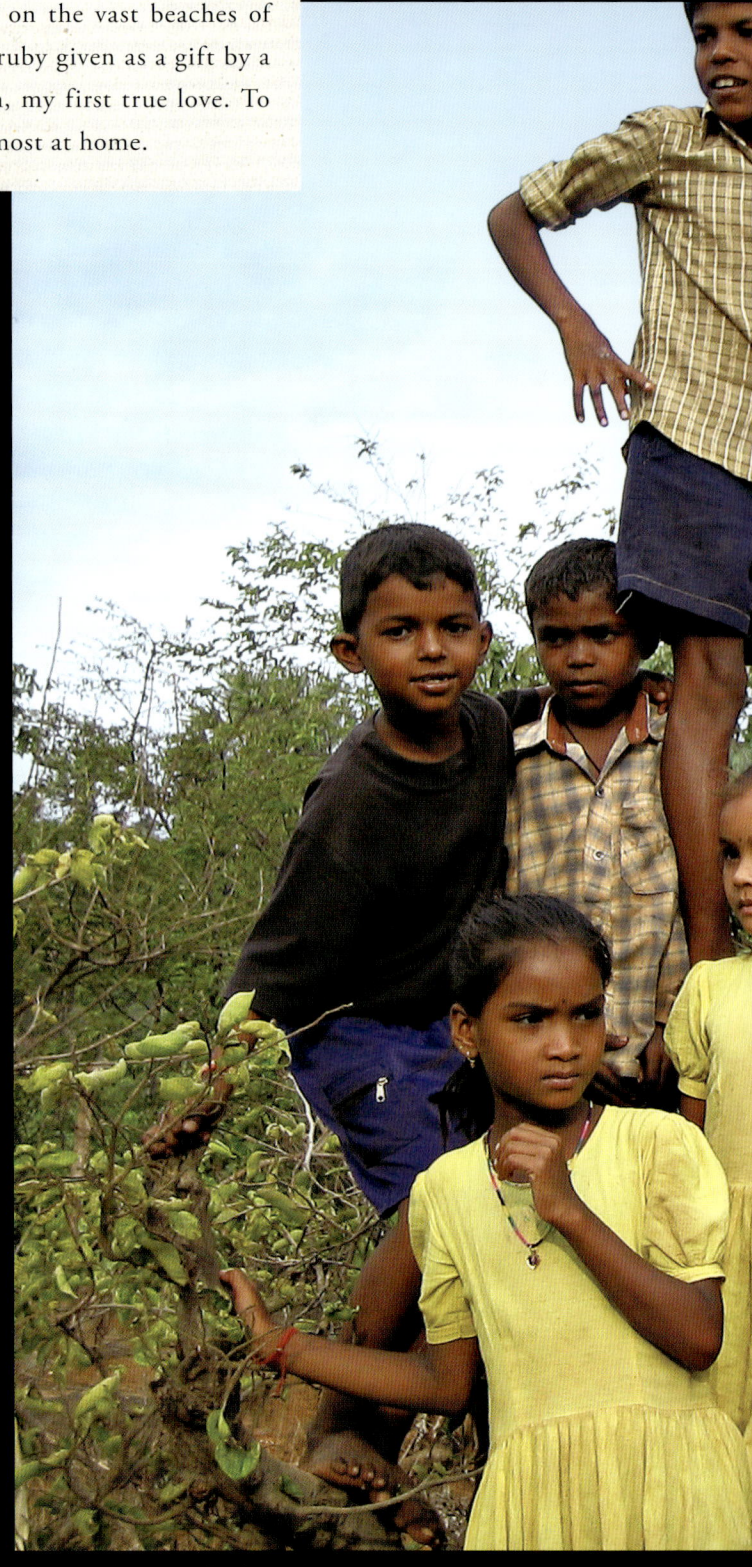

*A small village outside of Mumbai, May 2004*

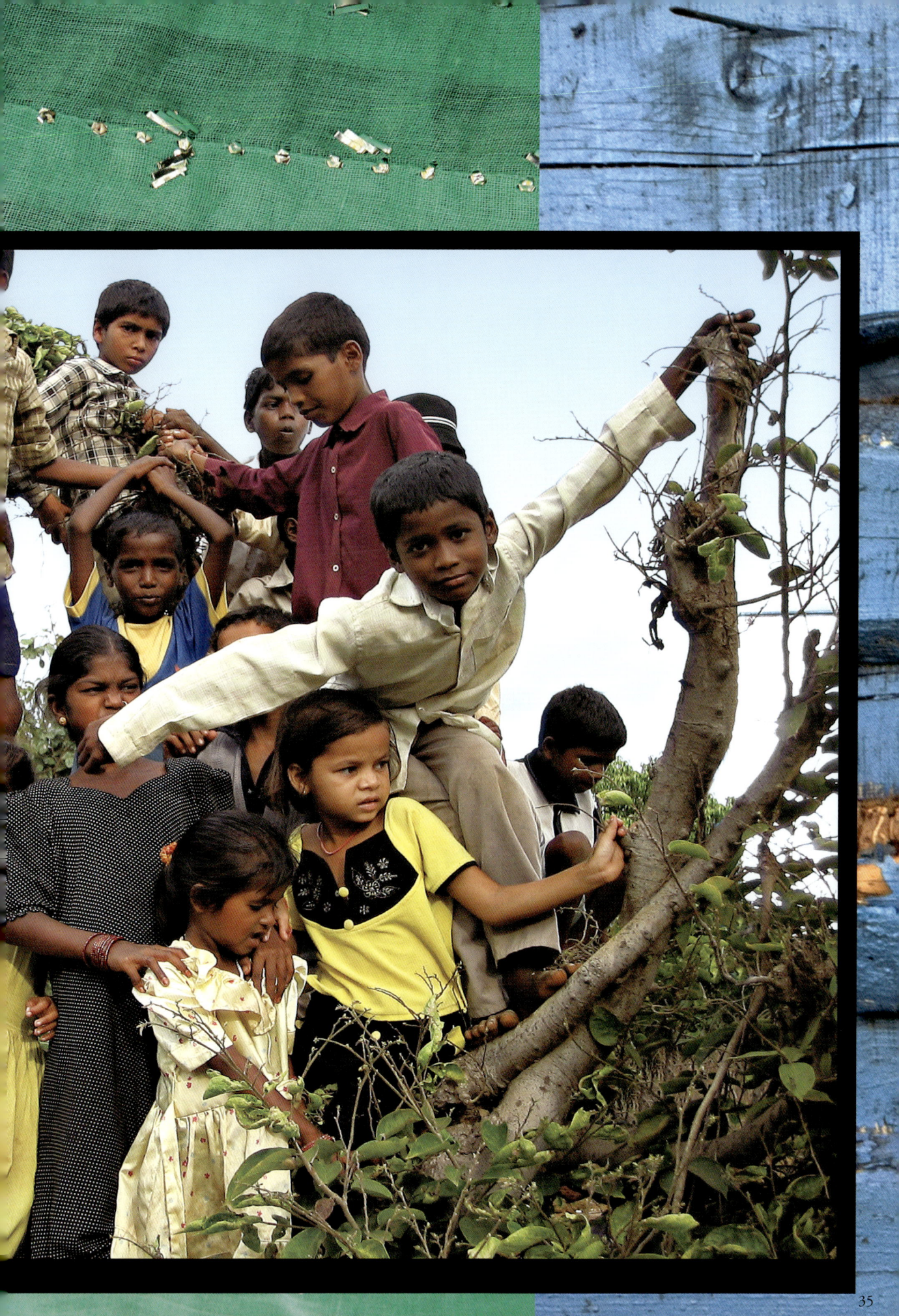

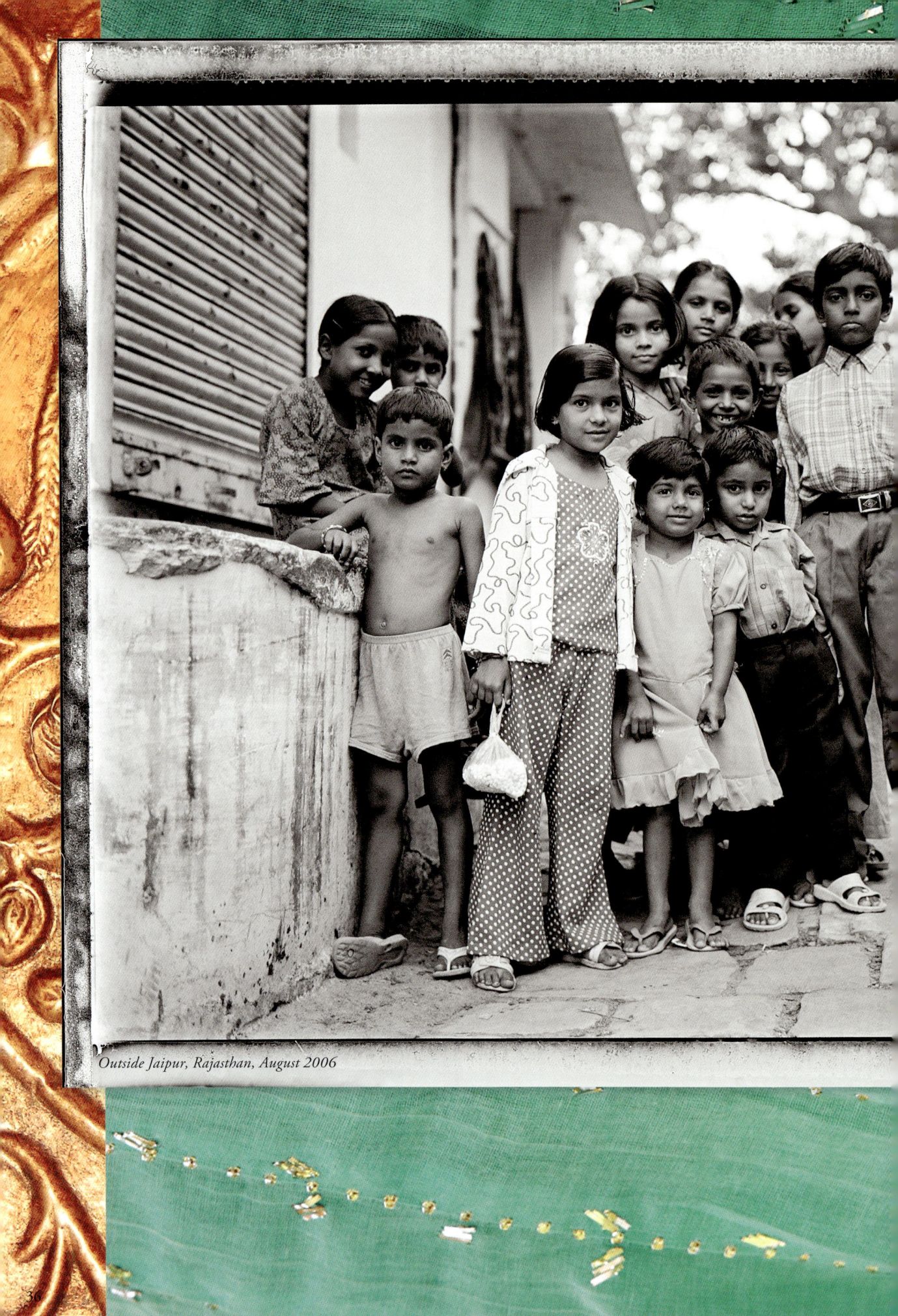

*Outside Jaipur, Rajasthan, August 2006*

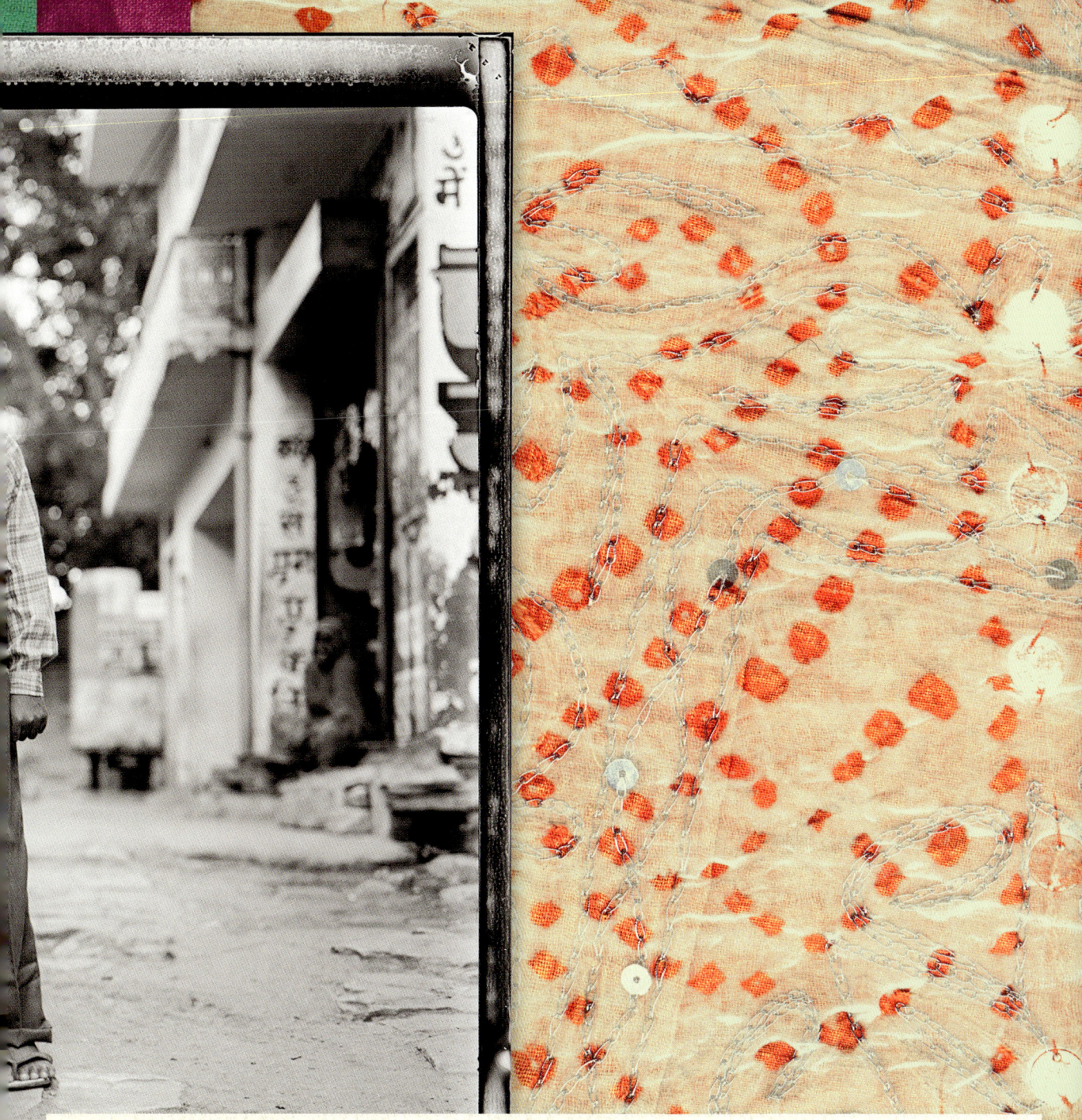

# Christopher Wray-McCann
*Photographer*

The children of India did something astounding to me. They made me feel like a kid again. In India, I turned corners and found myself on streets that children seemed to own, own in a way I remembered from the hours before dusk when we were told to go play outside. They are all the things we pray for children to be. They are saavy; they are curious; and they are excited. There is one thing they lack though, and that is fear, or at least fear of a stranger. When they see me come 'round their corner, they want to know "Where are you from?" and "How far away is that?" and "Why are you here?" And I think—these are a few good questions we all should ask out loud from time to time.

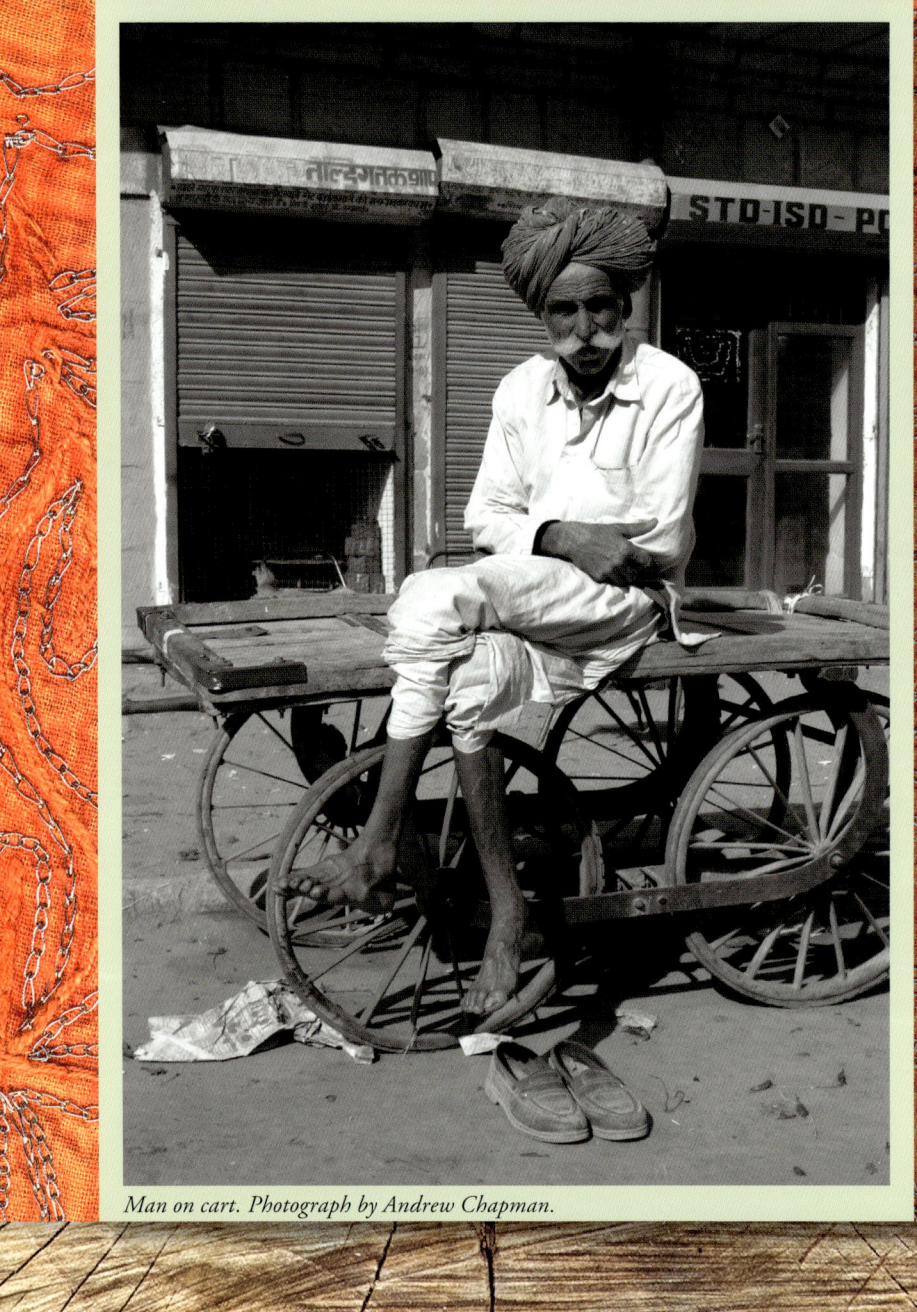

*Man on cart. Photograph by Andrew Chapman.*

# Dennis Freedman

## *Creative Director*, W *Magazine*

I made my first trip to India to do a fashion shoot for *W* magazine, and it was then that I fell in love with the country and its people. I knew I would return again and again to this place that captivated and inspired me.

*On the border between India and Nepal*

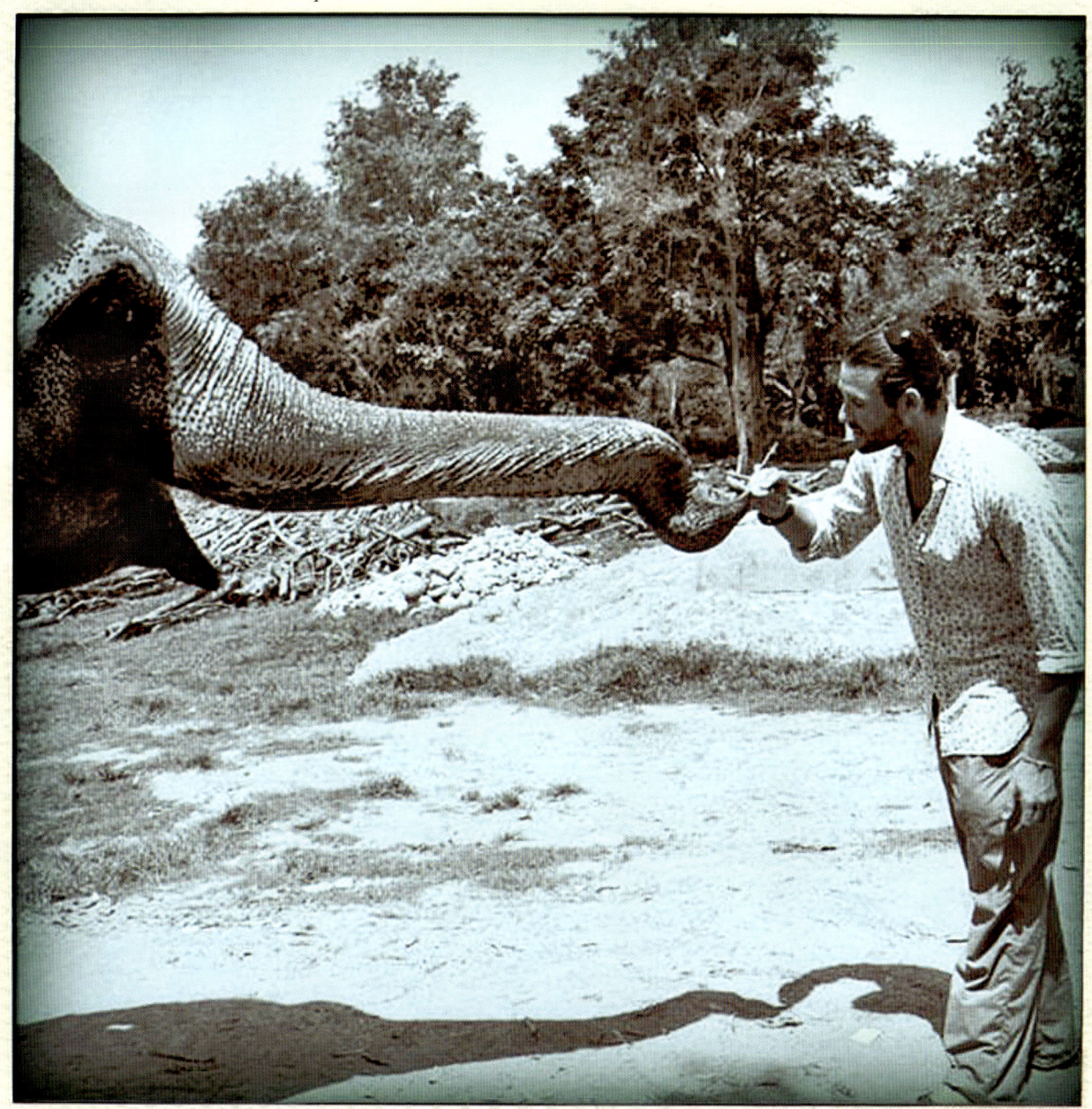

# David de Rothschild

*Environmentalist, Founder of the SMART Collective*

❝To truly understand, feel, and see India would require more than a thousand lifetimes, but its movement, smiles, and energy are so vibrant that one visit changes the spirit forever.❞

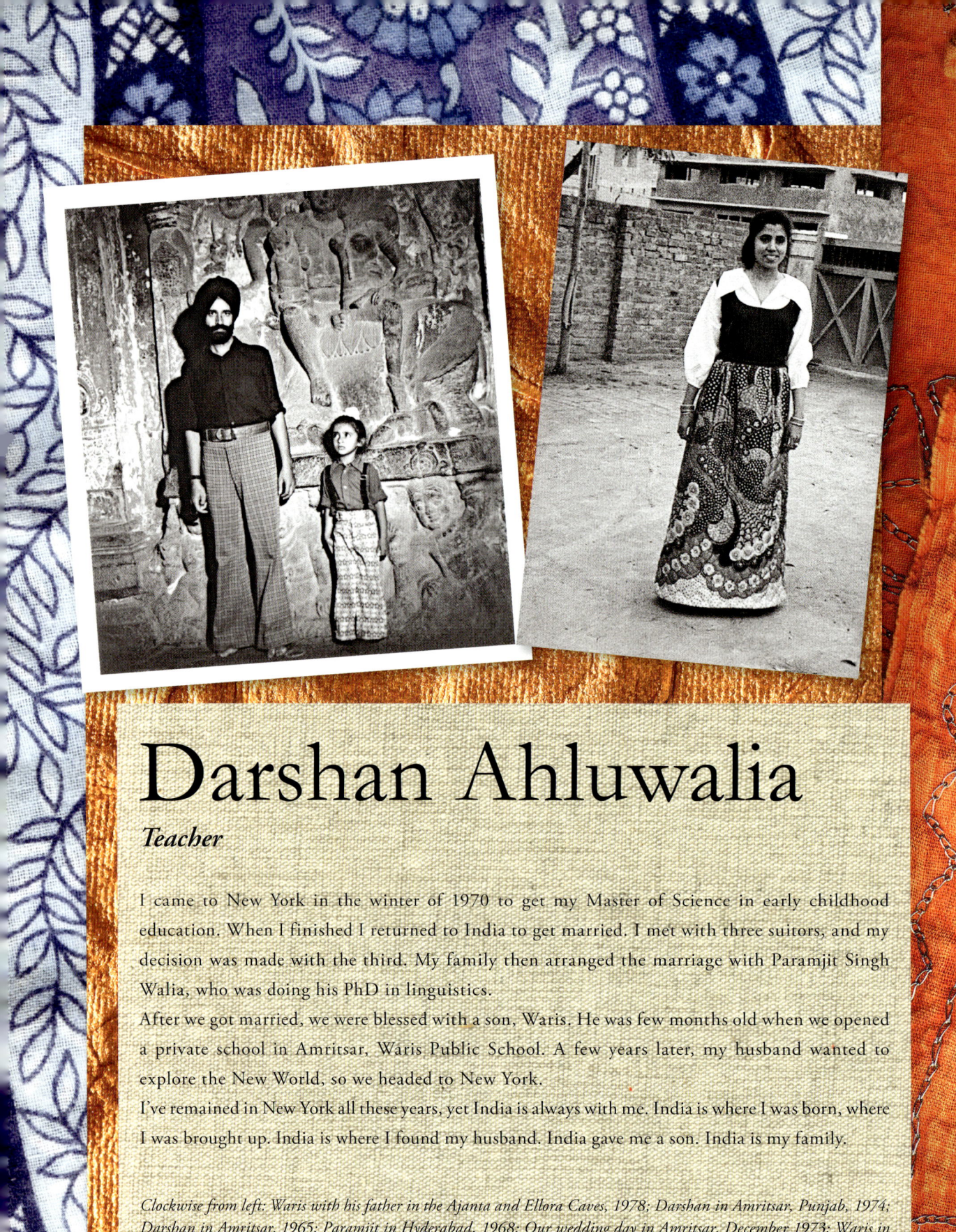

# Darshan Ahluwalia
*Teacher*

I came to New York in the winter of 1970 to get my Master of Science in early childhood education. When I finished I returned to India to get married. I met with three suitors, and my decision was made with the third. My family then arranged the marriage with Paramjit Singh Walia, who was doing his PhD in linguistics.

After we got married, we were blessed with a son, Waris. He was few months old when we opened a private school in Amritsar, Waris Public School. A few years later, my husband wanted to explore the New World, so we headed to New York.

I've remained in New York all these years, yet India is always with me. India is where I was born, where I was brought up. India is where I found my husband. India gave me a son. India is my family.

*Clockwise from left: Waris with his father in the Ajanta and Ellora Caves, 1978; Darshan in Amritsar, Punjab, 1974; Darshan in Amritsar, 1965; Paramjit in Hyderabad, 1968; Our wedding day in Amritsar, December 1973; Waris in Amritsar, December 1977.*

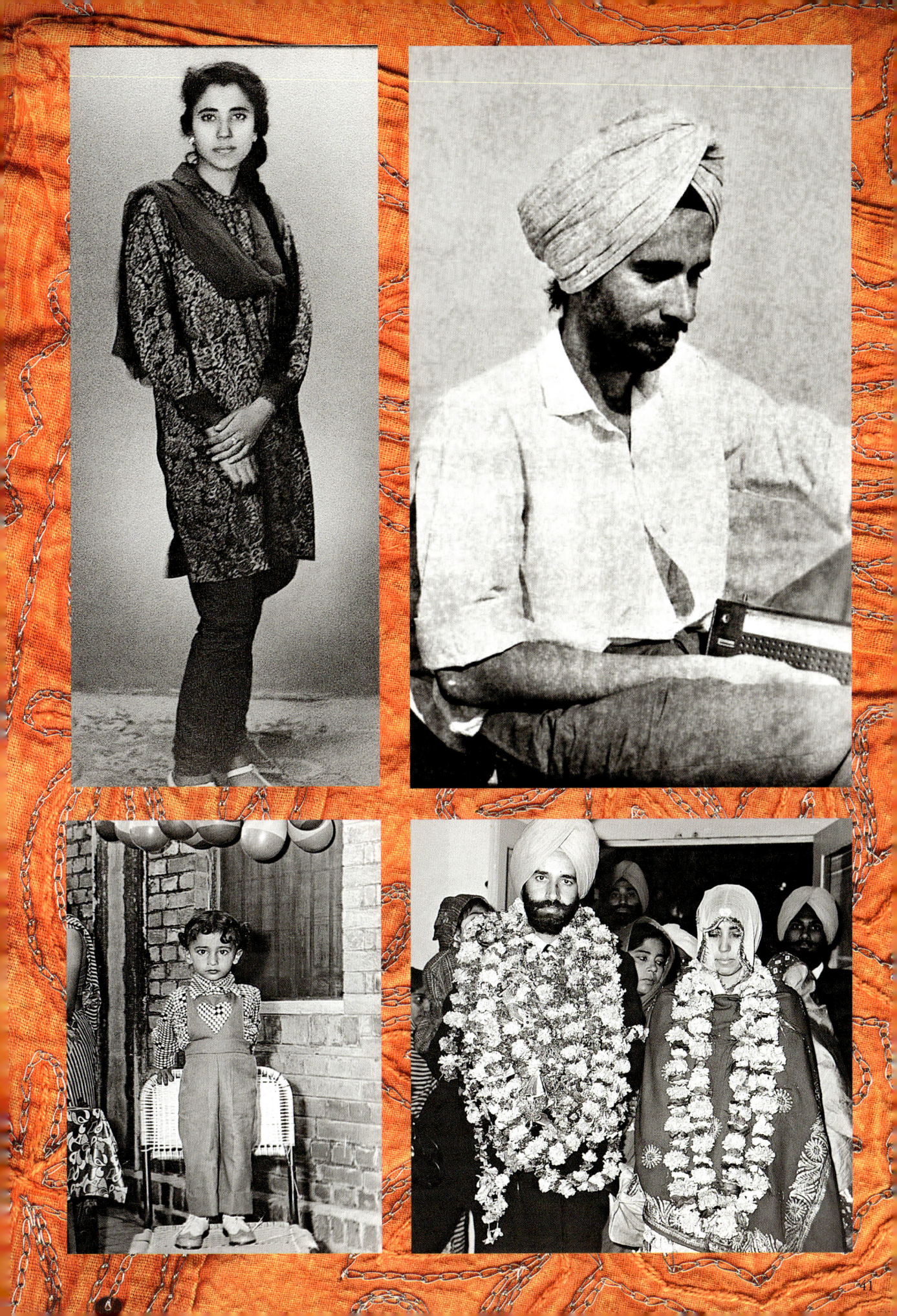

# Diane Pernet

*Founder,* A Shaded View on Fashion Film

My first introduction to India was through the films of Satyajit Ray, films like *Pather Panchali*, the entire *Apu* series, and more than any other, *The Salon of Music*. I had visions of a beautiful white horse running on a vacant beach at night. I never saw that horse, but I did attend a days-long Indian wedding where a white horse covered in marigolds and rose buds carried the bridegroom. Vibrant colors and intense fragrances assault one's senses at every corner in India. Early on I traveled to Darjeeling and stayed at the Hotel Windermere, in the foothills of the Himalayas. The air was thin, and when the mist cleared I could see the mountains. I'd never felt closer to God.

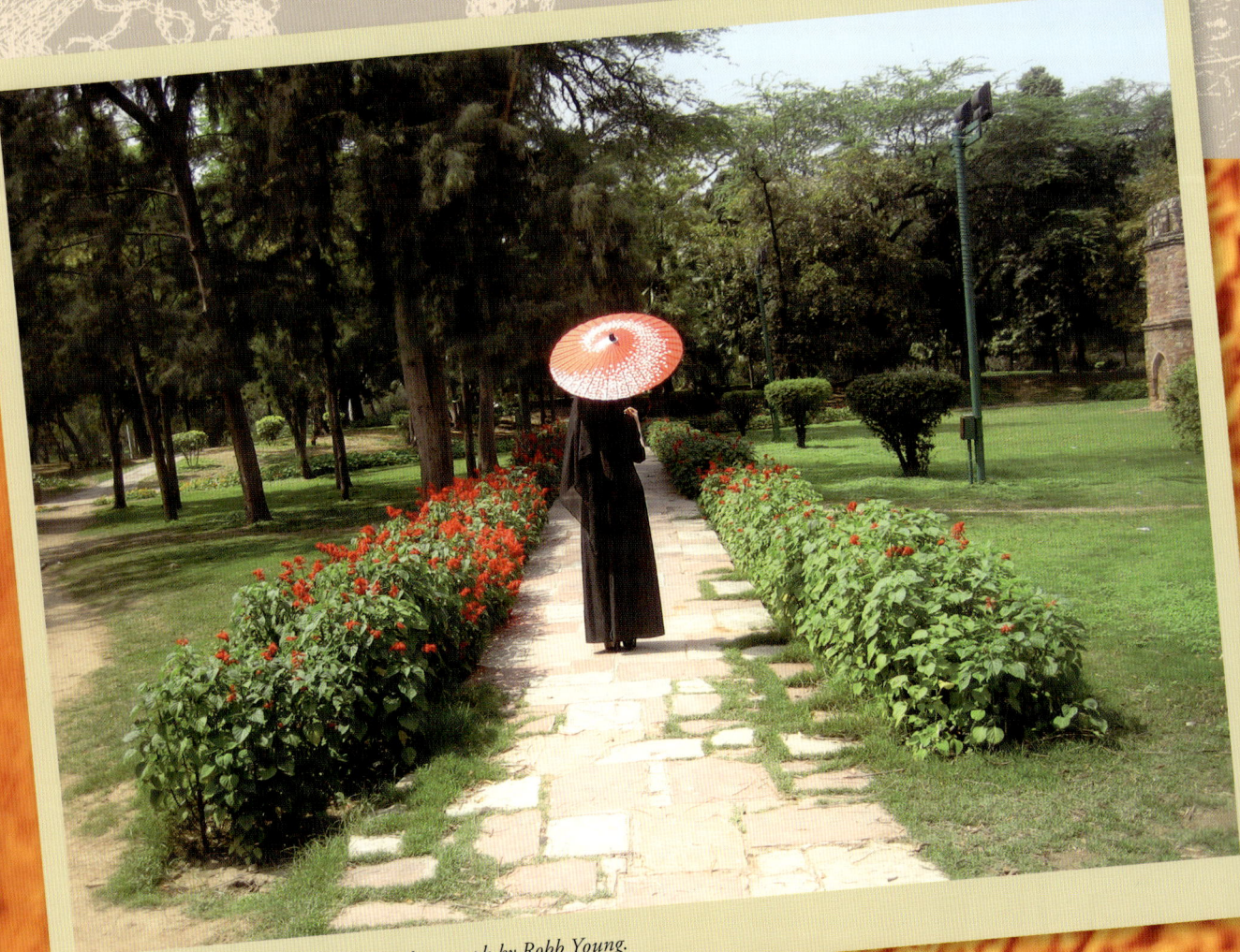

Lodhi Gardens, Delhi, March 2007. Photograph by Robb Young.

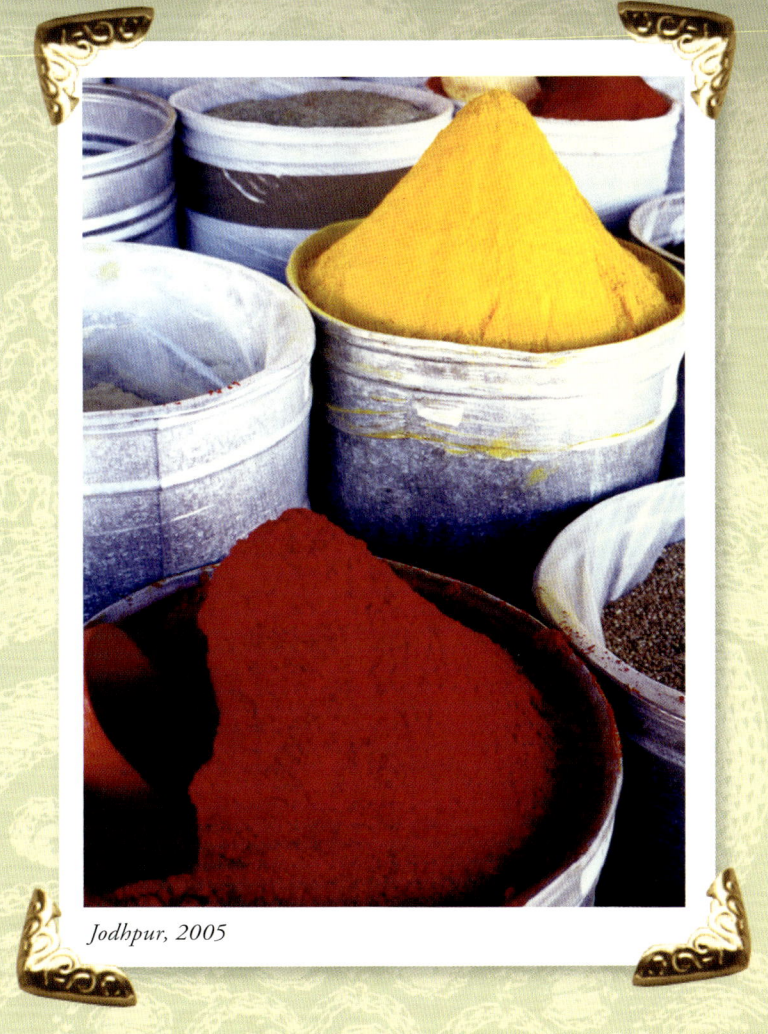

*Jodhpur, 2005*

# Diane von Furstenberg
**Fashion Designer**

❝*Color is more present in India than anywhere else… It explodes everywhere and creates an optimism and a faith in beauty that cannot be found anywhere else.*❞

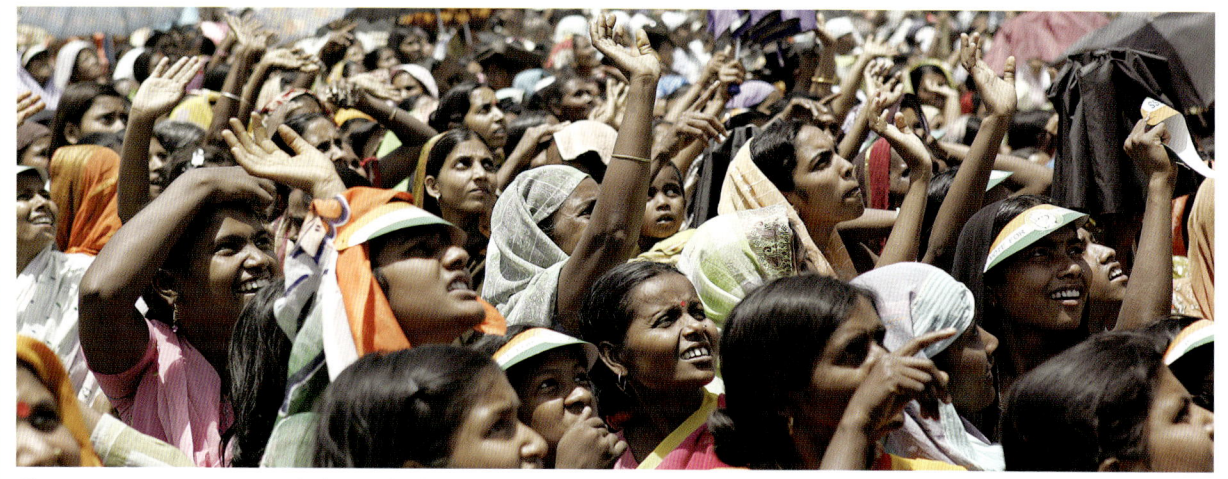
*Congress party supporters in Lalgola, north of Kolkata, wave at a helicopter carrying Sonia Gandhi to a campaign rally, April 2009.*

# Fareed Zakaria
*Editor,* **Newsweek International**

*"India is the greatest experiment in human history. Poverty, wealth, diversity, and democracy, all on a breathtaking scale, mixing and melding together. When it works—and it often works—it is a testament not to the strength of government, but to the power of ordinary people."*

# Evelyn Lauder
*Senior Corporate Vice President, the Estée Lauder Companies*

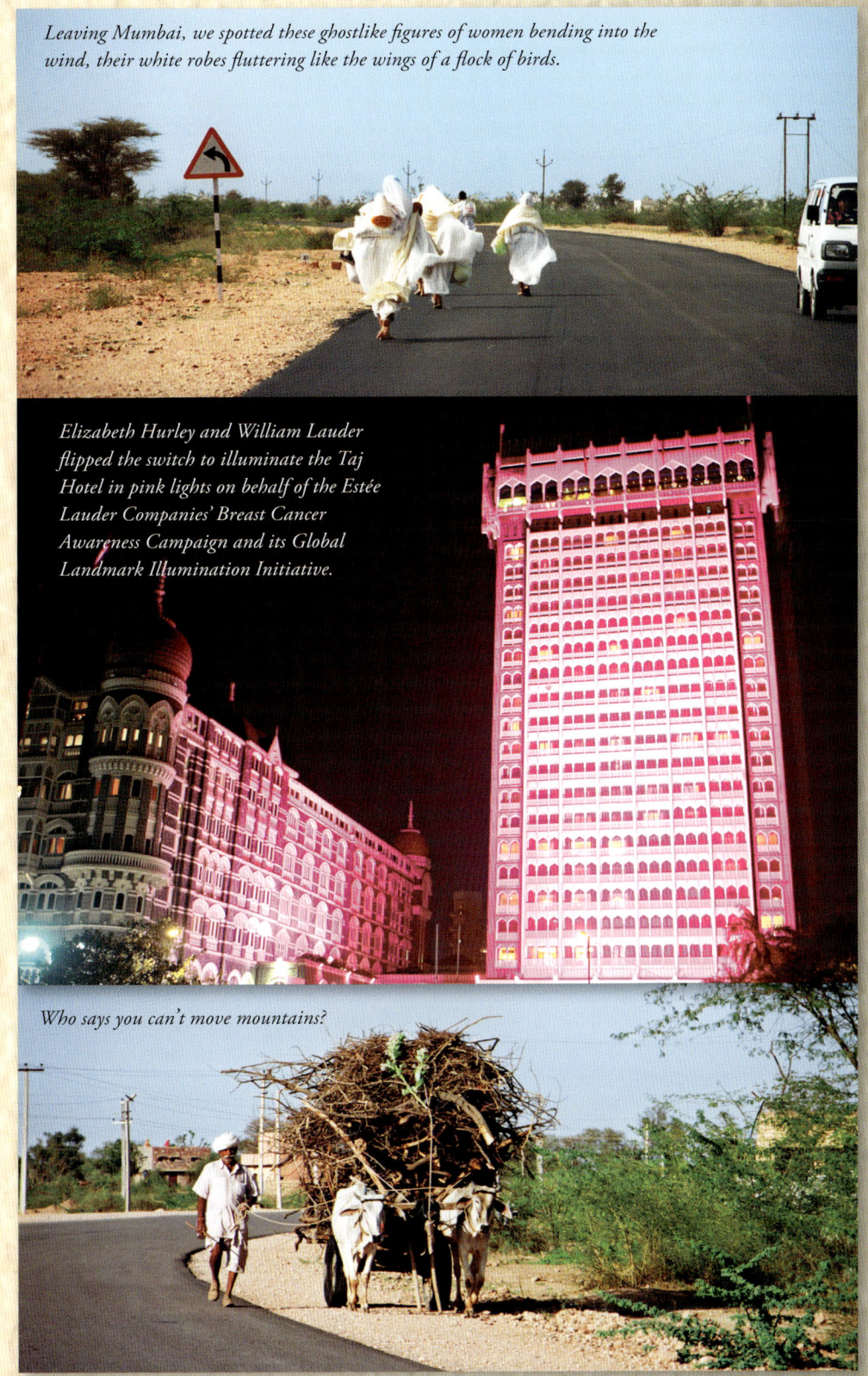

*Leaving Mumbai, we spotted these ghostlike figures of women bending into the wind, their white robes fluttering like the wings of a flock of birds.*

*Elizabeth Hurley and William Lauder flipped the switch to illuminate the Taj Hotel in pink lights on behalf of the Estée Lauder Companies' Breast Cancer Awareness Campaign and its Global Landmark Illumination Initiative.*

*Who says you can't move mountains?*

# Elizabeth Hurley
*Model, Actor, and Designer*

"*When I close my eyes and think of India, huge swaths of pink and orange flowers drift before me, and I can almost smell the sweet, intoxicating scent of jasmine and frangipani. I hear the trumpeting of elephants and the laughter of all my friends, because, in my dreams, I am often back in Jodhpur, amid the frenzy and the joy of my own Indian wedding. This photograph reminds me of the many happy times I have spent in my new, adopted country.*"

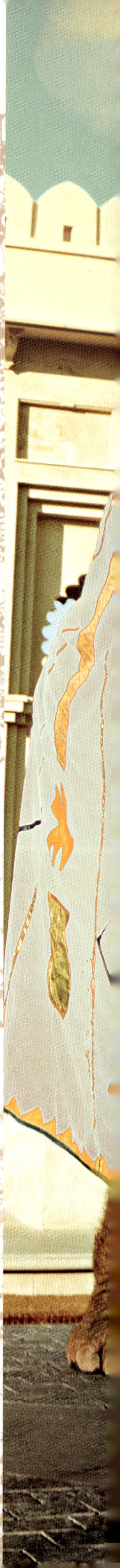

*Udaipur, 2006.*
*Photograph by*
*Daniela Federia.*

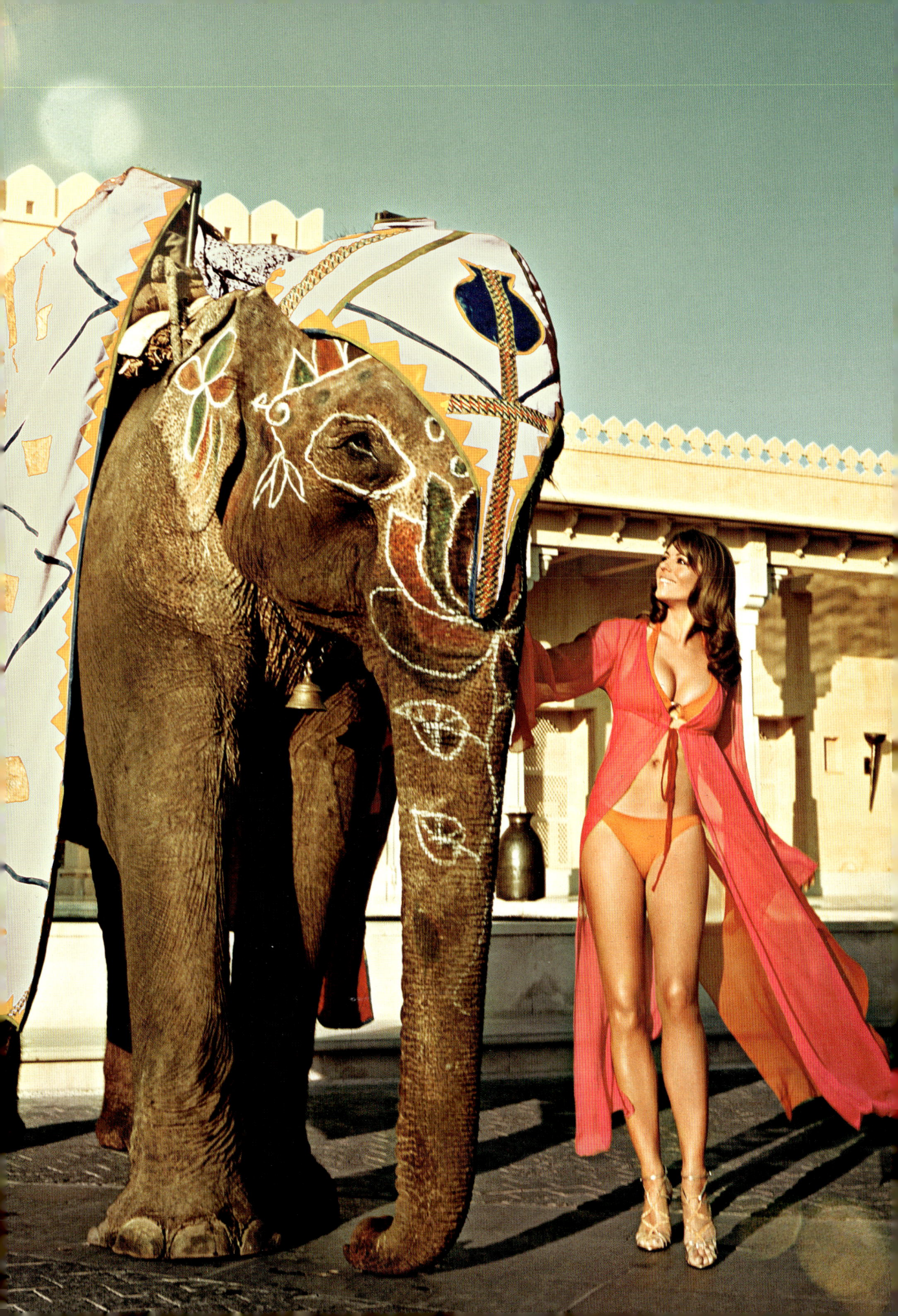

# Farzad S. Jehani

*Owner, Leopold Cafe*

We won, they lost. We always bounce back: Our shutters went up as soon as the curfew was lifted. We lost two of our staff, but the Cafe resurrected itself with Mumbai loyalists. The city is full of life and of cultures, and after this dastardly act it mobilized itself in grief—we all came back together. We hope this never happens again, but if it does, the next time we shall be prepared.

*Below: Siddharth Mallya sharing a beer at the Cafe, April 2009*

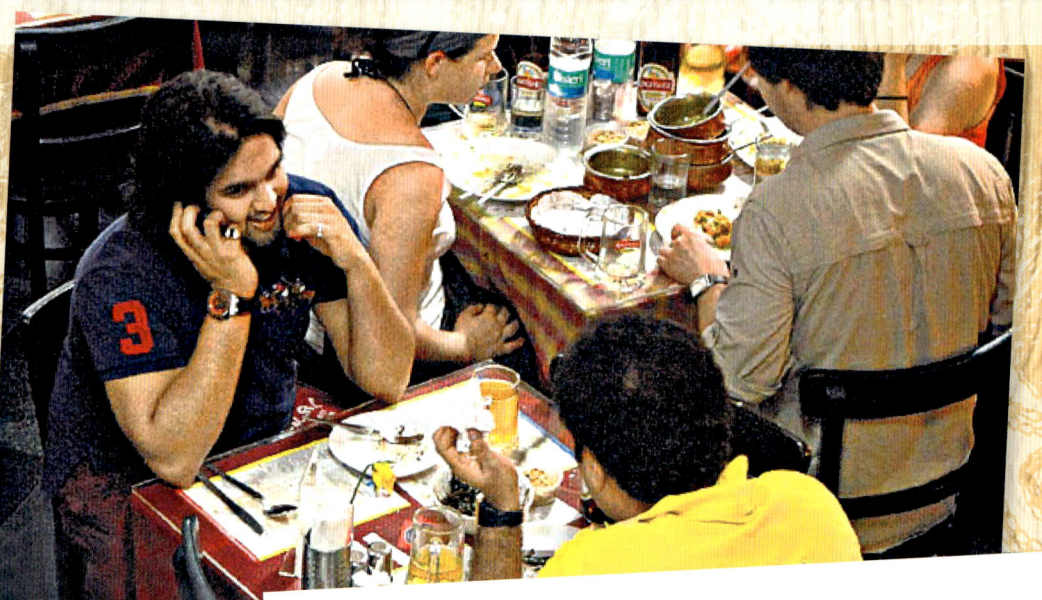

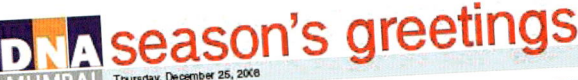
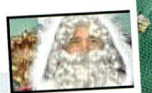
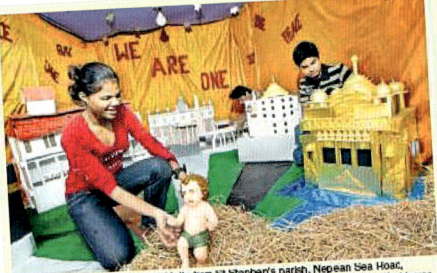
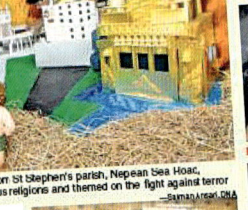
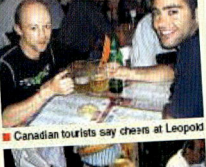
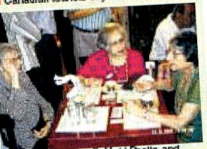

# Francesco Clemente

*Artist*

avijñatam vijānatam vijñātam avijānatām.

It is not understood by those who understand it;
it is understood by those who do not understand it.

*Below:* Map of What is Effortless, *1978*

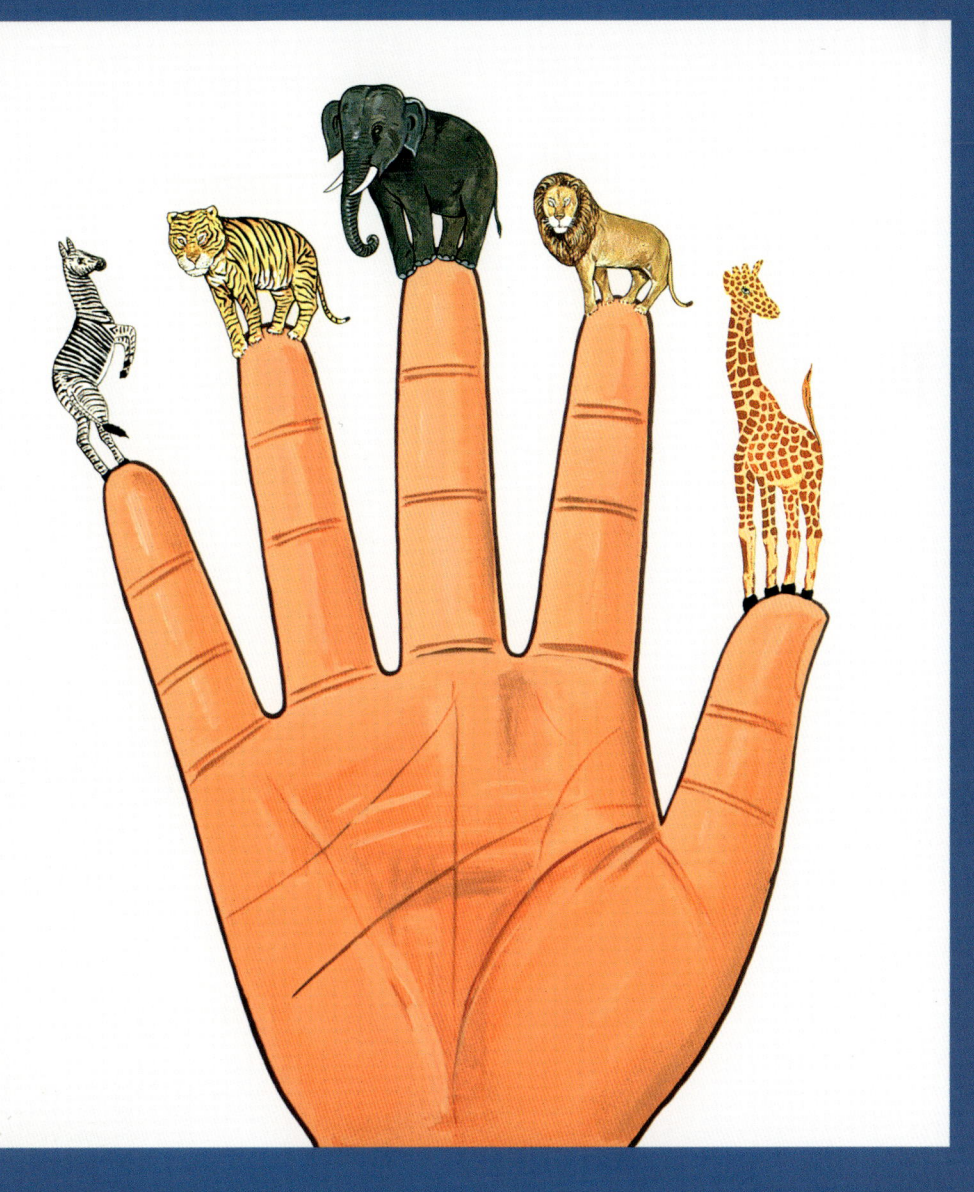

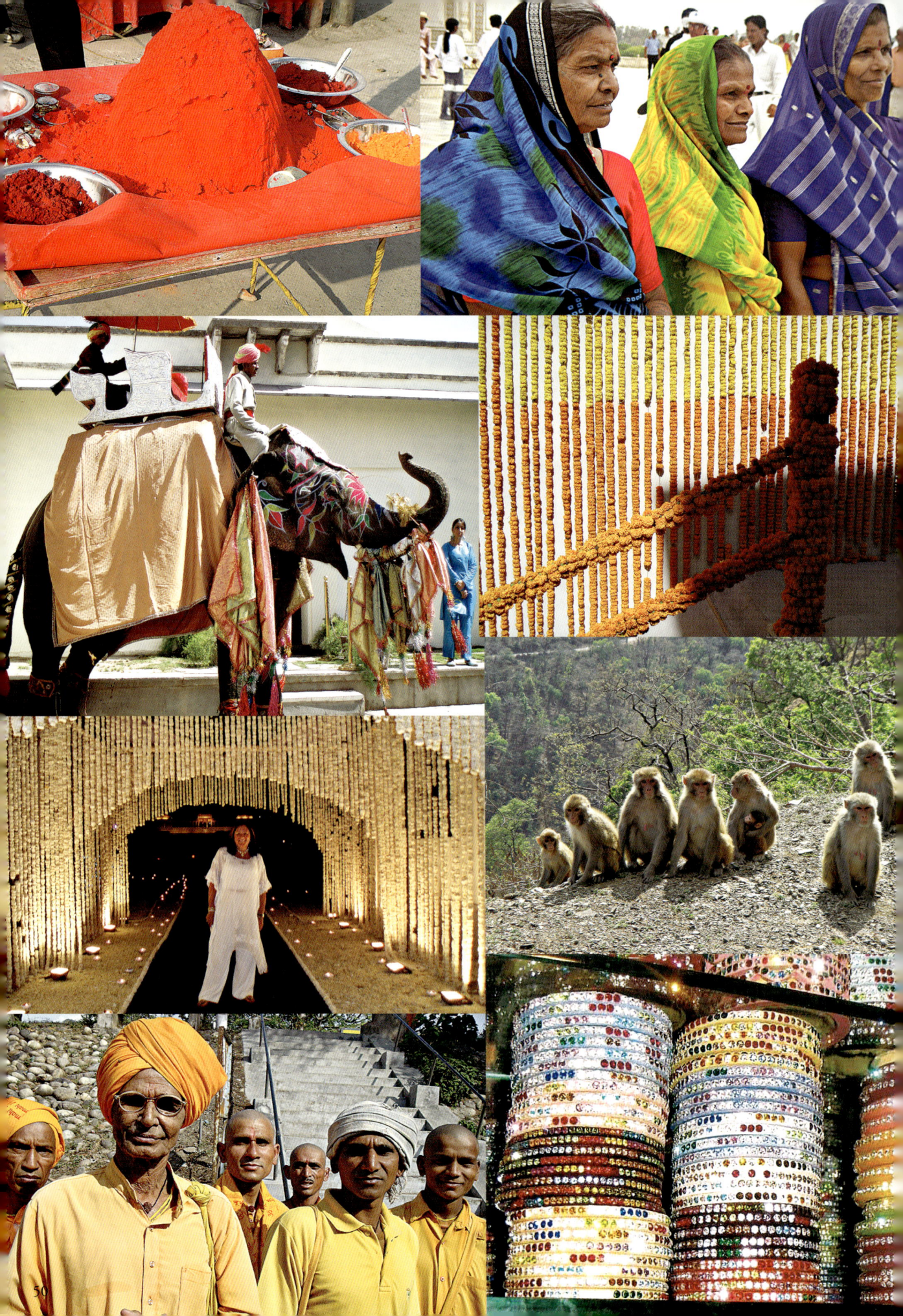

# Fern Mallis

*Senior Vice President, IMG Fashion*

India was basically love at first sight; I was completely taken by surprise. My first trip was in the summer of 2001, just after IMG acquired 7th on Sixth, the entity that created and produced Fashion Week in New York City. I was enlisted to go to Mumbai, where IMG India had just produced their first Lakme Fashion Week.

I was not anxious to go, and to give up a summer weekend at my house on the lake, but I was summoned, got my visa, some shots and malaria pills, and clearly packed way too much, as this was just the beginning of a radical shift in my closet and my wardrobe.

The number of people waiting at the airport at one a.m. was a shock, and the drive from the airport to the majestic Taj hotel across from the Gateway of India was a revelation. I was exhausted after more than twenty hours of travel, and it was late and dark, but I couldn't close my eyes or believe what they were seeing. And the smell—it stays with you forever; I stop and take a deep breath every time I arrive back on Indian soil.

During that drive I saw the slums, the countless people sleeping on streets, the men squatting in groups and carrying on conversations, the dogs, the cows, even an elephant, the children, the big deep eyes, the teeny-tiny shops selling all sorts of things all night long. And then we got closer to South Mumbai, Marine Drive, and the coastline, buildings, and hotels, where it felt more like Rio, or Miami, or another world-class city by the sea.

Arriving at the Taj hotel sometime between two and three a.m., I expected a quiet, sleepy lobby, but instead it felt like New Year's Eve in Times Square—lots of people, activity, and noise, and a city that never sleeps. The next morning I met my colleagues, had breakfast at the café outside—near the pool, with large wicker chairs and overhead fans, and black crows flying by—and after my first sweet lime juice I was hooked.

Lakme Fashion Week in India just celebrated its tenth anniversary, and over the past decade I've been back several times a year. I've had the great privilege and joy of shopping in Jaipur, sightseeing in Agra, partying in Udaipur, and working and playing in Delhi and Kerala. I broke my arm in Kovalam, lunched on a houseboat in the backwaters of Cochin, crossed the Ganges in Rishikesh and Haridwar, and relaxed in Goa and at a spa in the Himalayas. And there are still so many places I want to experience.

I have as many friends now in India as I do in New York; I know and love the designers, media, and fashion editors; and it feels like a second home. My closets are filled with kurtas and tunics and dresses and leggings and dhurry pants in pinks, blues, and rainbow-bright colors and prints, all perfectly balancing my black New York wardrobe. My baskets of accessories are filled with beads and necklaces, bracelets and earrings, shawls and scarves—all things Indian. Not a day goes by that I am not asked, "Is that from India, too?"

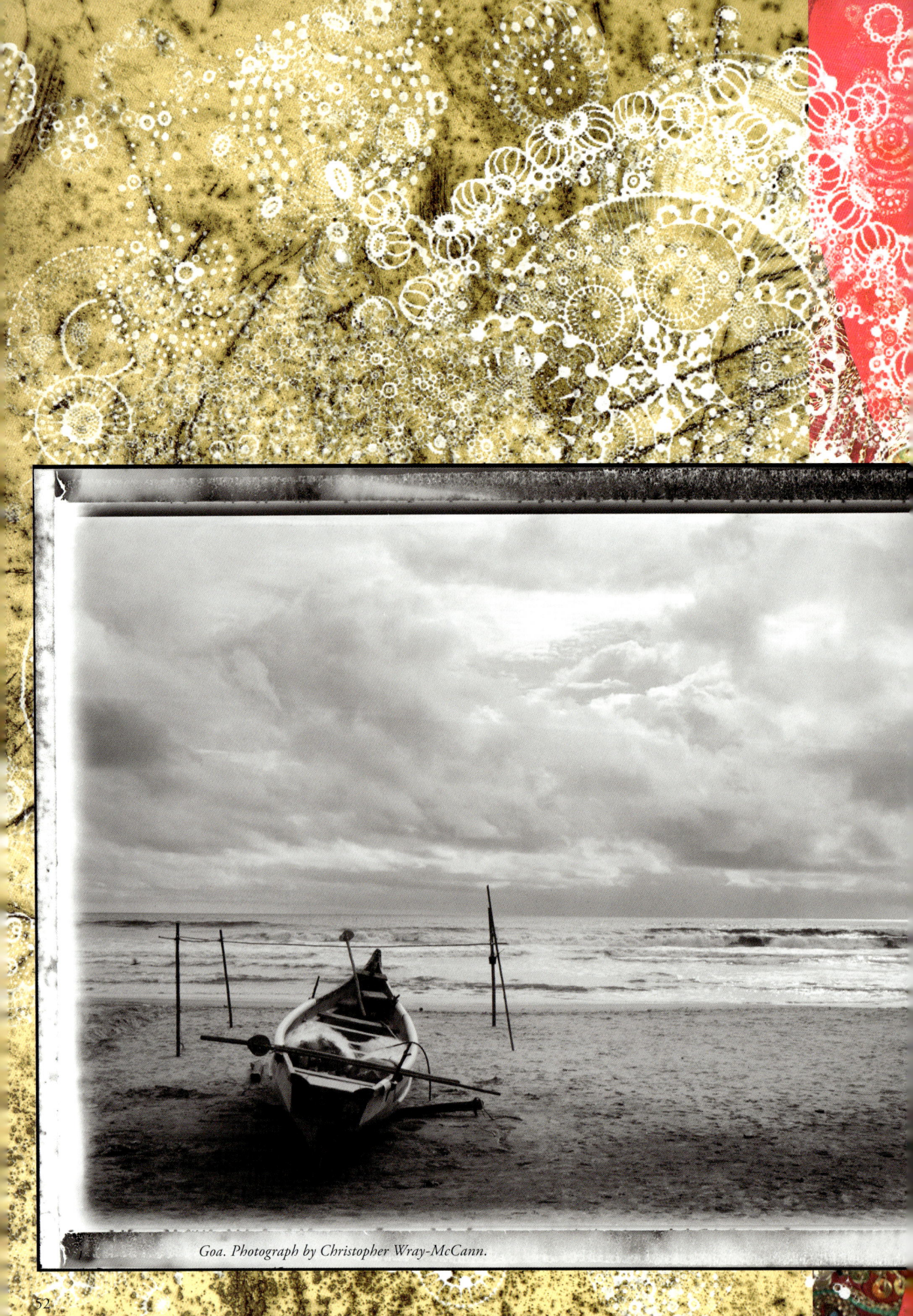

*Goa. Photograph by Christopher Wray-McCann.*

# Franca Sozzani

*Editor in Chief,* **Vogue Italia**

I was very young and completely free. India was my ideal destination. I flew there in a few hours and it took me a few months to get back.

I was totally fascinated by the colors, the people, the architecture, the richness, and the poverty. I couldn't think of living anywhere else. I spent time in Delhi, Jaipur, Benares, and Bombay, but where I felt at home was in the south: from Madras to Pondicherry to Cape Comorin, from Trivandrum to Cochin. I used to travel by bus, so I had plenty of time to admire the nature around me and the calm of the women along the rivers, washing their colorful clothes. Then I finally arrived in Goa. That place was absolutely a dream. I remember a desert and an immeasurable beach with a few cabins where young people used to live. In those days there wasn't any sign of civilization. With few rupees you could live by eating fish and drinking tea, and we were very happy. The sunrise and the sunset were the key moments of the day, and nobody was in a rush or cared about money or social relations.

Goa, that Goa, will always be my India.

Today it is a very fashionable place where you can stay in the most sumptuous hotels. But nobody can ever destroy my dream!

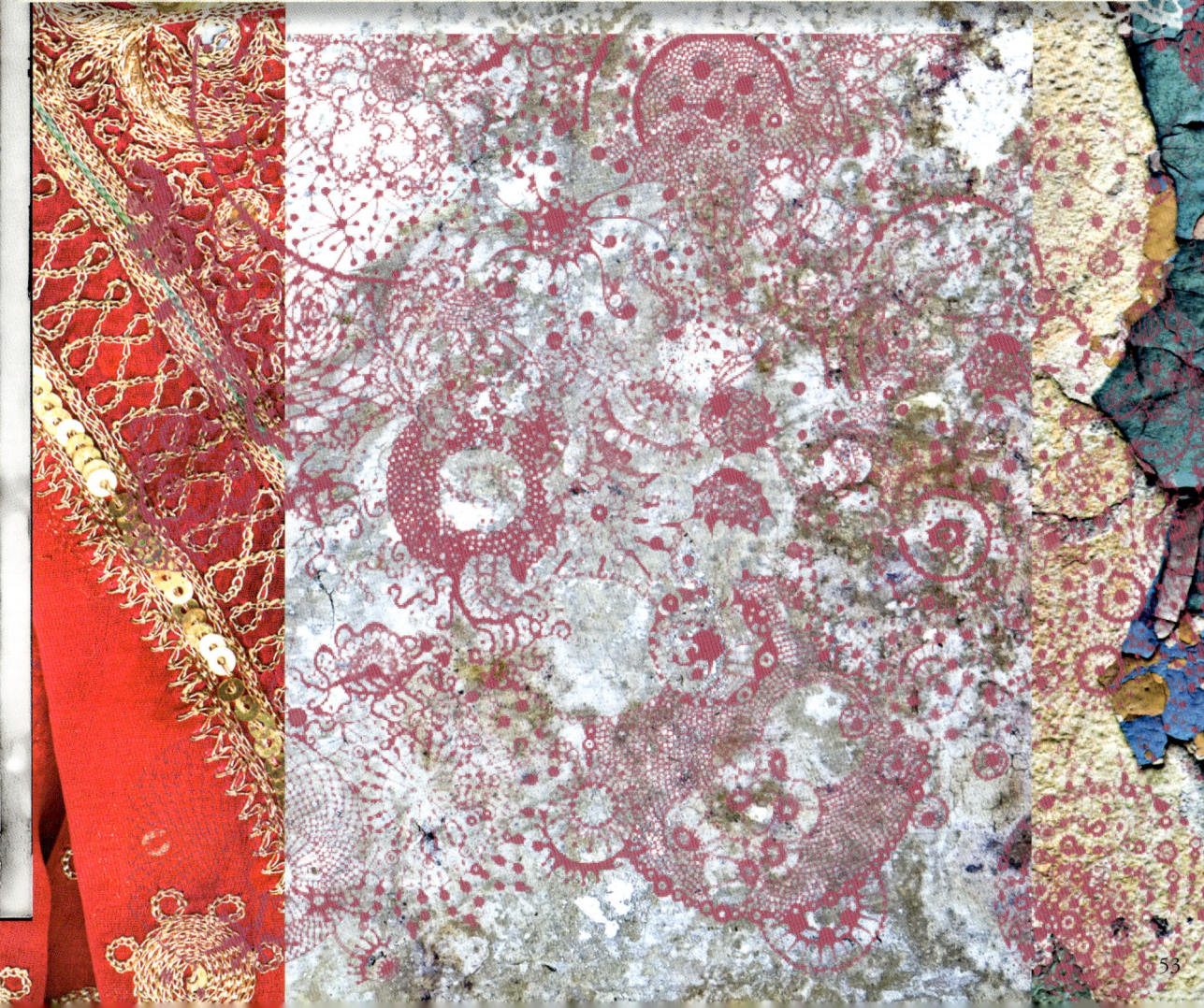

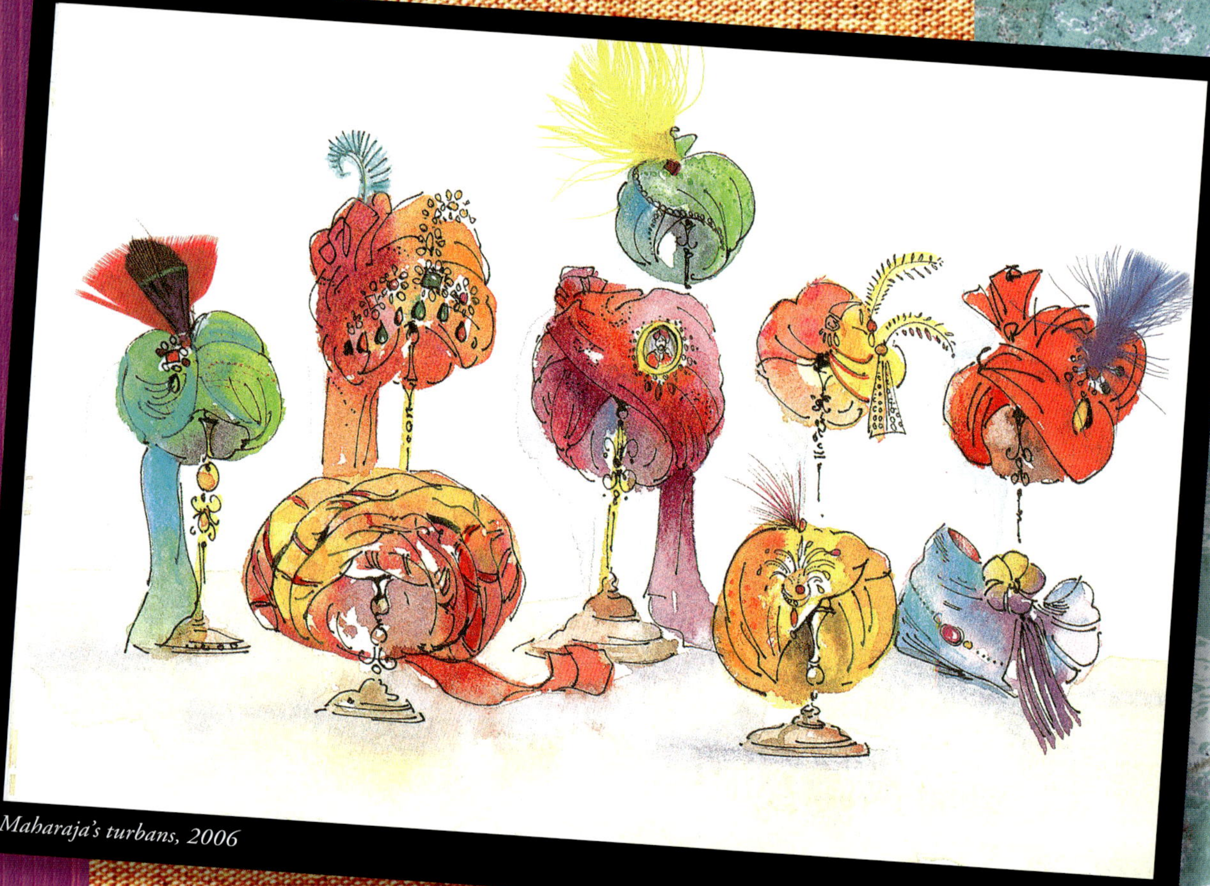

*Maharaja's turbans, 2006*

*Jain temple, Bombay 2006*

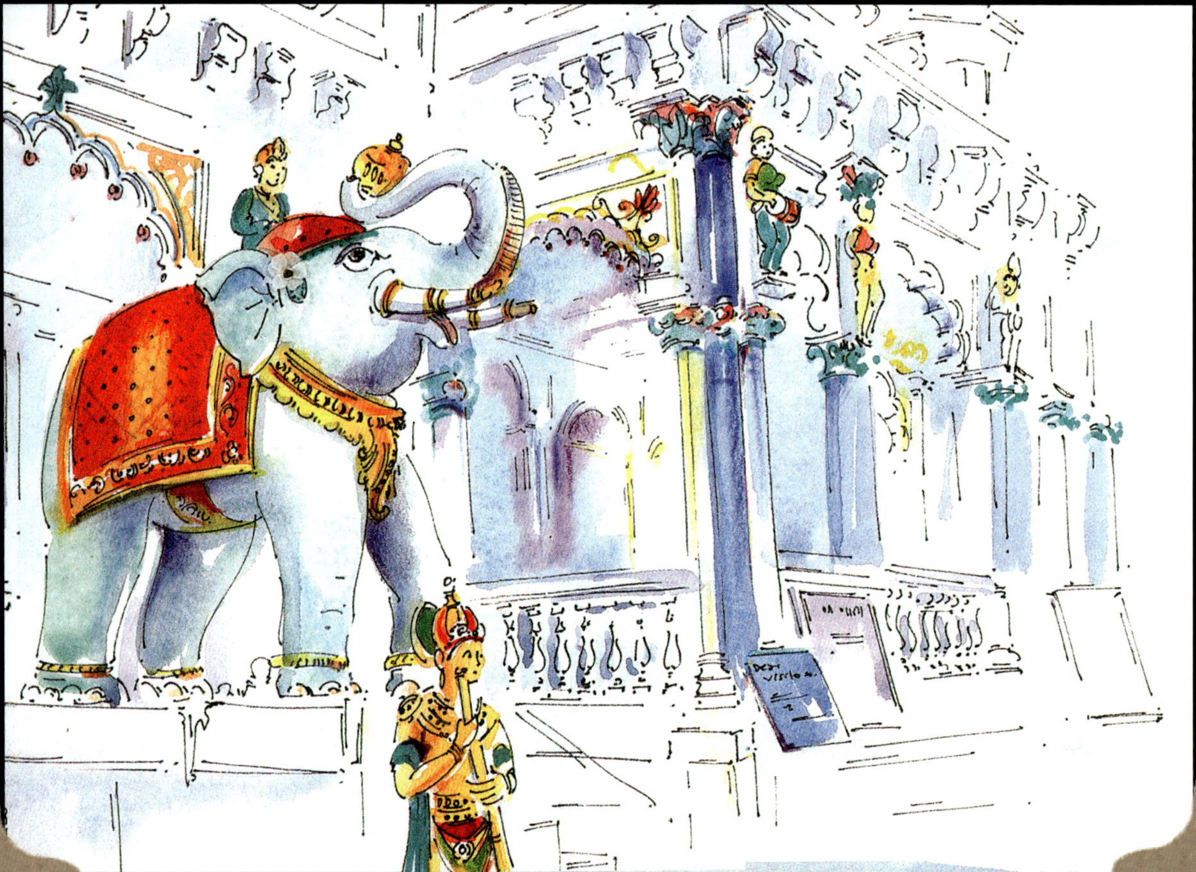

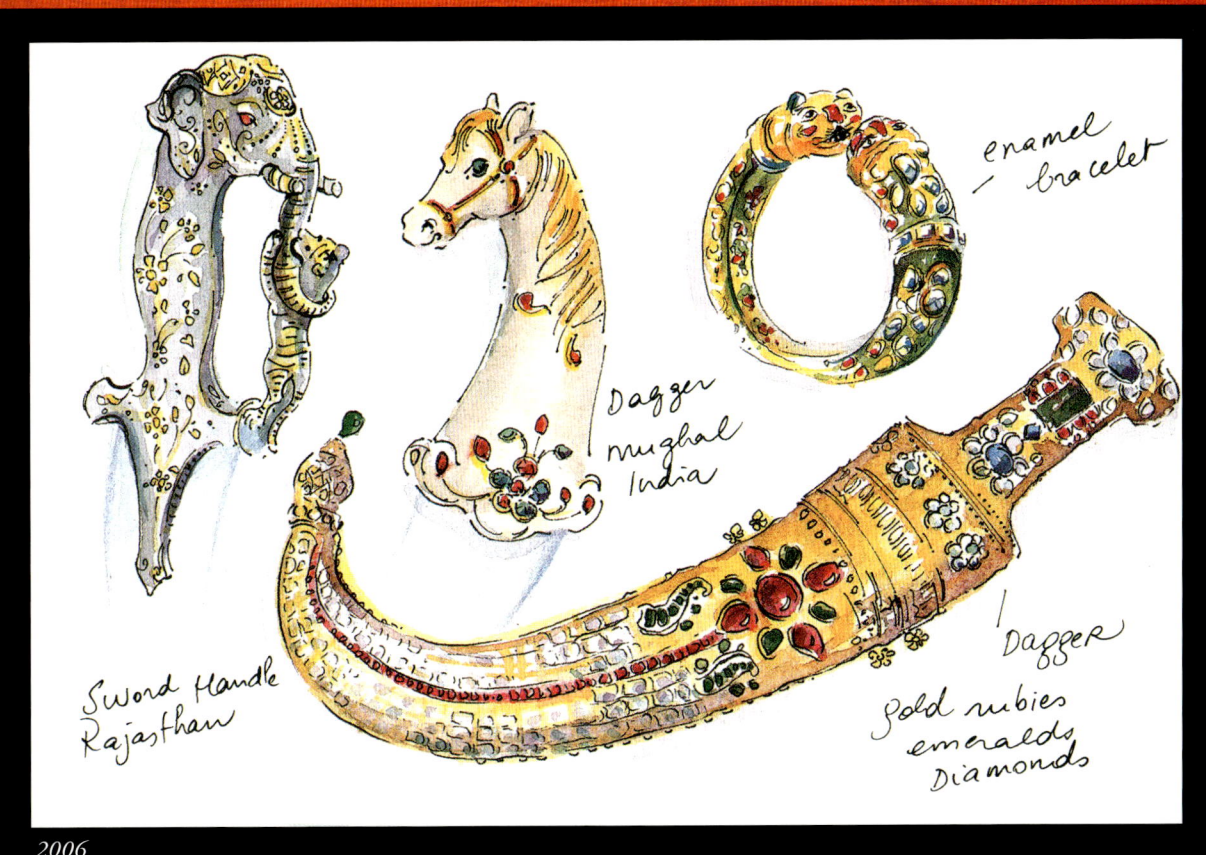

2006

# Florine Asch

*Illustrator, Vuitton* Carnet de voyage Mumbai

For me, as a watercolorist, India was a wonderful source of inspiration and constant emotion, a place where beauty met spirituality. I was touched by the kindness of the people and the refinement of their clothes, even in the middle of the countryside; the brightness of the colors moved me very much.

# Harsh Goenka

*Chairman, RPG Enterprises*

When Baiju Parthan and I did this collaborative painting, *Indie Ascensus*, my contribution was largely conceptual; little did I foresee that our six-by-four piece of canvas would go on to capture the intense emotions, sentiments, and spirit of not only the nation in general but Mumbai itself during and after those terrible days of darkness. Undoubtedly 26/11 has changed the way we think, feel, and express ourselves. In fact, even as they rebuild the damaged wings of the two marquee hotels, the unlit towers stand quiet to remind us of wounds that are still healing—in stark contrast to the pigeons opposite, at the Gateway of India, who have begun to soar again.

*Indie Ascensus* reflects the resurrection of the city's soul. For a painting done before the 26/11 attacks, the work has become near prophetic. The soaring pigeons take up with them the undying spirits of millions in the city as the white dove hovers within, bringing peace once again to a peace-loving people. The background imagery gives glimpses of the grandeur of yesteryear, history and geography. And finally there is the central figure, the man, phoenixlike, breaking free from the past, moving forward into the future—a determined, confident run, on the ascent.

Our memories will fade. *Indie Ascensus* and the spirit of Mumbai will live on.

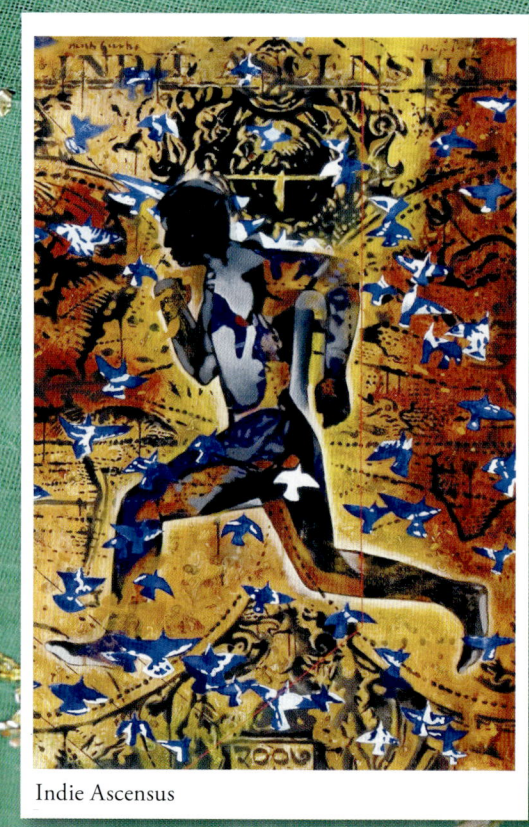

Indie Ascensus

# Hugo Guinness
*Artist*

"*India is trippy. It's all a blur. The past, the present, the future is India. We got your back.*"

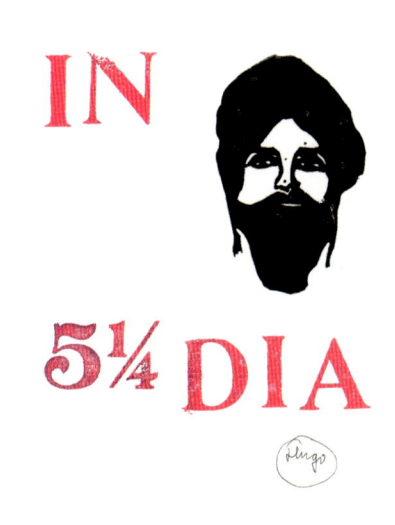
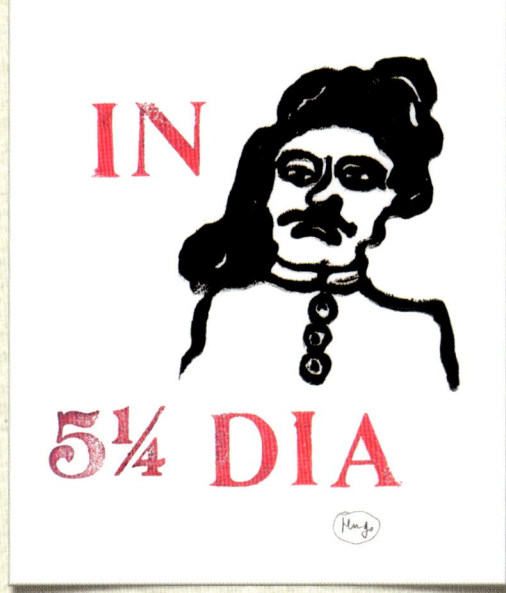
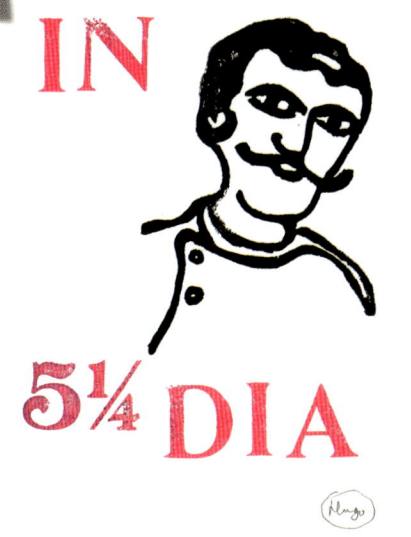

*Left: Waris Ahluwalia;*
*Right: unidentified subjects.*
*All art 2007.*

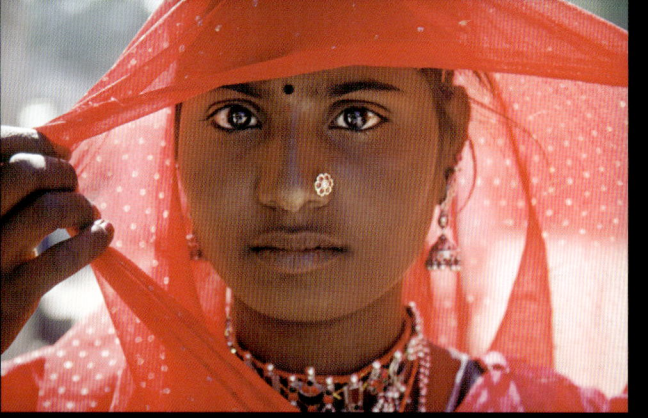

Girl in Town Market, *2003*

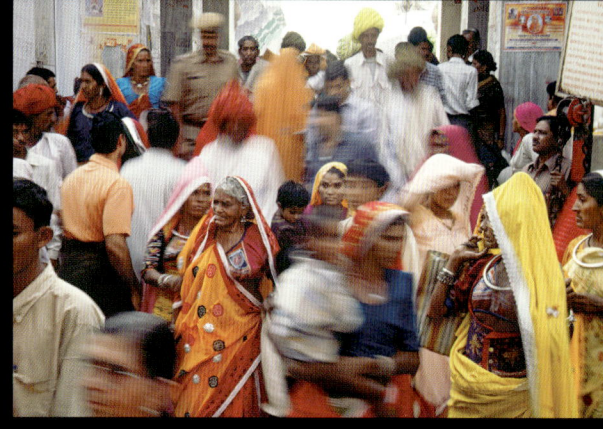

Gau Ghat, *2003*

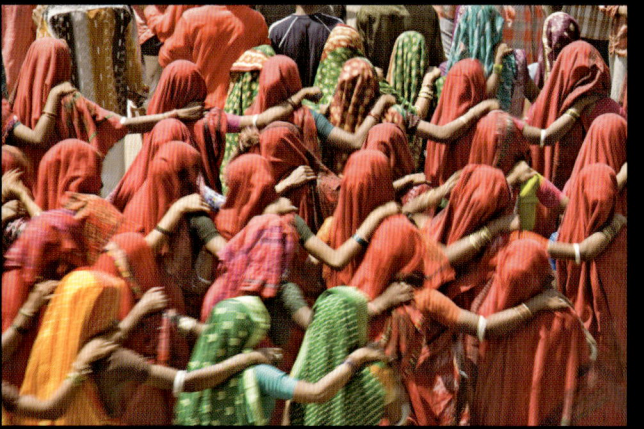

Kawant Gher Dancers

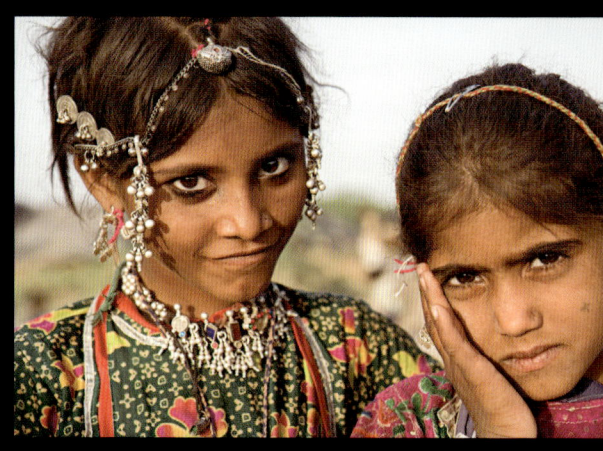

Sweet Faces

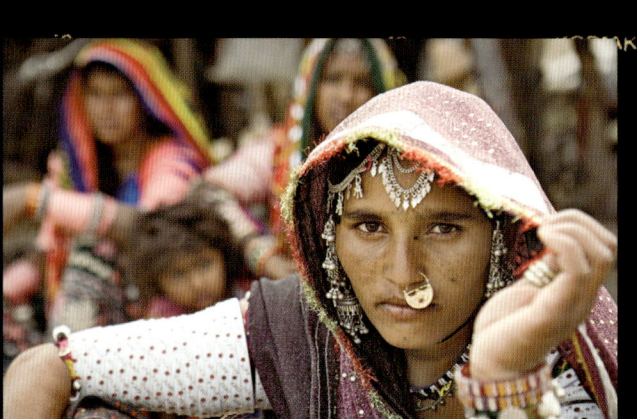

Dasada Mother

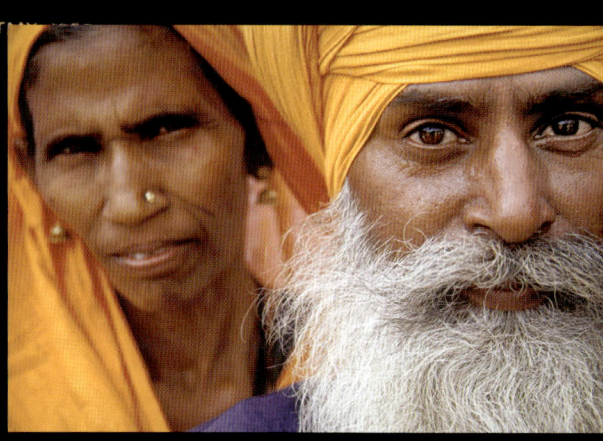

Sikh Couple, *2003*

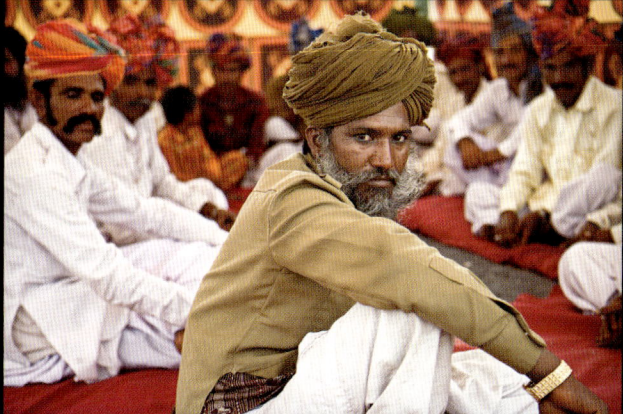
Dasada Banquet

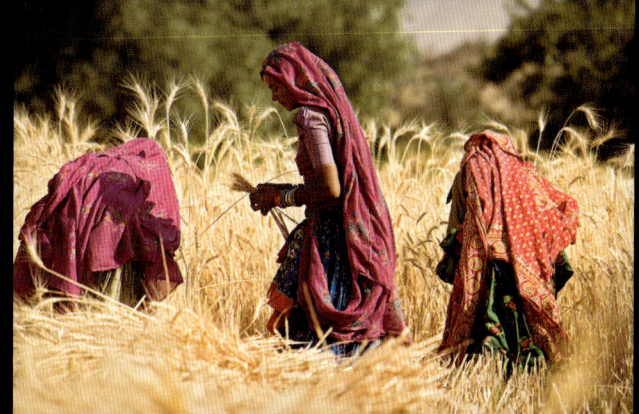
Wheat Harvesters

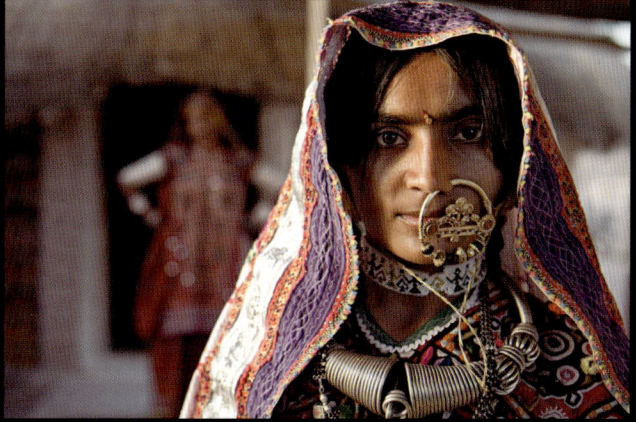
Harijan Beauty

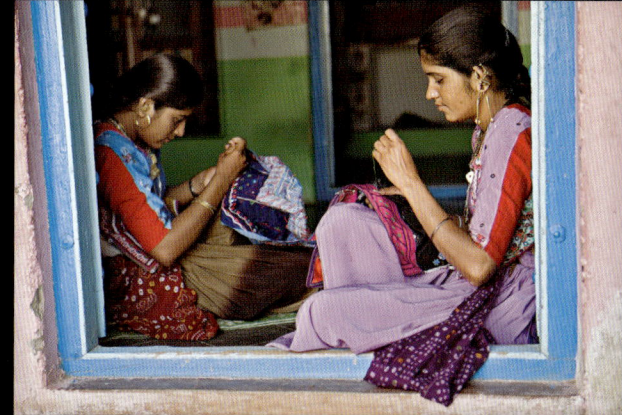
Embroidering

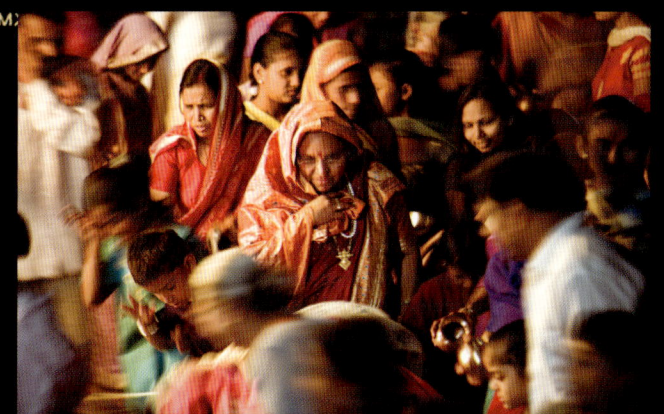
Holi Bonfire

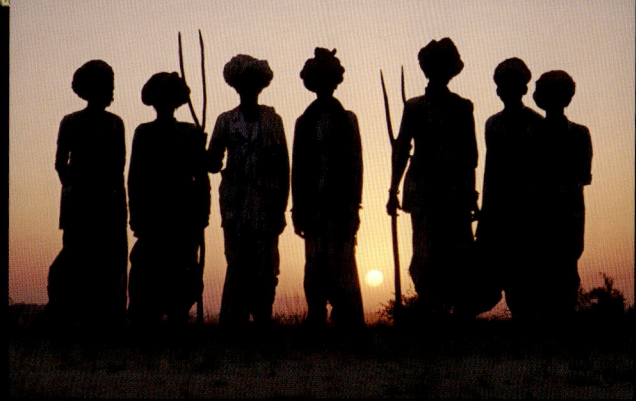
Nabi Sunset, *2003*

# Fredric Roberts
*Photographer*

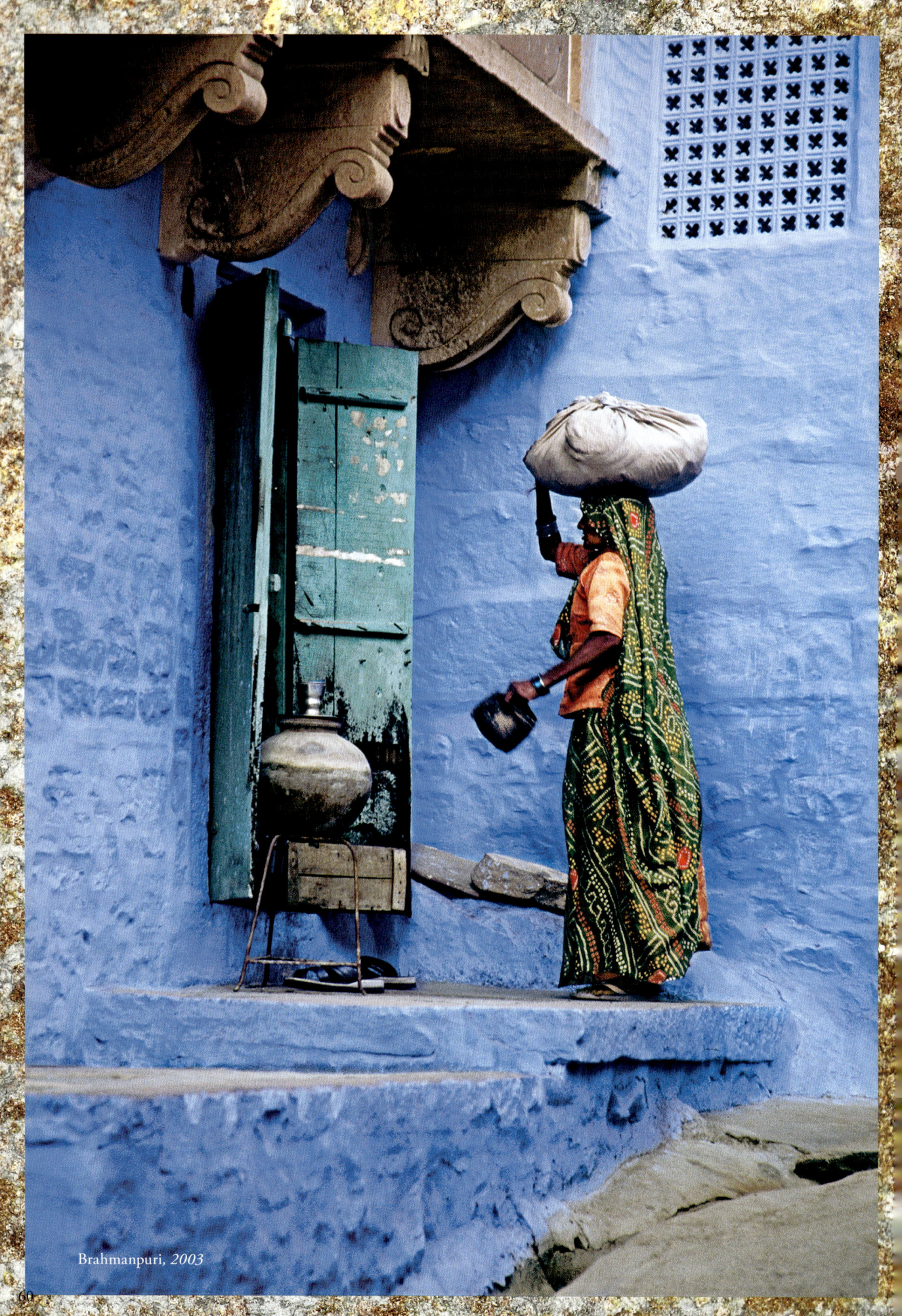
Brahmanpuri, *2003*

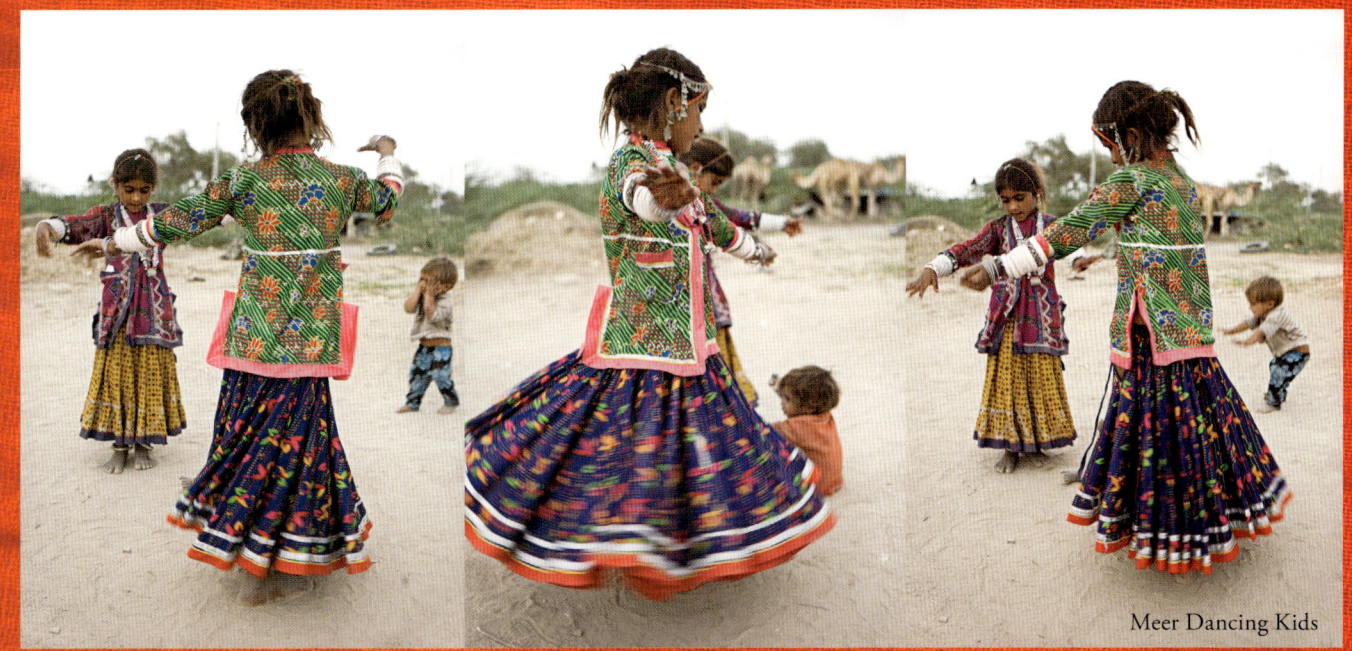
Meer Dancing Kids

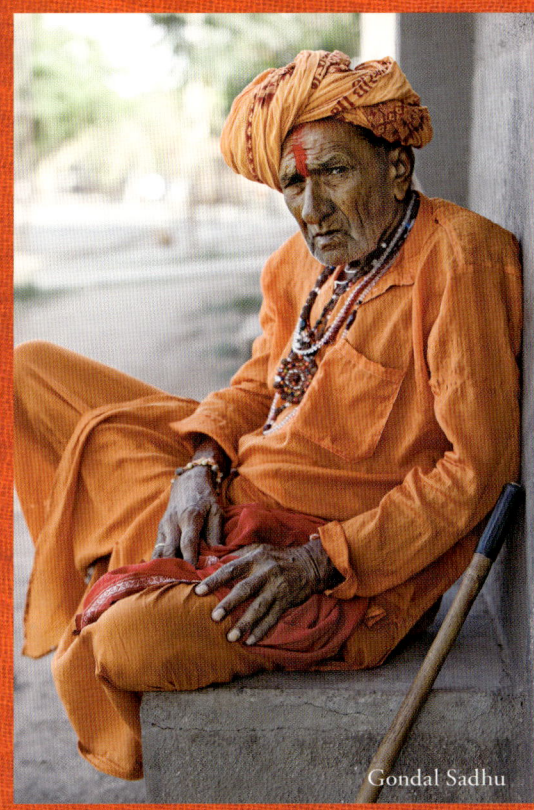
Gondal Sadhu

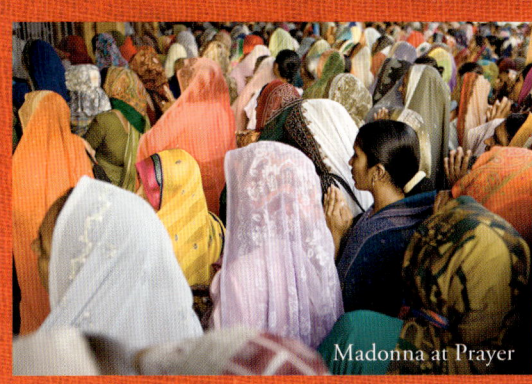
Madonna at Prayer

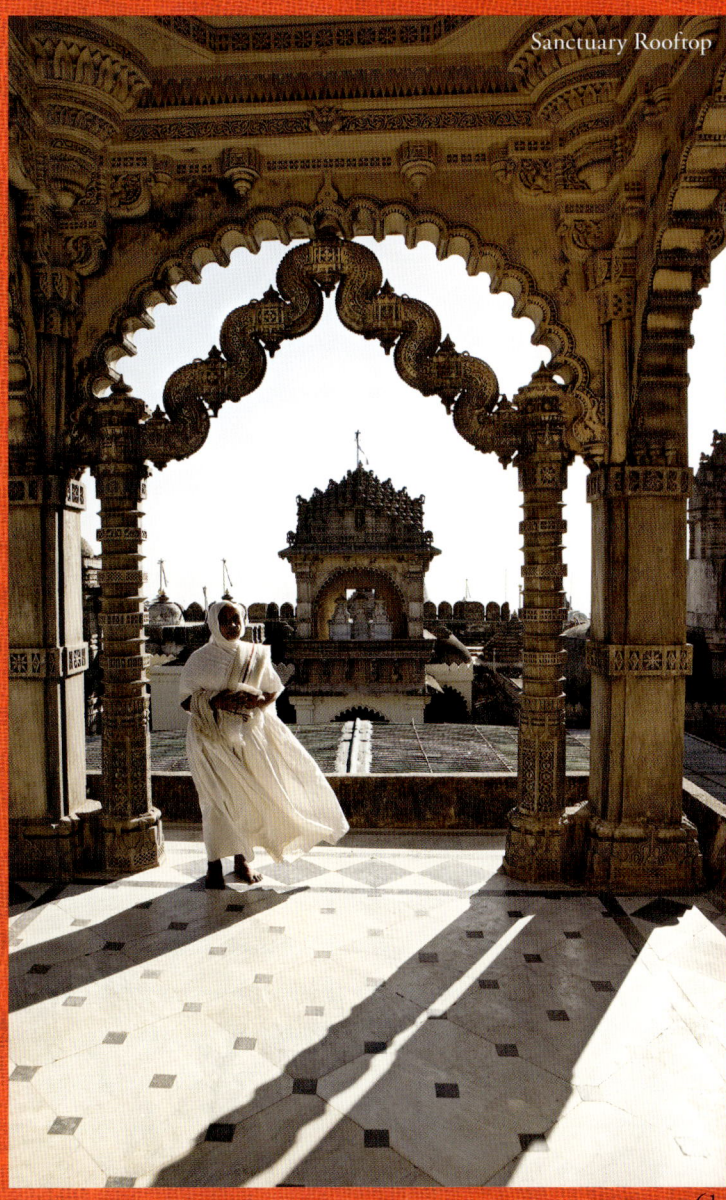
Sanctuary Rooftop

# Giambattista Valli
*Fashion Designer*

*"A veil, as the smoke of stunning incense or a raga that swaths you with the music of a sitar and the unexpected caress of a voice, which grazes your face like lint shaken by a lukewarm, light wind. A blow, a bird's song, a smell, a dream, a state of grace... like a glance hidden by a sudden magic spell capable of fulfilling yet-unexpressed desires."*

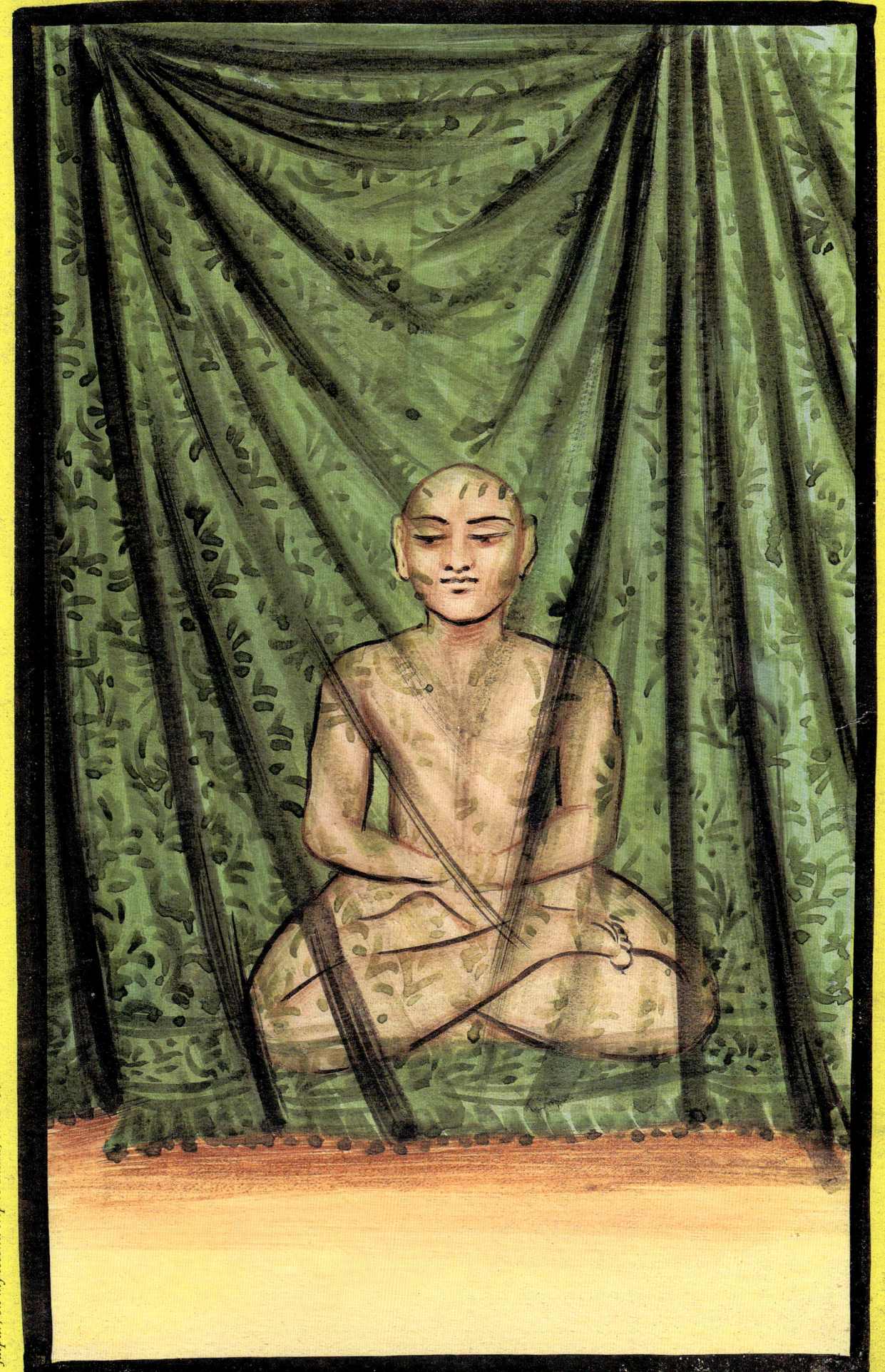

*Jaipur, on my second trip to India, circa 1991*

# Graham Nash

*Singer, Songwriter, and Photographer*

I have been lucky enough to travel around this planet many times, but I have never experienced a place quite so rich in religion and culture. The dichotomy between the rich and the poor, the shadows and the sparkling colors, the peace and the chaos, is thrilling to behold. I am all the richer in spirit because of my journey to India.

*Rajasthan, summer 2007*

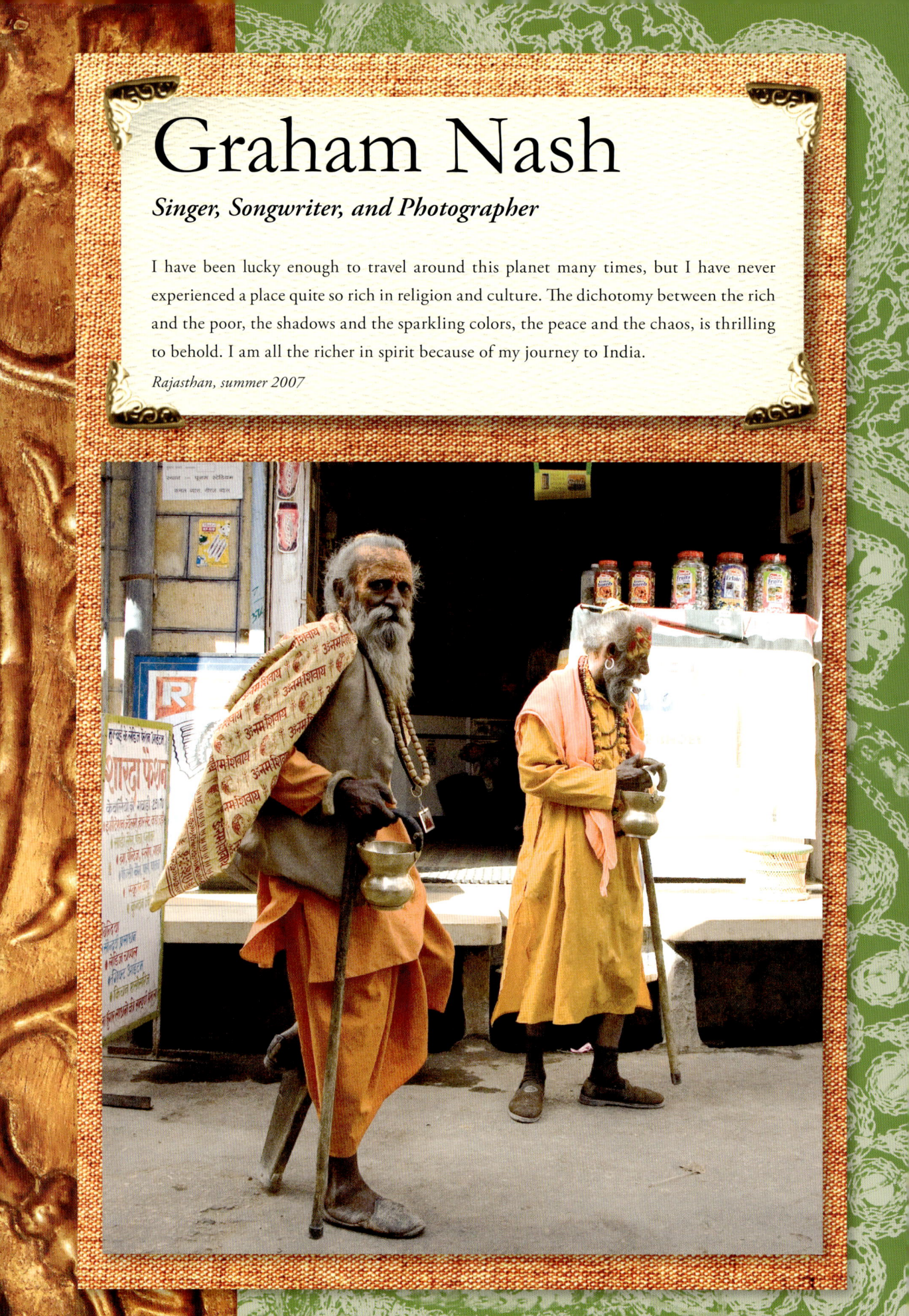

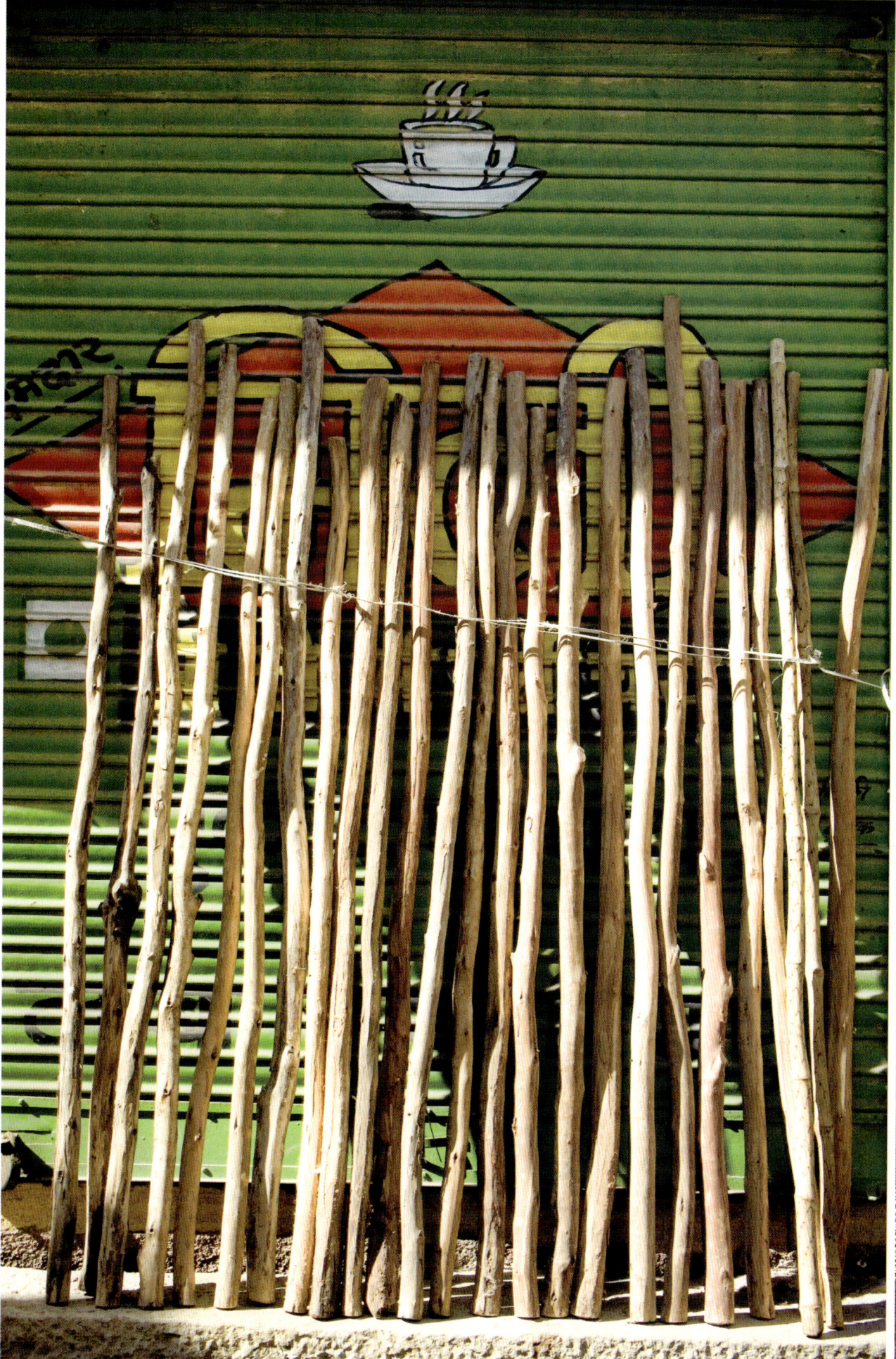

# Hemant Oberoi

*Executive Chef, Taj Hotels*

I am moved by the beauty of the Taj Mahal in Agra, and my heart beats for the Taj Mahal Palace & Tower. The Taj Mahal Palace & Tower is not a hotel but an institution, and my life revolves around it.

For the millions of Indians who make their way to Mumbai, this is the city where they realize their dreams: It is a tough place, but it has a heart, and it has proved it time and again. Its people take crisis in stride and just keep moving. The Taj Mahal Palace & Tower epitomizes the spirit and essence of this cosmopolitan city, a melting pot of cultures.

India is incredible and has to be experienced to be understood and appreciated. I am extremely proud to be an Indian.

*Twenty years as executive chef! A surprise party at the Taj Mahal Palace & Tower, August 2006.*

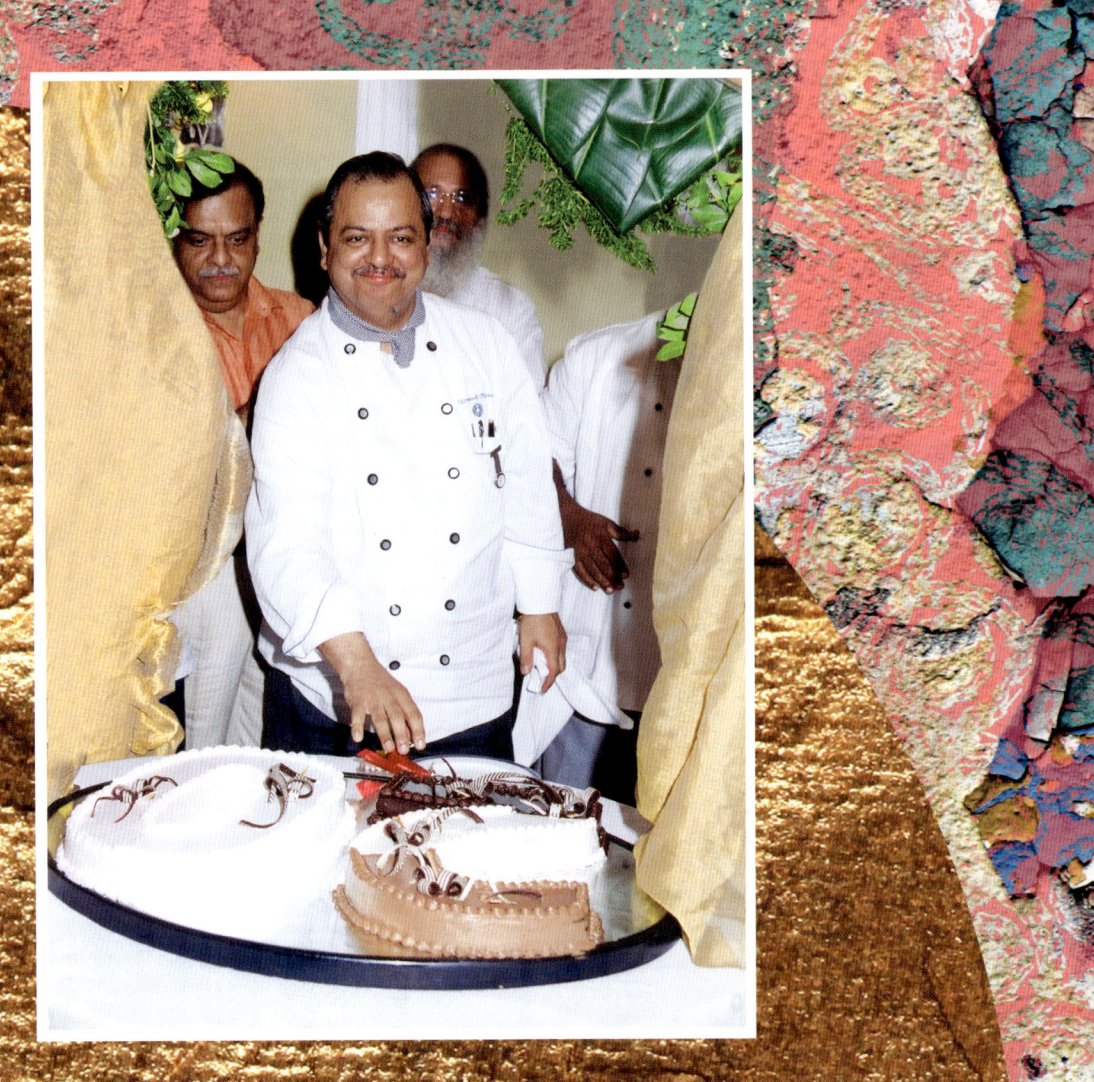

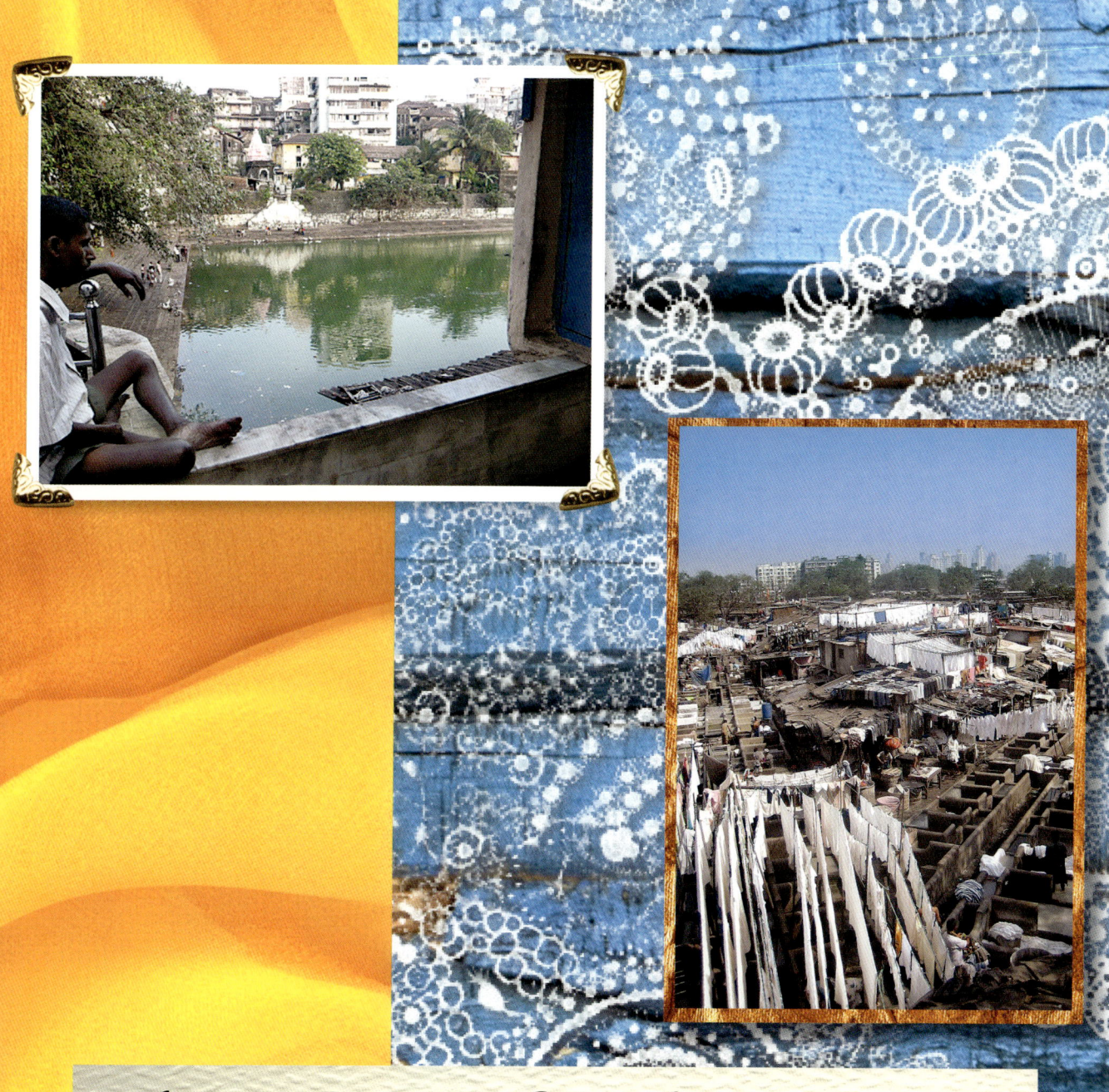

# Ilse Crawford
*Decorator and Director, Studioilse*

What inspires me about Mumbai are the practical and poetic systems that have been developed to attend to the needs of the teeming population. There are the incredible tiffin wallahs, who deliver hundreds of thousands of lunches daily without misplacing a single one; the laundry where, again, millions of pieces of laundry are washed in open-air pools and returned in perfect order to their owners; and the Banganga tank, built in 1127, which is beautiful, sociable, practical, and mystical. All are so far from the image usually portrayed of Mumbai, as a chaotic, conflicted city.

*Banganga tank (top) and Dhobi Ghat, Mumbai, November 2007*

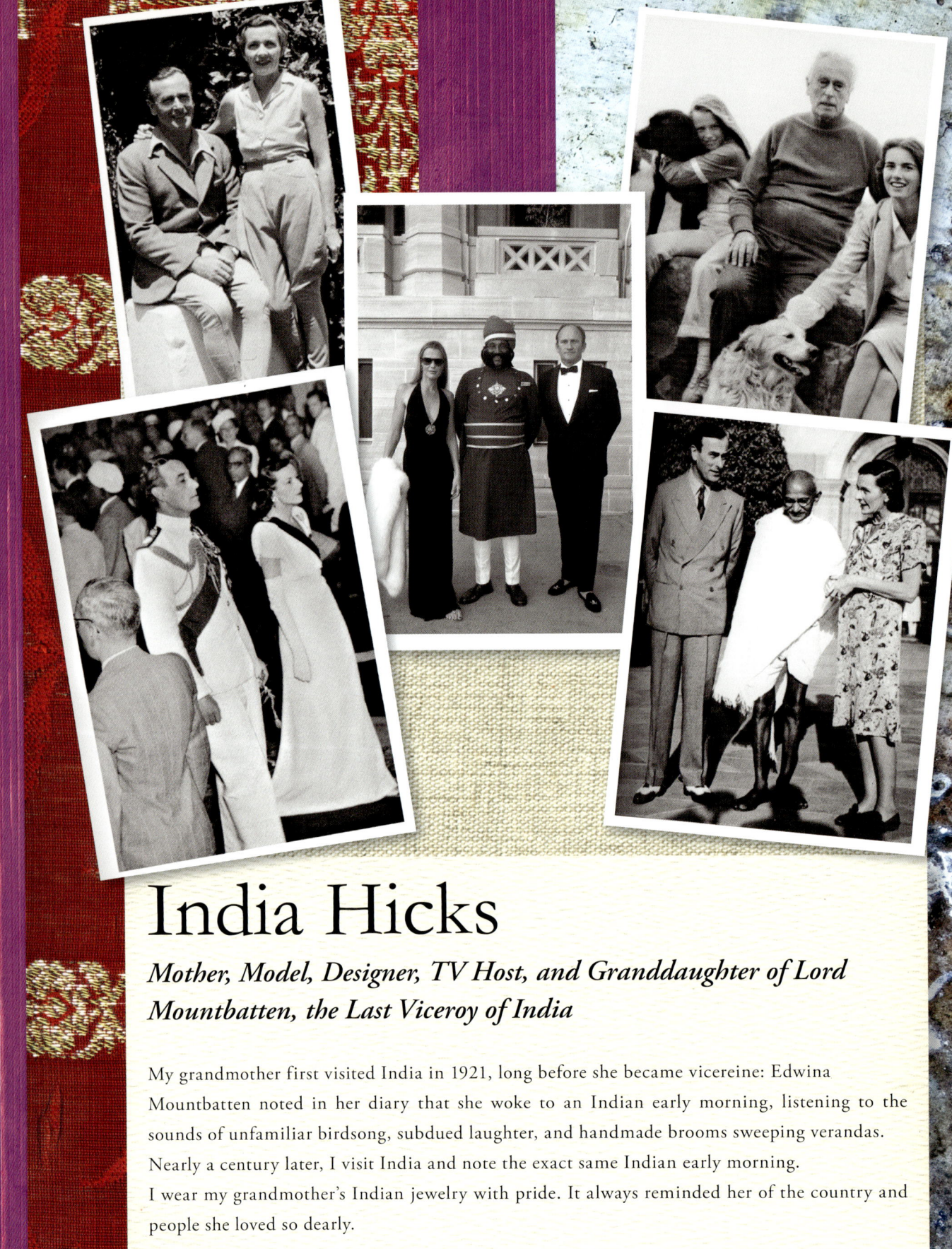

# India Hicks

*Mother, Model, Designer, TV Host, and Granddaughter of Lord Mountbatten, the Last Viceroy of India*

My grandmother first visited India in 1921, long before she became vicereine: Edwina Mountbatten noted in her diary that she woke to an Indian early morning, listening to the sounds of unfamiliar birdsong, subdued laughter, and handmade brooms sweeping verandas. Nearly a century later, I visit India and note the exact same Indian early morning. I wear my grandmother's Indian jewelry with pride. It always reminded her of the country and people she loved so dearly.

*Clockwise from top right: India (at left) with her grandfather, Louis Mountbatten, and a family friend; Gandhi's first visit to the Viceroy's; The Viceroy and Vicereine processing out of Durbar Hall after the swearing-in ceremony; Lord and Lady Mountbatten in a relaxed moment before going riding; India with David Flint Wood at Elizabeth Hurley and Arun Nayar's wedding, Jodhpur, 2007.*

# India Mahdavi

*Architect and Designer*

India and I have always had a special relationship: a very close mutual understanding and bond. I was conceived in India, hence my first name, and my Persian family name, Mahdavi, means "goddess" in Hindi. So I very well could have been an Indian goddess protected by amazing karma in another life.

Not long ago, a taxi driver in Mumbai decided otherwise. He was instructed to pick me up at my hotel with a sign reading "Miss India." After he had confirmed my identity, as we drove on to the Taj Mahal, he kept looking in the rearview mirror and asking me "Are you really Miss India?" Seeing the disappointment in his eyes, I finally understood that he was expecting to meet the real Miss India, the beauty queen, and not a casual-looking architect, who, by a twist of fate, just happened to be called India!

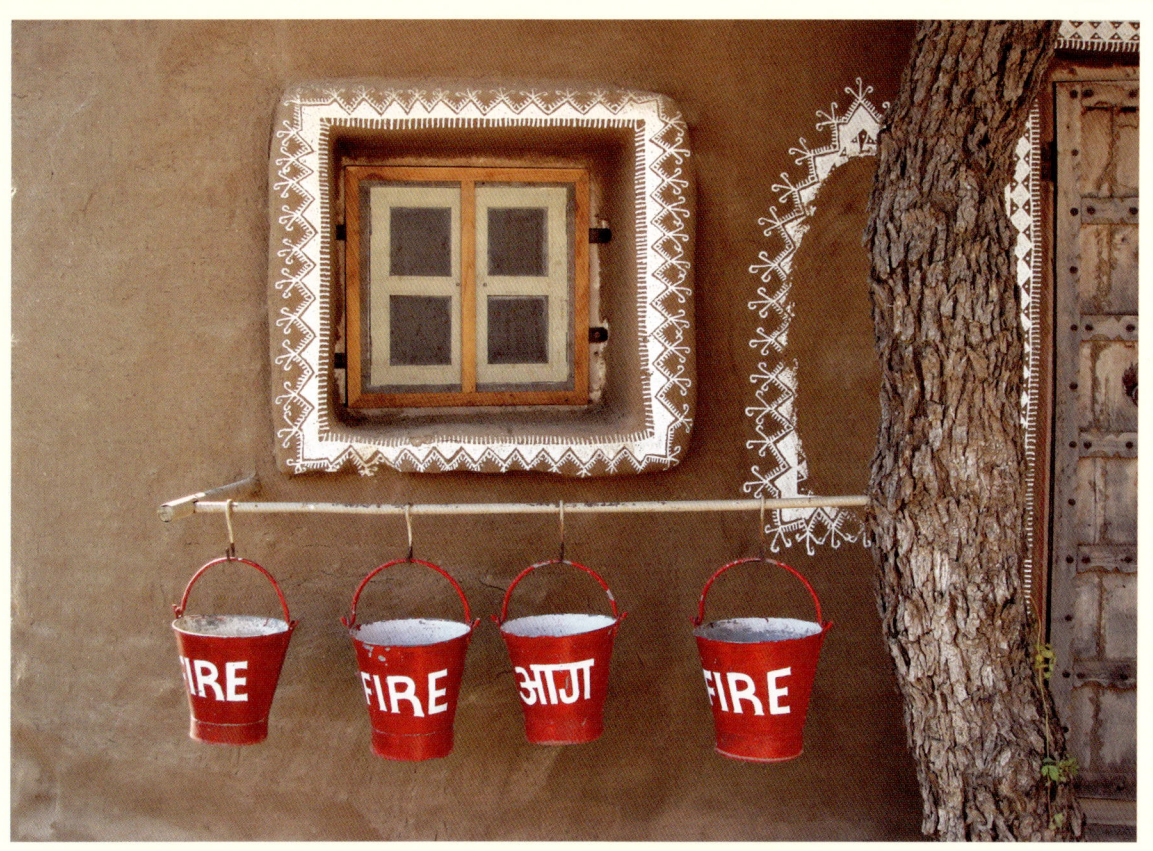

# Inez van Lamsweerde and Vinoodh Matadin

*Photographers*

The family in Deogarh, Rajasthan, who owned this tent couldn't believe we preferred to shoot Christy with it instead of in front of the ancient temple that stood right behind it. We traveled all around the area to take pictures for *Vogue Paris*, while the maharaja and his family spent the day watching us work from their rattan chairs, which they brought, along with tea and french fries for the crew.

*Christy Turlington in Rajasthan for* Vogue Paris, *2001*

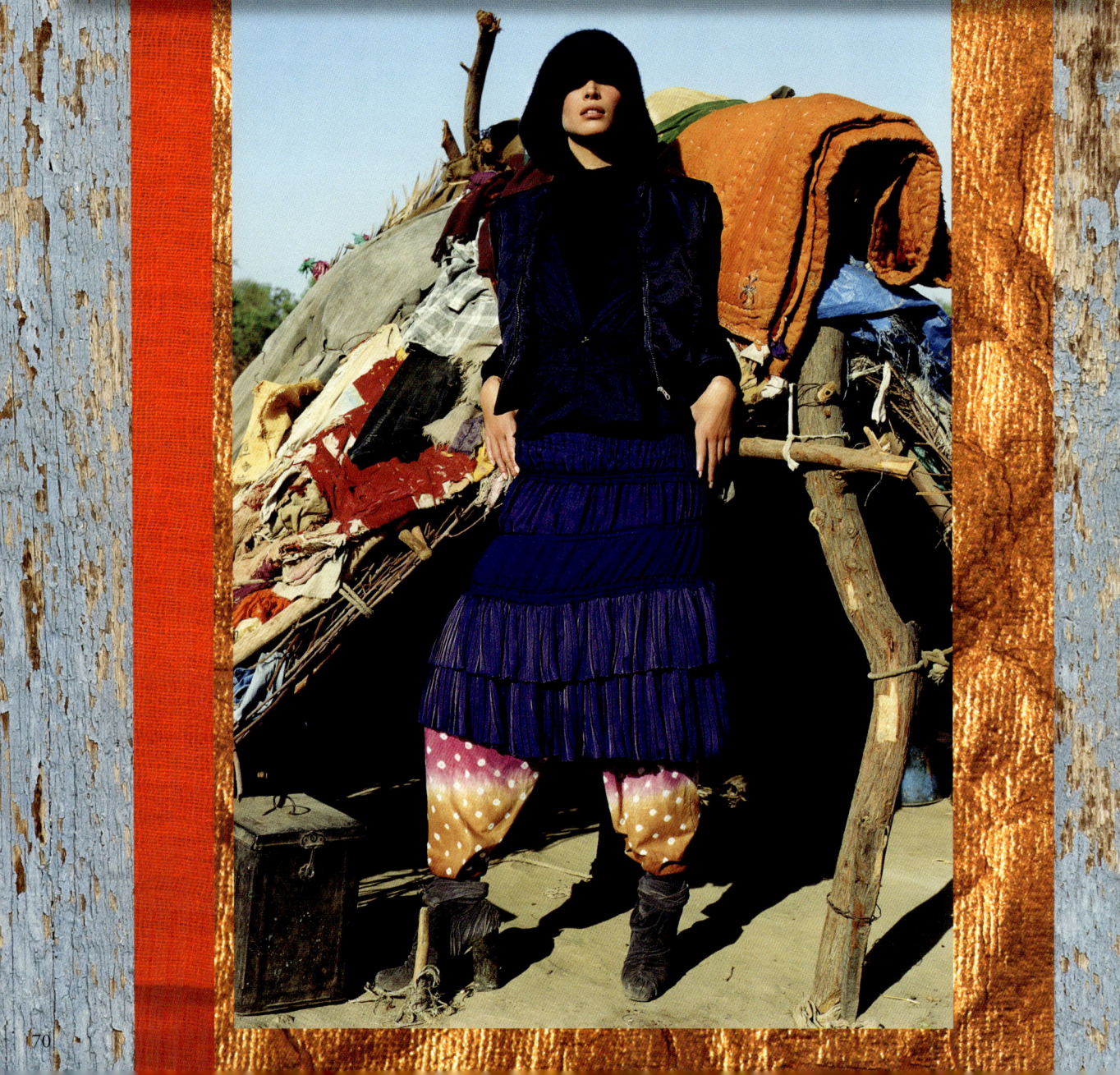

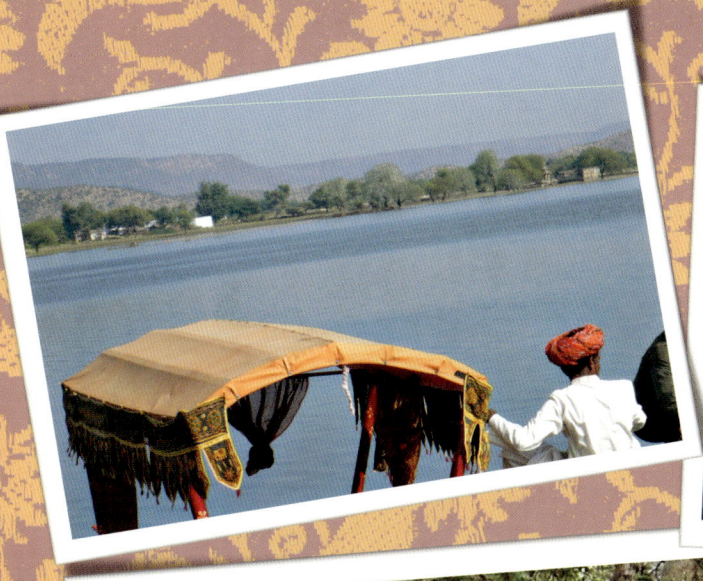
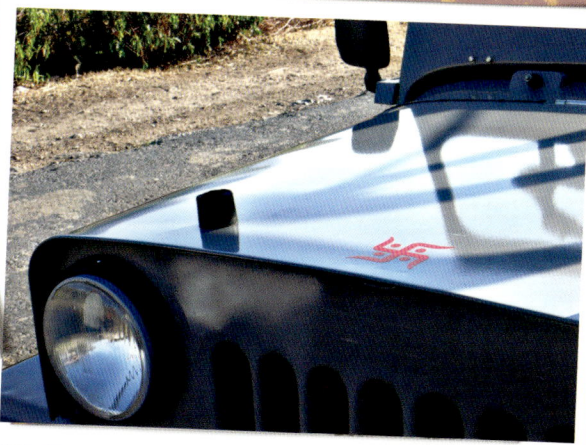
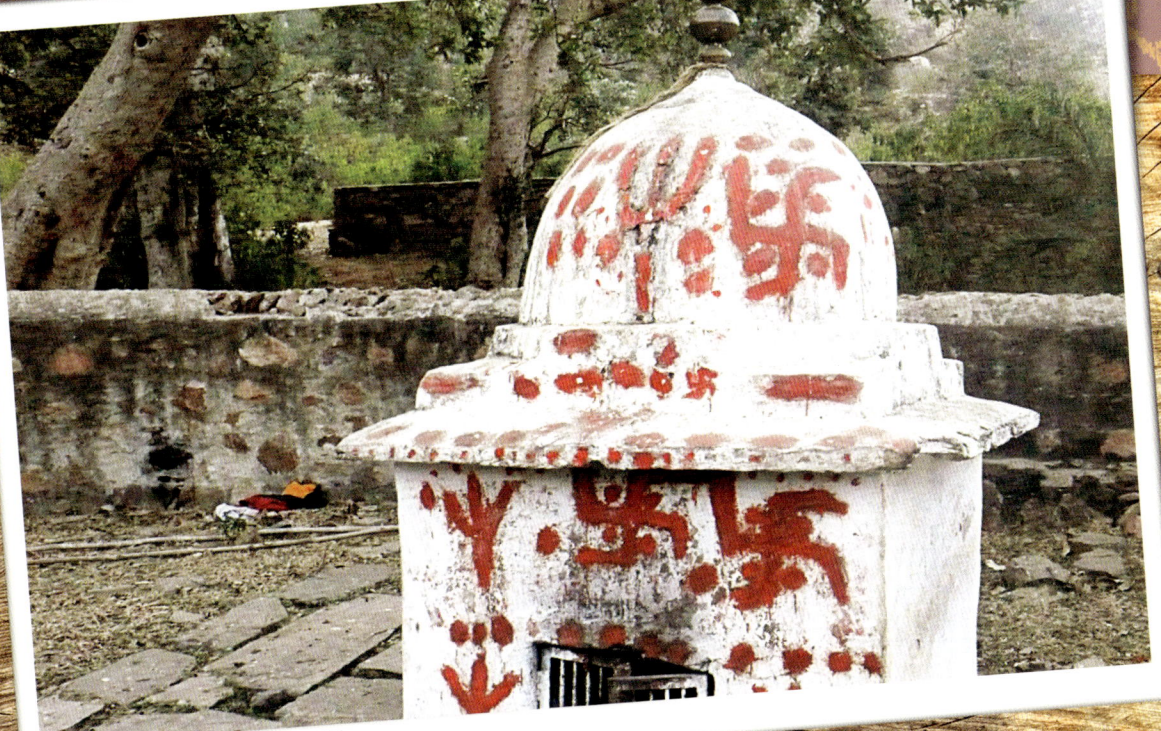

*All photographs Rajasthan, 1997*

# Jean Touitou

*Founder and Designer, A.P.C.*

I dream of driving a red, four-hundred-horsepower, six-cylinder SUV on the road from Delhi to Rajasthan. And you know, of driving just like them—I'm jealous of their crazy ways with vehicles. I want to be part of that game. Hell, it's always the driver who's having all the fun.

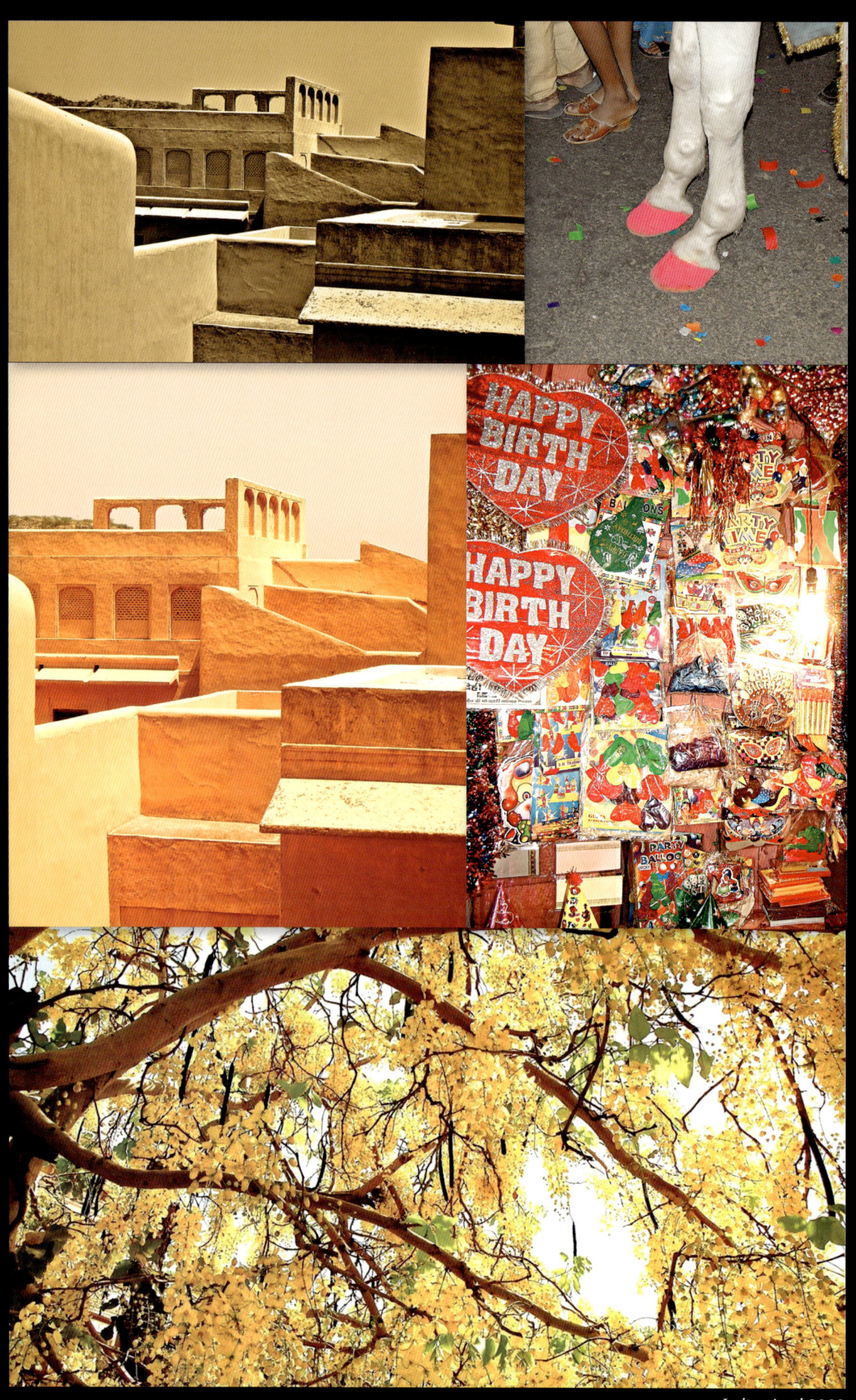

*India, April 2008*

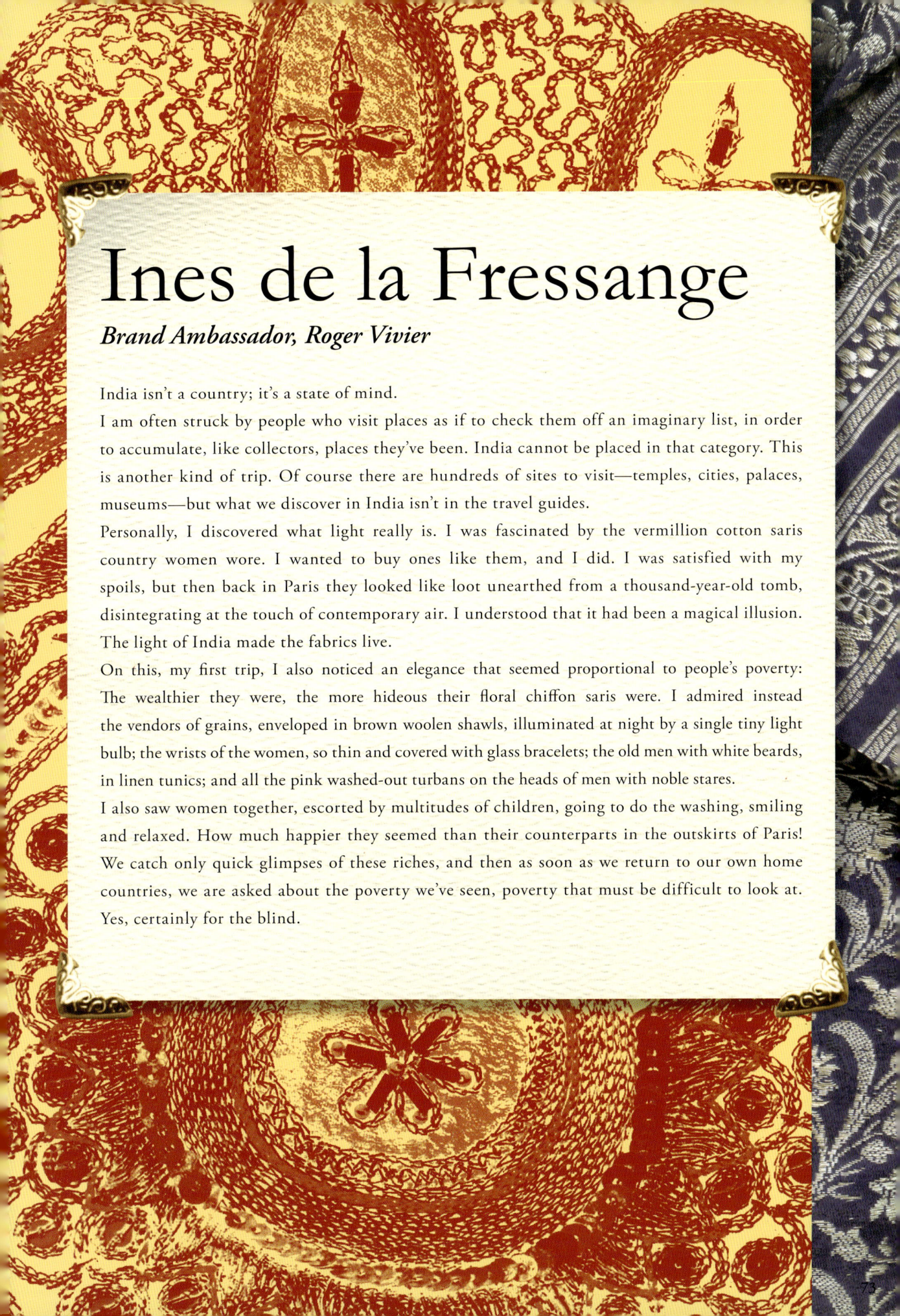

# Ines de la Fressange
*Brand Ambassador, Roger Vivier*

India isn't a country; it's a state of mind.

I am often struck by people who visit places as if to check them off an imaginary list, in order to accumulate, like collectors, places they've been. India cannot be placed in that category. This is another kind of trip. Of course there are hundreds of sites to visit—temples, cities, palaces, museums—but what we discover in India isn't in the travel guides.

Personally, I discovered what light really is. I was fascinated by the vermillion cotton saris country women wore. I wanted to buy ones like them, and I did. I was satisfied with my spoils, but then back in Paris they looked like loot unearthed from a thousand-year-old tomb, disintegrating at the touch of contemporary air. I understood that it had been a magical illusion. The light of India made the fabrics live.

On this, my first trip, I also noticed an elegance that seemed proportional to people's poverty: The wealthier they were, the more hideous their floral chiffon saris were. I admired instead the vendors of grains, enveloped in brown woolen shawls, illuminated at night by a single tiny light bulb; the wrists of the women, so thin and covered with glass bracelets; the old men with white beards, in linen tunics; and all the pink washed-out turbans on the heads of men with noble stares.

I also saw women together, escorted by multitudes of children, going to do the washing, smiling and relaxed. How much happier they seemed than their counterparts in the outskirts of Paris! We catch only quick glimpses of these riches, and then as soon as we return to our own home countries, we are asked about the poverty we've seen, poverty that must be difficult to look at. Yes, certainly for the blind.

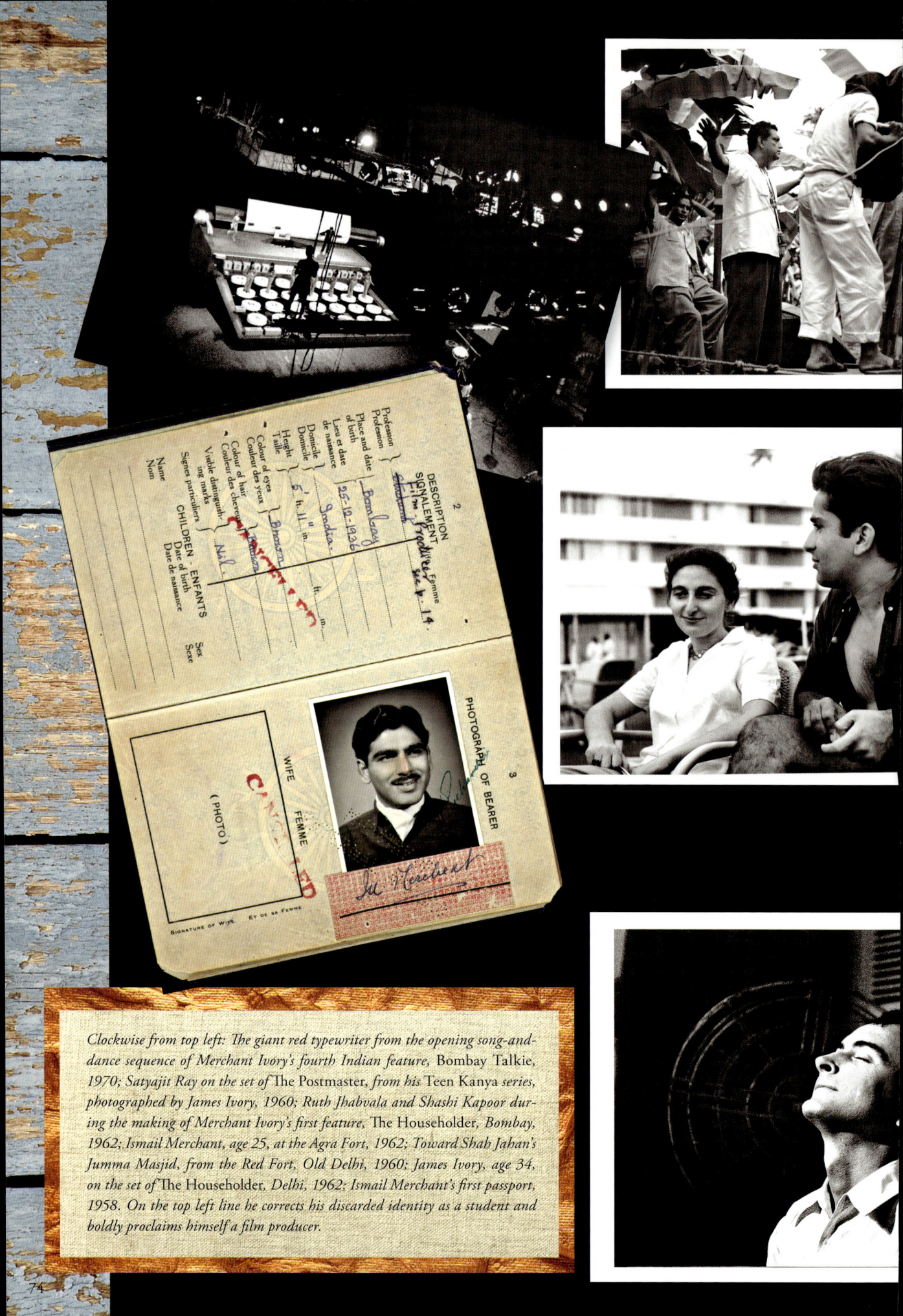

*Clockwise from top left: The giant red typewriter from the opening song-and-dance sequence of Merchant Ivory's fourth Indian feature,* Bombay Talkie, *1970; Satyajit Ray on the set of* The Postmaster, *from his* Teen Kanya *series, photographed by James Ivory, 1960; Ruth Jhabvala and Shashi Kapoor during the making of Merchant Ivory's first feature,* The Householder, *Bombay, 1962; Ismail Merchant, age 25, at the Agra Fort, 1962; Toward Shah Jahan's Jumma Masjid, from the Red Fort, Old Delhi, 1960; James Ivory, age 34, on the set of* The Householder, *Delhi, 1962; Ismail Merchant's first passport, 1958. On the top left line he corrects his discarded identity as a student and boldly proclaims himself a film producer.*

# James Ivory
## *Film Director*

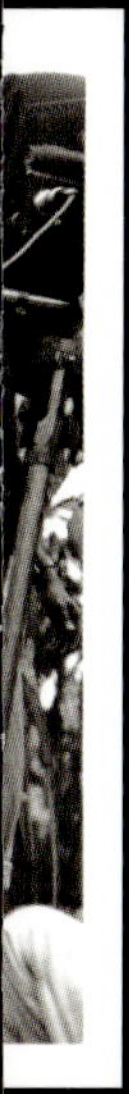

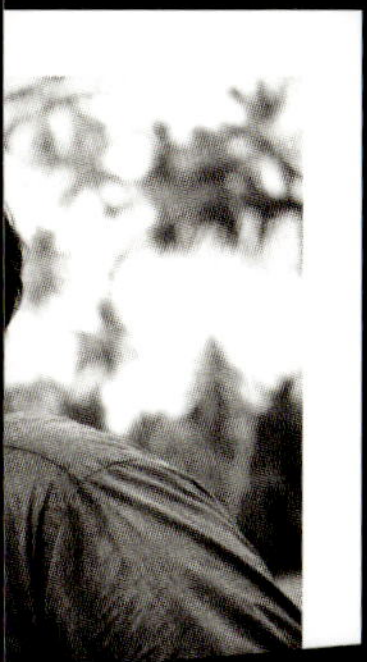

For me, at first, India was a never-ending feast of strange and beautiful new sights, tastes, and sounds, to which I was at once drawn—a place inhabited by people I was ready to love at first sight. I couldn't speak their languages and often they had trouble with mine, but that never mattered. When I went back to New York I remained passionately faithful to New Delhi, the only city I knew well in India, and I made a film about it. Or rather, about the two Delhis, New and Old.

Then I met Ismail Merchant; and soon after Ruth Jhabvala and her husband, Cyrus; and then our first star, Shashi Kapoor. Their combined strengths formed the resilient superstructure of my life to come. They were joined by Satyajit Ray, who already was my filmmaking mentor, or guru. Every Indian artist finds a mentor, and by this time I thought of myself as Indian. I had been born again, into another life. It was these five people, over the many decades of our friendship, who turned me into that man called James Ivory.

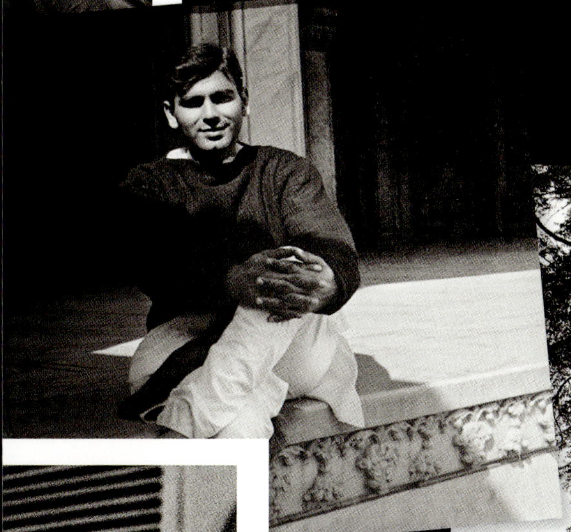

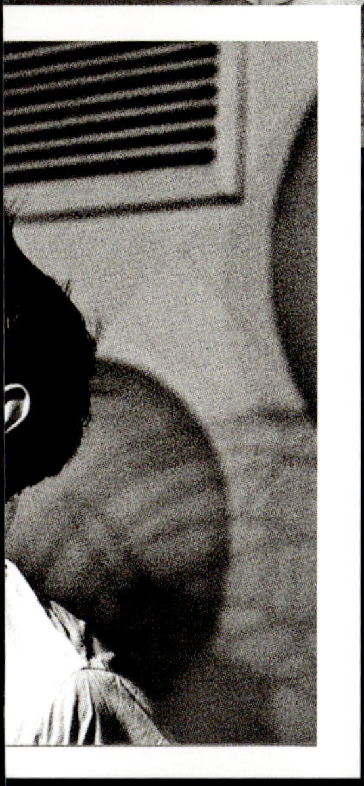

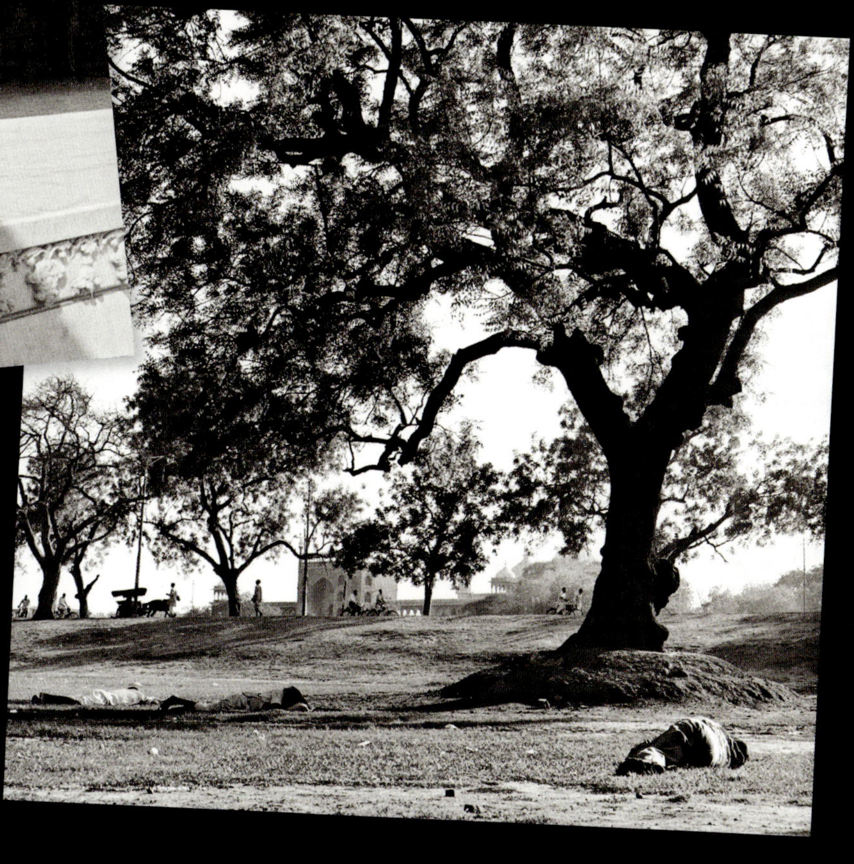

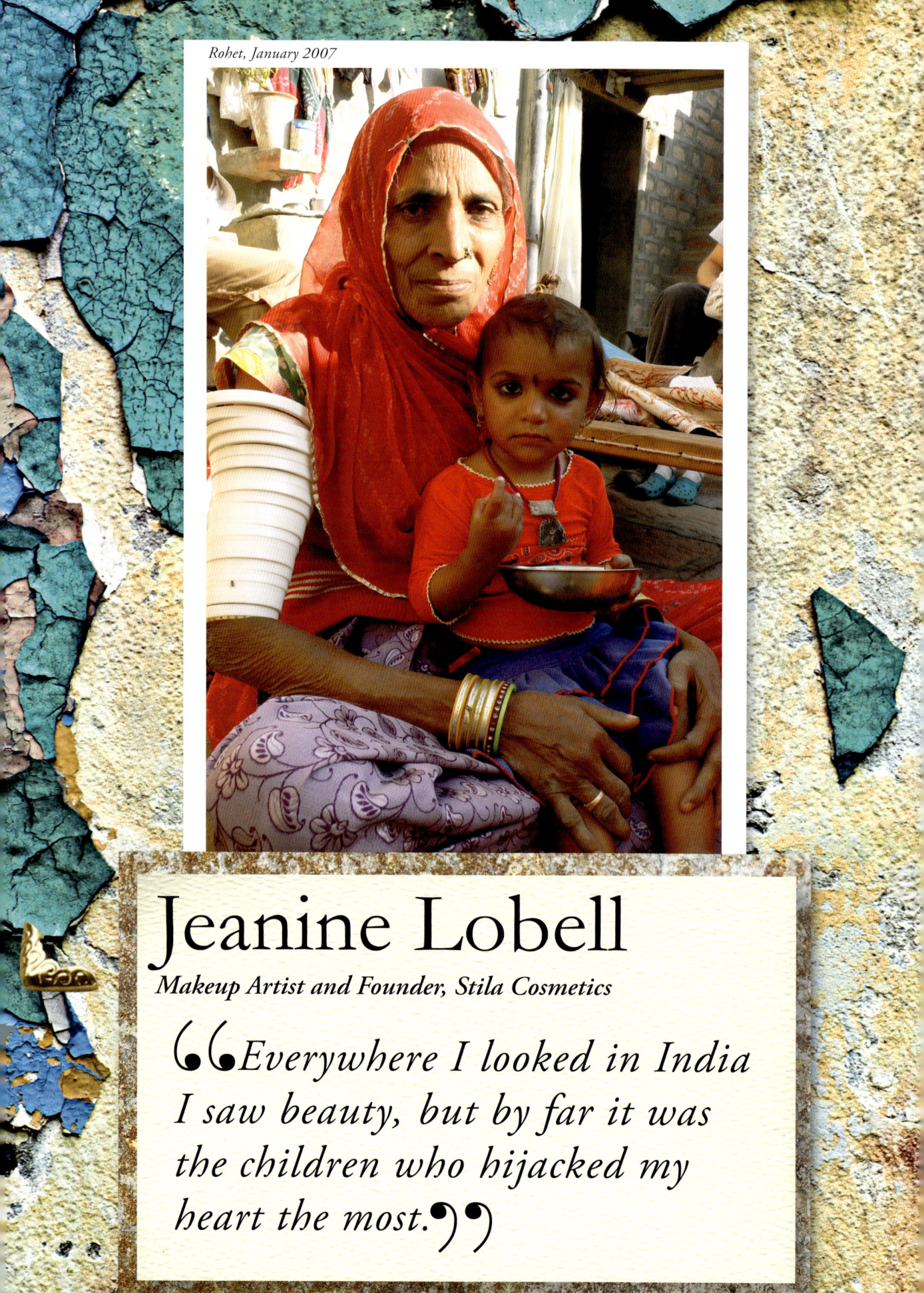

*Rohet, January 2007*

# Jeanine Lobell
*Makeup Artist and Founder, Stila Cosmetics*

❝*Everywhere I looked in India I saw beauty, but by far it was the children who hijacked my heart the most.*❞

# Jeffry Aronsson
*Founder, the Aronsson Group, LLC*

I love India as an oasis of diversity that excites the senses in a world otherwise overtaken by blandness and homogeneity. I love its unique mosaic of rich colors, aromas, tastes, textures, and humanity, and the juxtaposition of ancient with modern. I love how it inspires my quest for adventure while awakening my senses.

I will never forget the time I was driven to a meeting by a man named Rattan Lal. Rattan drove straight into what appeared to be an impenetrable mass of fast-moving traffic, circling simultaneously in opposite directions. It seemed like a miracle that we got in, got through, and arrived unscathed at our destination. I asked him in complete disbelief: "How, Rattan, did you do that? You are amazing!" His response: "In India, all you need is a good horn, a good brake, and good luck." Thinking back, in the context of Mumbai today, I cannot help but see the wisdom in such a simple response: This book is evidence that Mumbai has more than a good horn. India's measured response is a testament to a good brake. And the package is complete with an incredible people as its good luck. As Mumbai progresses, it will become even stronger.

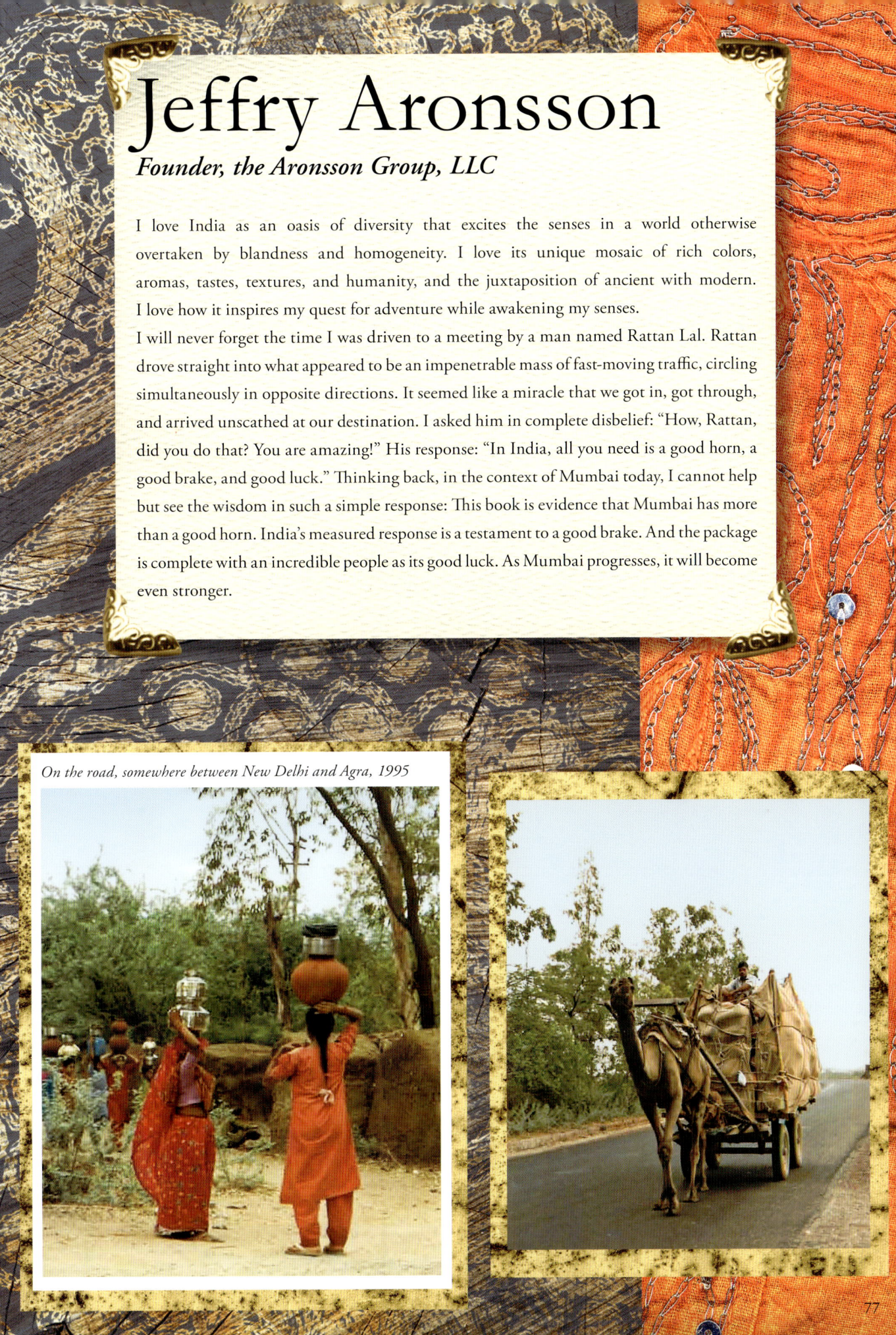

*On the road, somewhere between New Delhi and Agra, 1995*

# Jean François Lesage
*Embroiderer, Designer*

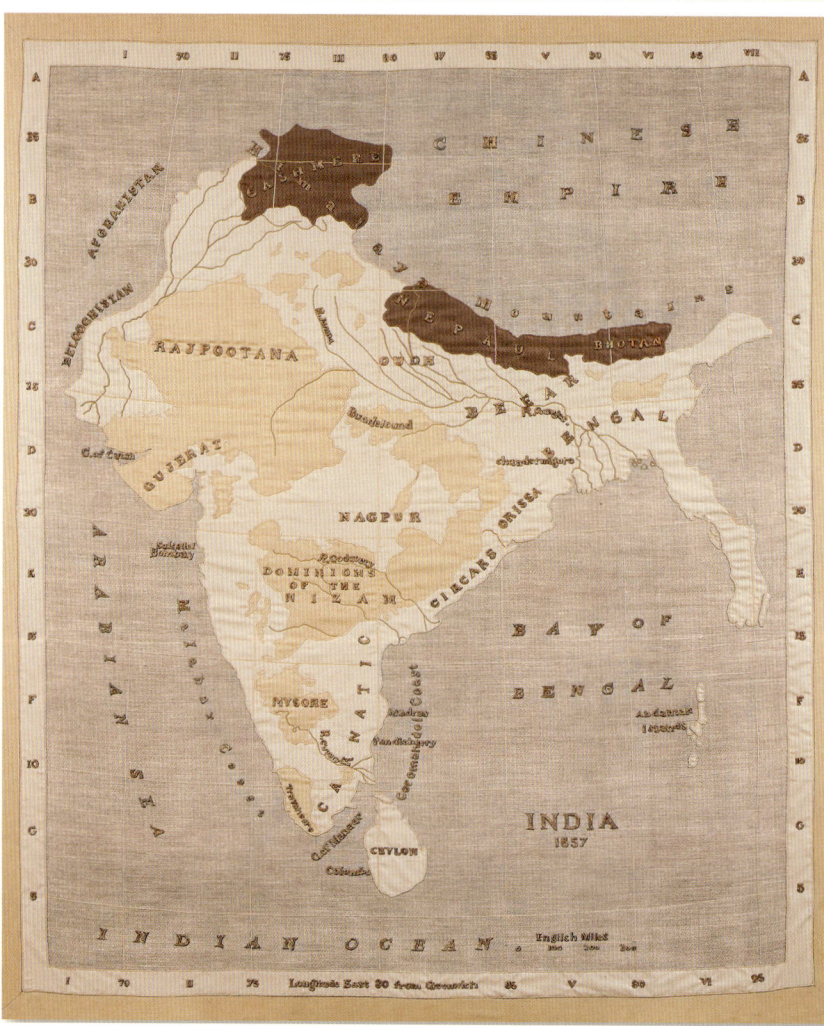

*This piece was made in Madras in 2009 for the opening of the shop at 7bis rue des Saints Pères, sixth arrondisement, Paris. The embroidery required more than five hundred hours of work.*

For me, India is the most special place in the world to be, to exist, and to feel alive. It is where the most ancient lives alongside a way of life reinvented every day. In India, I have my feet on the ground and my head in the sky—a place where fifty percent of the population is younger than twenty-five, a place where the same word is used to say yesterday and tomorrow, a place where God is alive and amazingly human, a place where embroiderers practice their art like yoga asanas. India has been the chance of my life.

# Mark Friedberg
*Production Designer*

India still runs on human power. In today's digital world this is considered backward, but for me it was a revelation. I am a designer, so I fancy myself close to the essence of inanimate objects. I never realized how programmed my world was, how horribly, perfectly, dehumanizingly same.

There is a little bit of art in everything Indian. Every glass, every sign, all slightly off but all brought to being by someone's hands. It means that a collection of same things becomes a society, not an army.

For the sets of *The Darjeeling Limited* we needed huge quantities of same things, but since they were all made by hand, everything was individual, no two actually the same. When we couldn't find something, we simply made it: door hinges, stencils, moldings were all made by our crew with their hands. We were never stopped because a store had closed or run out of something. We had hands, and that was all we needed.

There are histories of the work of generations in those hands, masters teaching the next— all individuals, all with personalities. Such a treat to see all the things dancing together, being themselves.

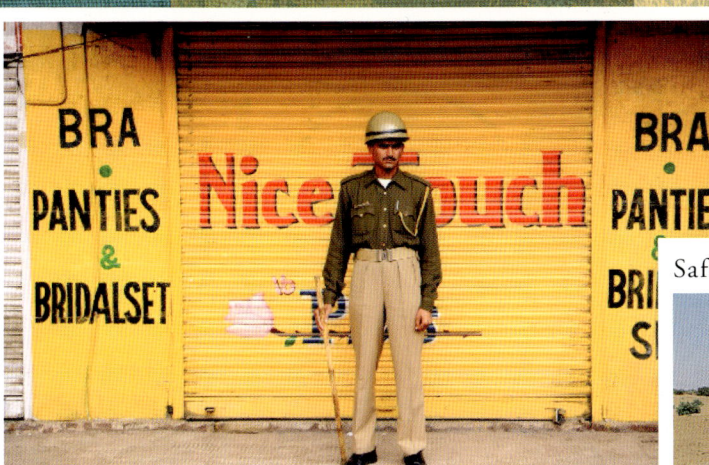

Nice Touch, *Jodhpur, October 2007*

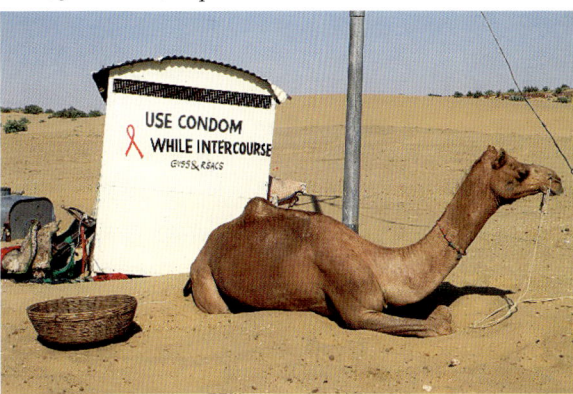

Safe, *Jaisalmer, September 2007*

# Karan Johar
*Film Producer and Director*

What fascinates me most about Mumbai is its paradoxes: No other city I know accords more or less the same respect to ambition and drive as it does to lack of direction and bohemia. No other place provides equal platforms for the jingoistic cries of religious zealots and the moderate voices of secularism. No other corner of the world turns a blind eye to blatant gender inequality even as it provides a diverse playground for expressions of sexuality. No other part of the globe, as far as I've seen, has the ability to absorb communal clashes, violent upheavals, and climatic extremities with the same panache with which it celebrates infrastructural development, economic progress, and religious differences. Scores of such examples form the kaleidoscope of contradictions that represents my city, but what really shines through this prism is the city's greatest virtue: acceptance. Acceptance courses incessantly through every nook and corner of the city, eventually seeping into the veins of its inhabitants to turn them into true-blue "Bombayites."

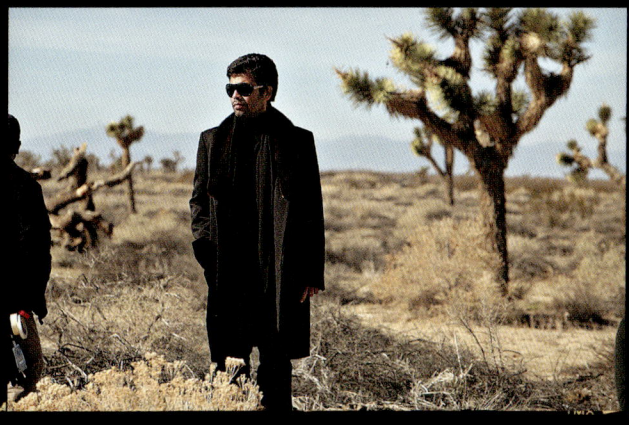
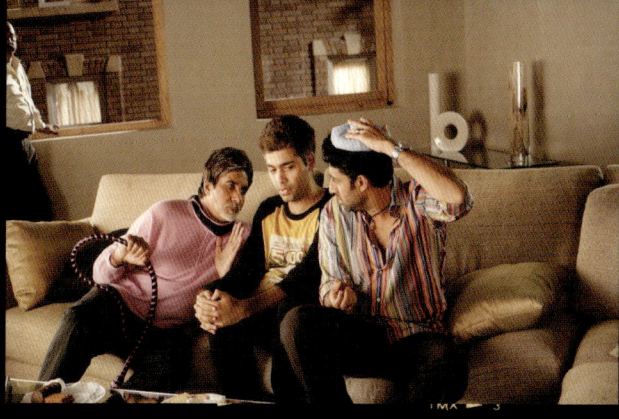
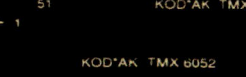
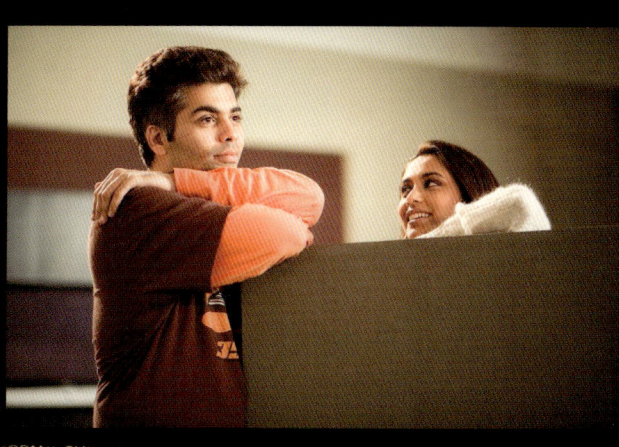
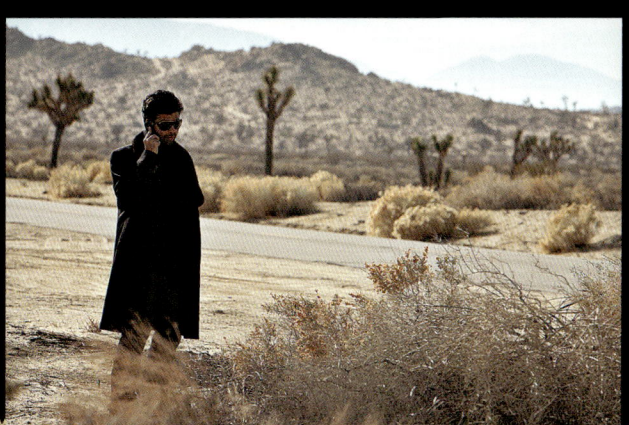
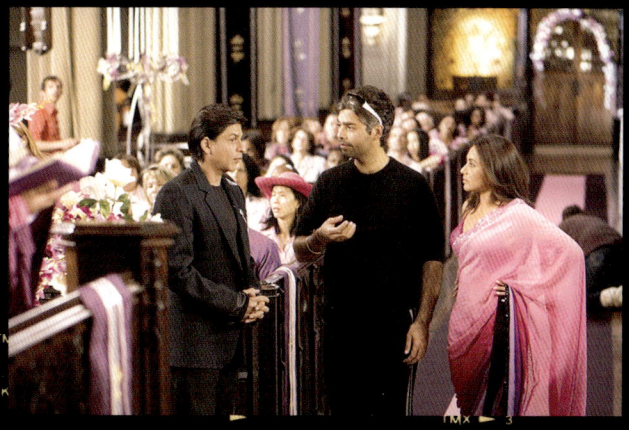

*Clockwise from top right: Amitabh Bachchan, Karan Johar, and Abhishek Bachchan; Karan Johar with Rani Mukherjee; and Shah Rukh Khan, Jaran Johar, and Rani Mukherjee, all photographed on the set of* Kabhi Alvida Naa Kehna, *2006; Karan Johar on the set of* My Name is Khan, *in production; Karan Johar on the set of* Kabhi Khushi Kabhie Gham, *2001; and Karan Johar on the set of* My Name is Khan.

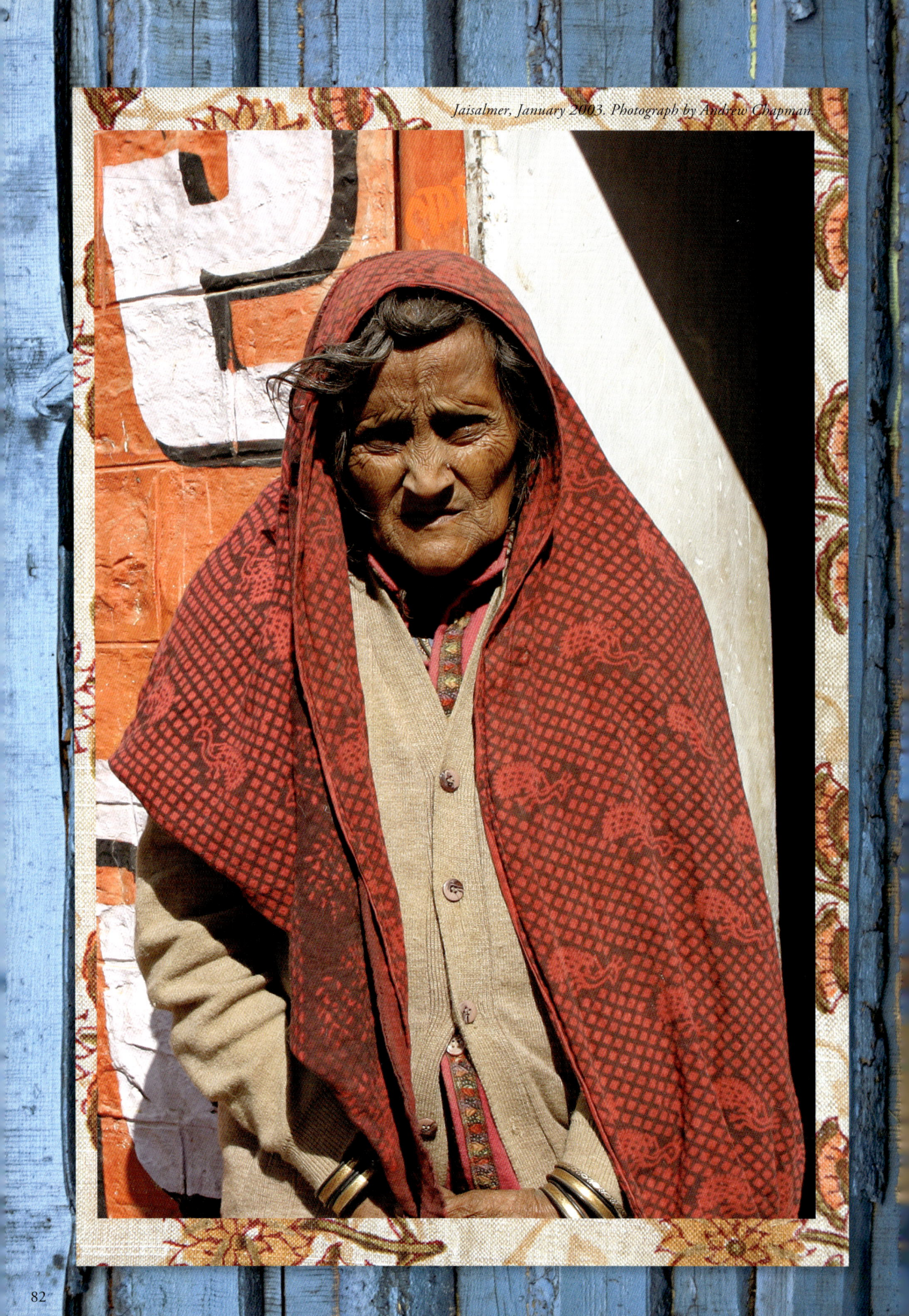
*Jaisalmer, January 2003. Photograph by Andrew Chapman.*

# Kenneth Cole
*Footwear and Fashion Designer*

*"As the most populous democracy in the world, India is immensely diverse in religion, government, people, and culture. As the world's fourth-largest purchasing power, India stands as one of our fastest-growing economies. It has quickly become a refreshing and inspiring fashion frontier, one that has influenced other nations and is not opposed to being influenced itself. However, it still suffers from high levels of poverty, illiteracy, and malnutrition.*

*To the extent that I can aid in providing new wardrobe alternatives for the fashionable, inspired citizens of India, I look forward to being afforded the privilege of contributing socially as well as culturally, if and when the opportunity presents itself.*

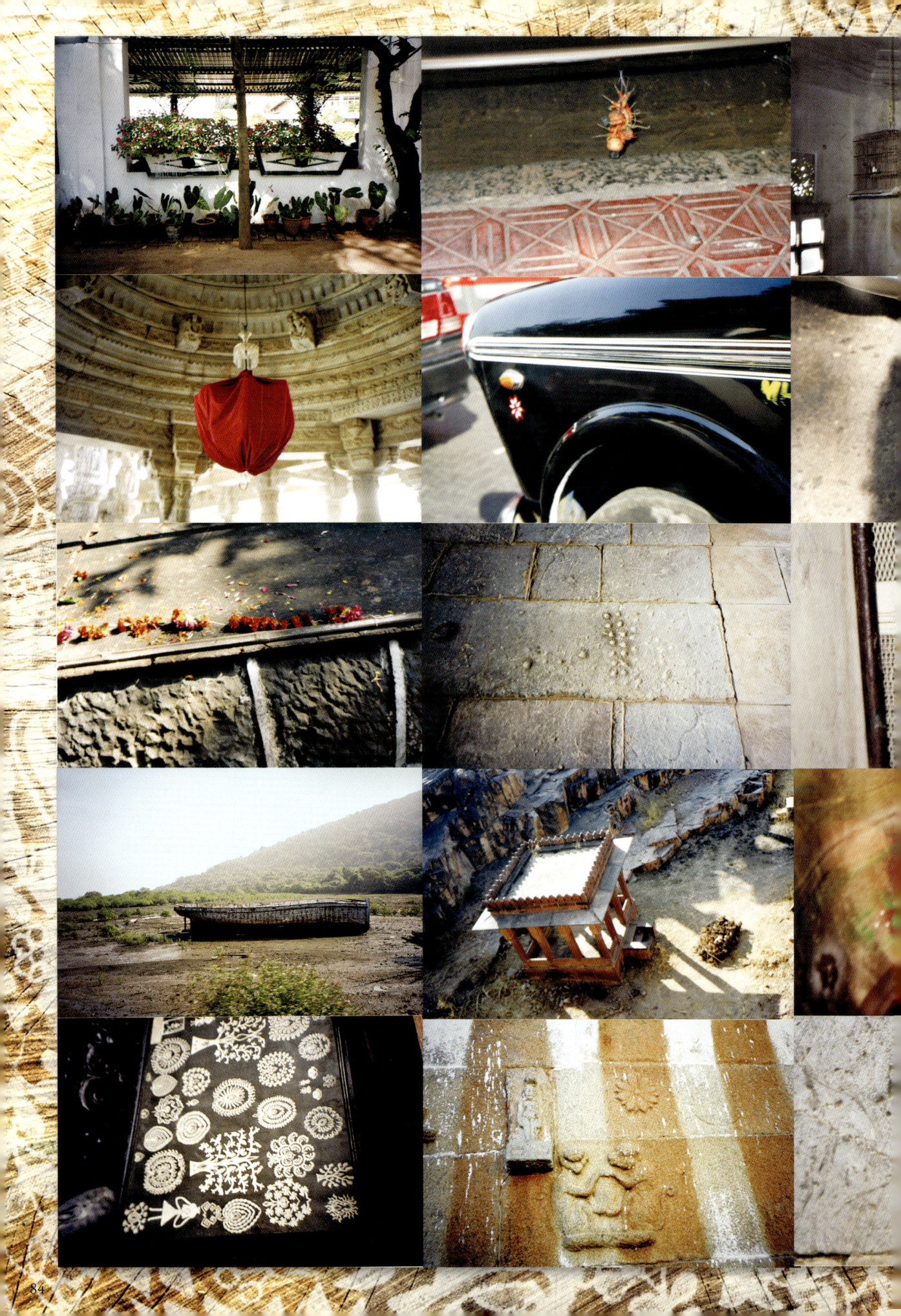

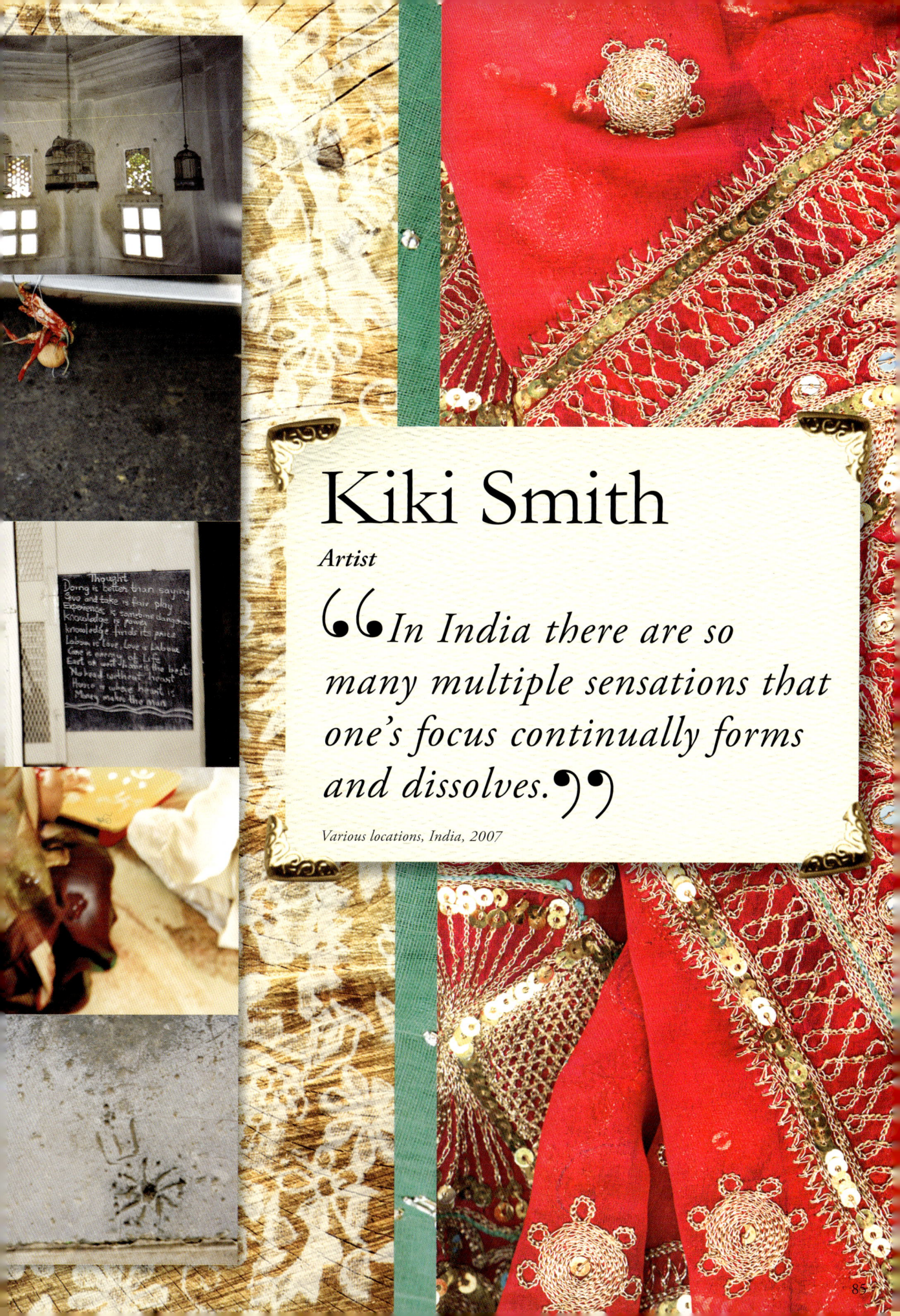

# Kiki Smith

*Artist*

"*In India there are so many multiple sensations that one's focus continually forms and dissolves.*"

*Various locations, India, 2007*

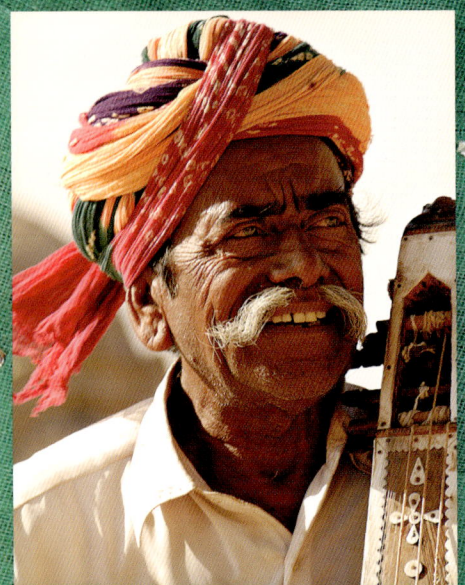
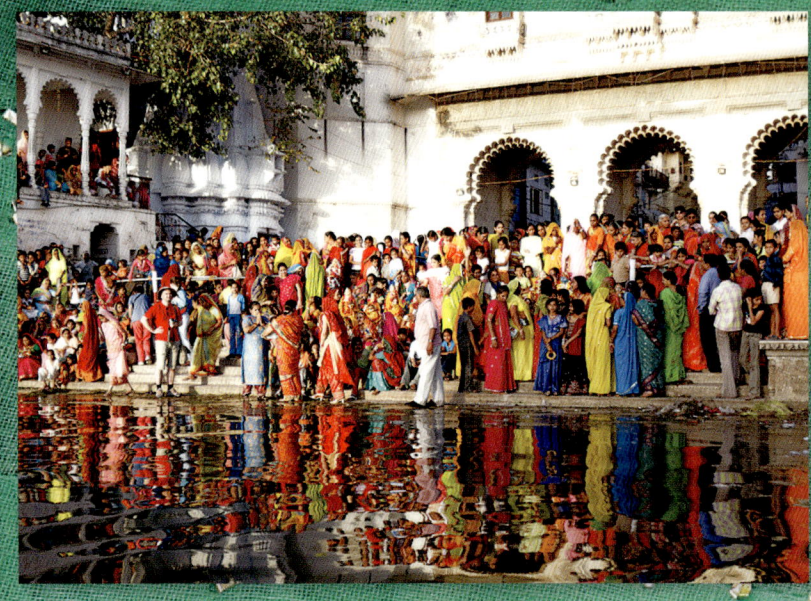
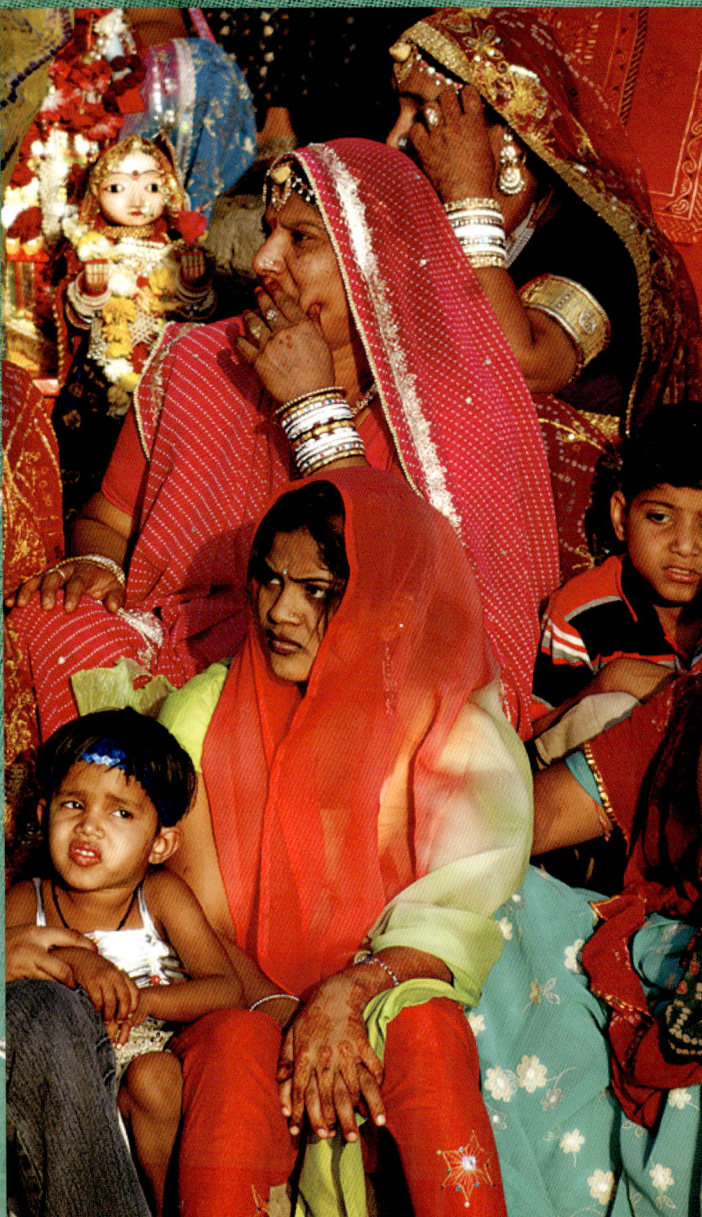
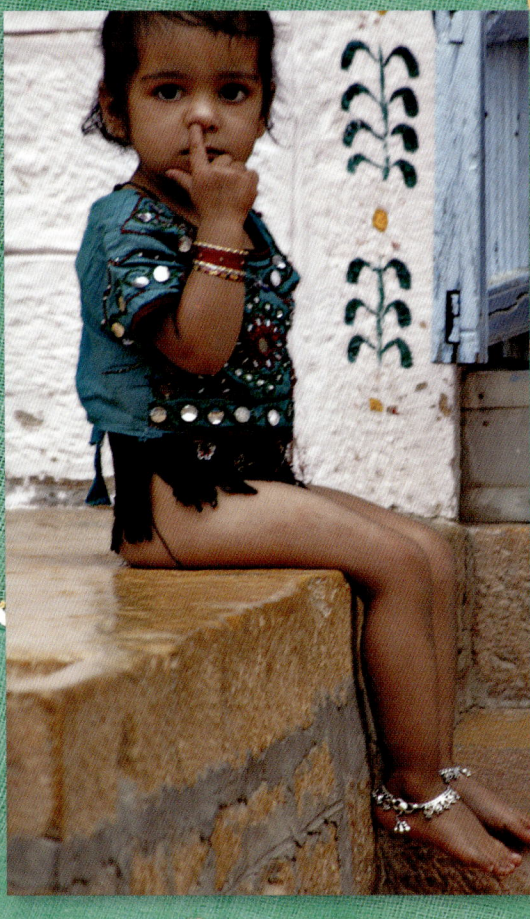
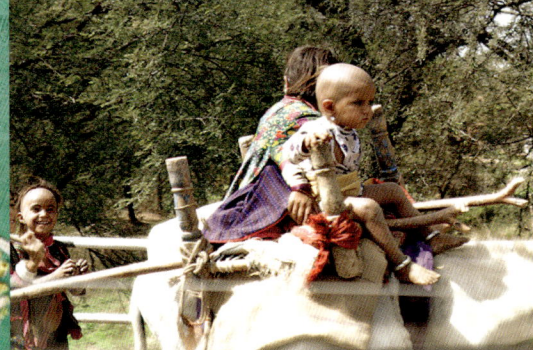

# Kilian and Melonie Hennessy

*Founder of the* By Kilian *Fragrance Line (Kilian) and Photographer (Melonie)*

❝*We went to India for the very first time two years ago. We arrived in Delhi and went to Mandawa, Bikaner, Jaisalmer, Udaipur, Jodhpur, Jaipur, and Fatehpur Sikri, ending up in Agra—of course at the Taj Mahal! But for me, India will remain a very specific image: I remember an old man in Jaisalmer, playing the tanpura beautifully, with his back facing a lake. I remember the beauty of the site, the temple. I remember a friend mesmerized by a man taking a bath at a far distance. I remember us turning slowly into stone; we stayed there for hours. When we finally left, we thought all day about coming back. But at the end of the day we decided not to, so that we could keep this image in our heads alive forever.*

—Kilian Hennessy

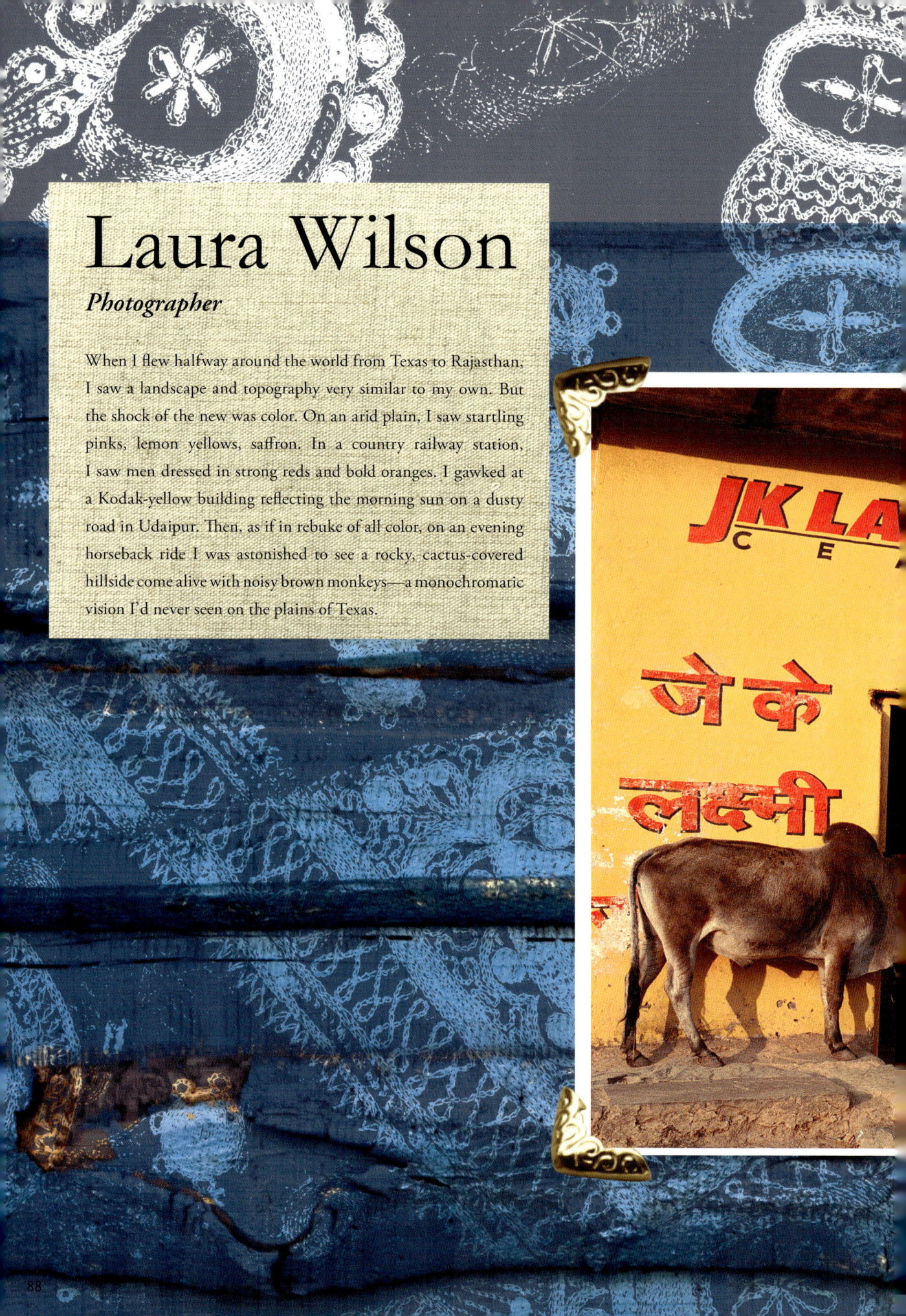

# Laura Wilson

*Photographer*

When I flew halfway around the world from Texas to Rajasthan, I saw a landscape and topography very similar to my own. But the shock of the new was color. On an arid plain, I saw startling pinks, lemon yellows, saffron. In a country railway station, I saw men dressed in strong reds and bold oranges. I gawked at a Kodak-yellow building reflecting the morning sun on a dusty road in Udaipur. Then, as if in rebuke of all color, on an evening horseback ride I was astonished to see a rocky, cactus-covered hillside come alive with noisy brown monkeys—a monochromatic vision I'd never seen on the plains of Texas.

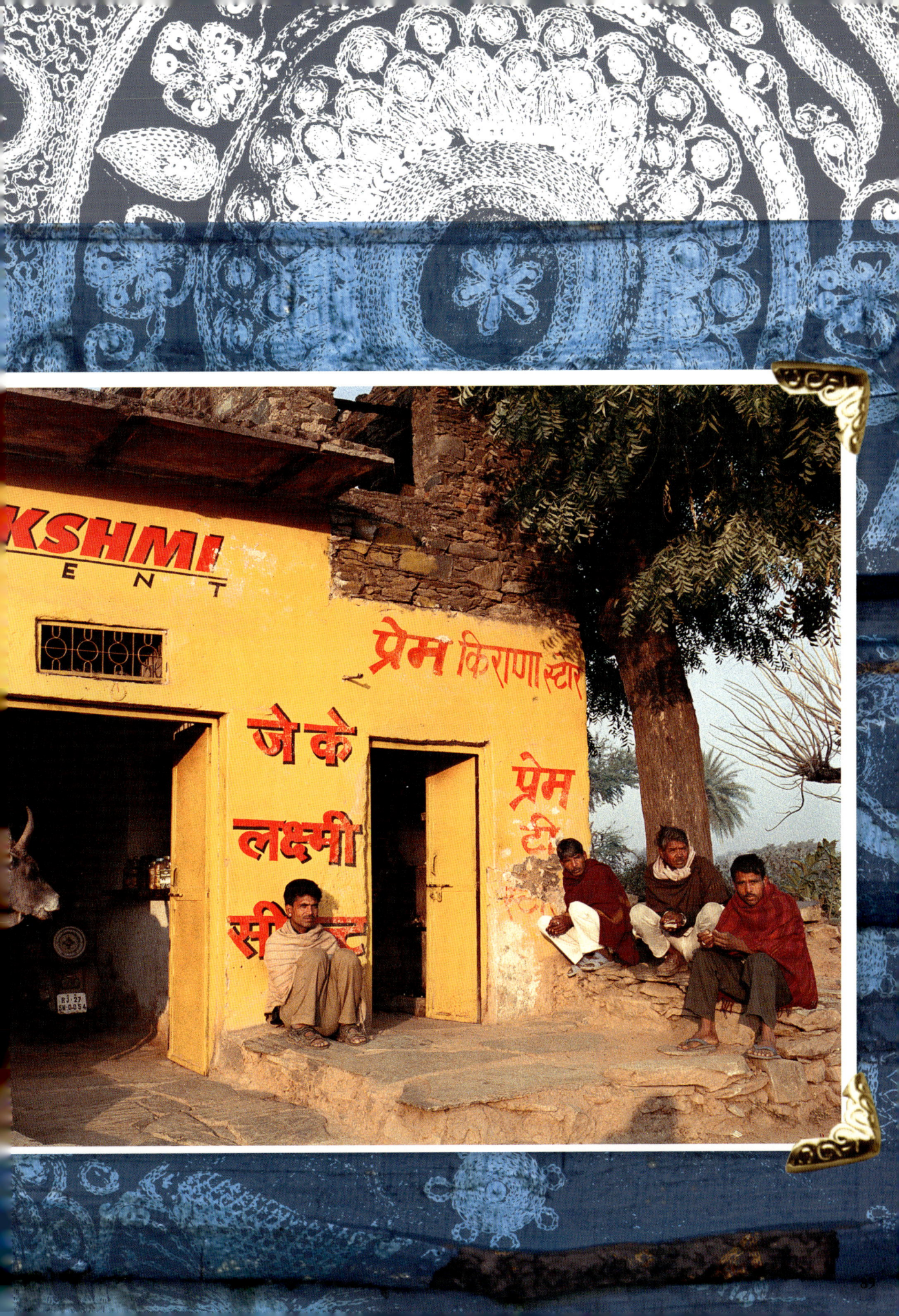

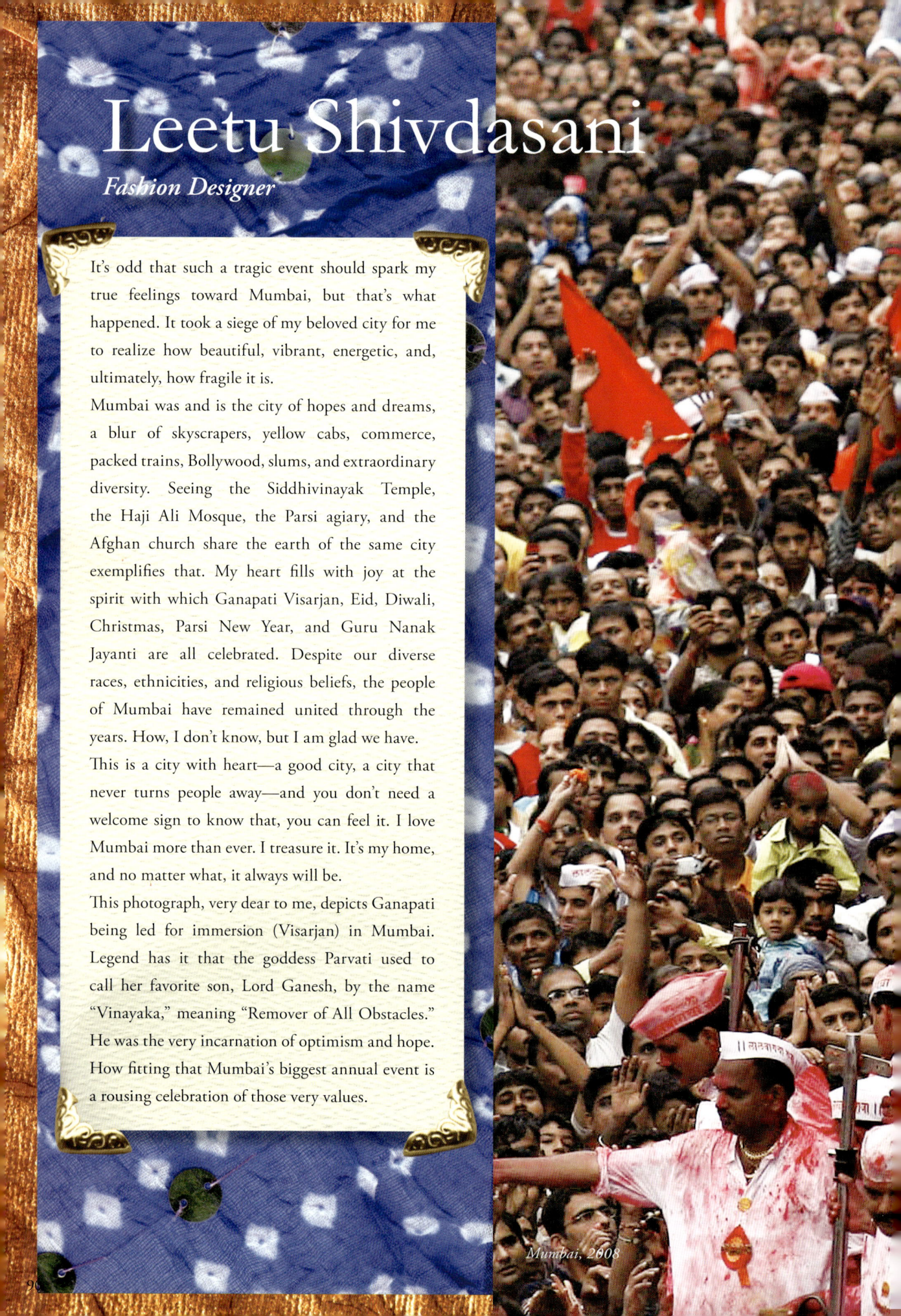

# Leetu Shivdasani
*Fashion Designer*

It's odd that such a tragic event should spark my true feelings toward Mumbai, but that's what happened. It took a siege of my beloved city for me to realize how beautiful, vibrant, energetic, and, ultimately, how fragile it is.

Mumbai was and is the city of hopes and dreams, a blur of skyscrapers, yellow cabs, commerce, packed trains, Bollywood, slums, and extraordinary diversity. Seeing the Siddhivinayak Temple, the Haji Ali Mosque, the Parsi agiary, and the Afghan church share the earth of the same city exemplifies that. My heart fills with joy at the spirit with which Ganapati Visarjan, Eid, Diwali, Christmas, Parsi New Year, and Guru Nanak Jayanti are all celebrated. Despite our diverse races, ethnicities, and religious beliefs, the people of Mumbai have remained united through the years. How, I don't know, but I am glad we have.

This is a city with heart—a good city, a city that never turns people away—and you don't need a welcome sign to know that, you can feel it. I love Mumbai more than ever. I treasure it. It's my home, and no matter what, it always will be.

This photograph, very dear to me, depicts Ganapati being led for immersion (Visarjan) in Mumbai. Legend has it that the goddess Parvati used to call her favorite son, Lord Ganesh, by the name "Vinayaka," meaning "Remover of All Obstacles." He was the very incarnation of optimism and hope. How fitting that Mumbai's biggest annual event is a rousing celebration of those very values.

*Mumbai, 2008*

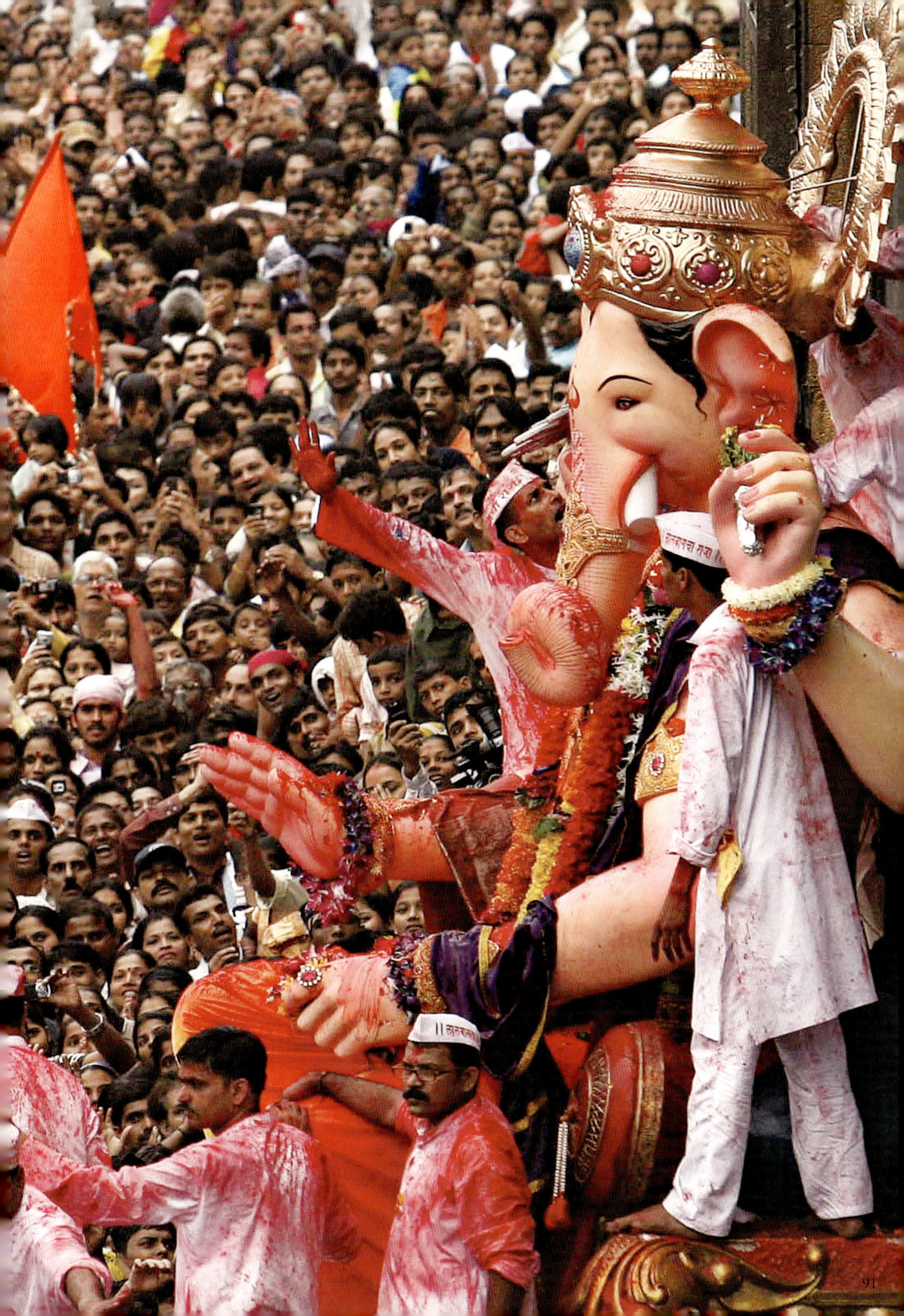

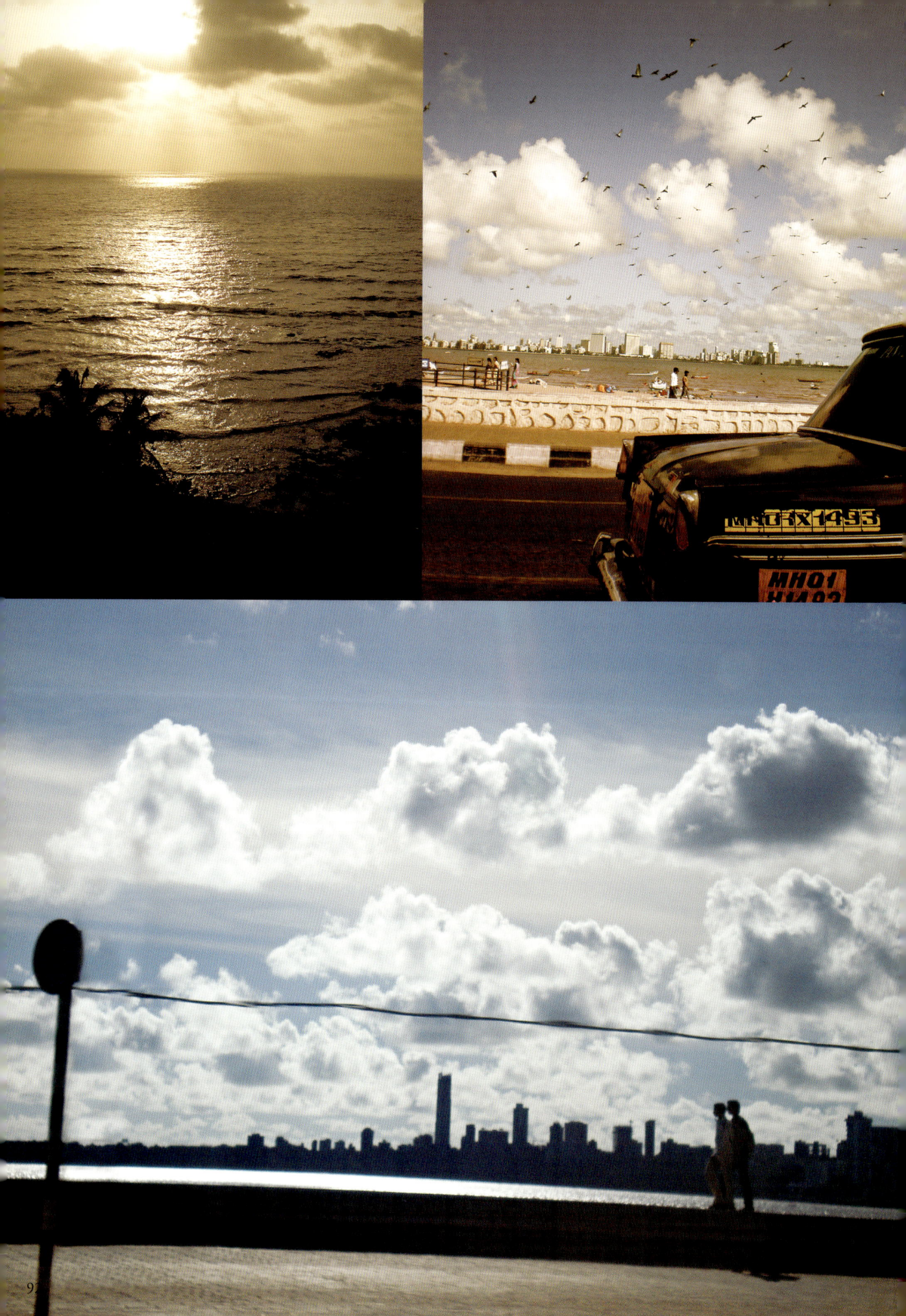

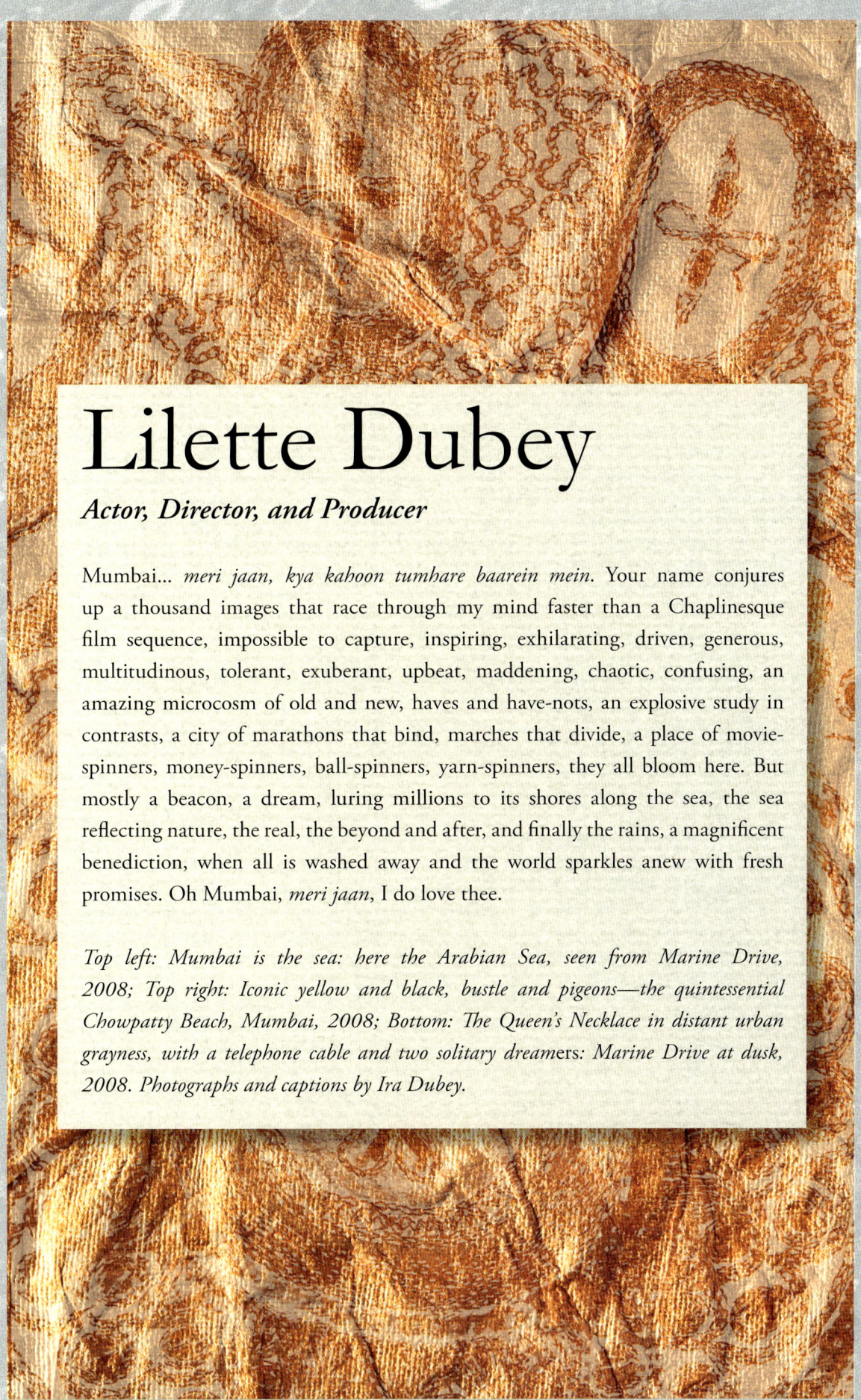

# Lilette Dubey
*Actor, Director, and Producer*

Mumbai... *meri jaan, kya kahoon tumhare baarein mein.* Your name conjures up a thousand images that race through my mind faster than a Chaplinesque film sequence, impossible to capture, inspiring, exhilarating, driven, generous, multitudinous, tolerant, exuberant, upbeat, maddening, chaotic, confusing, an amazing microcosm of old and new, haves and have-nots, an explosive study in contrasts, a city of marathons that bind, marches that divide, a place of movie-spinners, money-spinners, ball-spinners, yarn-spinners, they all bloom here. But mostly a beacon, a dream, luring millions to its shores along the sea, the sea reflecting nature, the real, the beyond and after, and finally the rains, a magnificent benediction, when all is washed away and the world sparkles anew with fresh promises. Oh Mumbai, *meri jaan*, I do love thee.

*Top left: Mumbai is the sea: here the Arabian Sea, seen from Marine Drive, 2008; Top right: Iconic yellow and black, bustle and pigeons—the quintessential Chowpatty Beach, Mumbai, 2008; Bottom: The Queen's Necklace in distant urban grayness, with a telephone cable and two solitary dreamers: Marine Drive at dusk, 2008. Photographs and captions by Ira Dubey.*

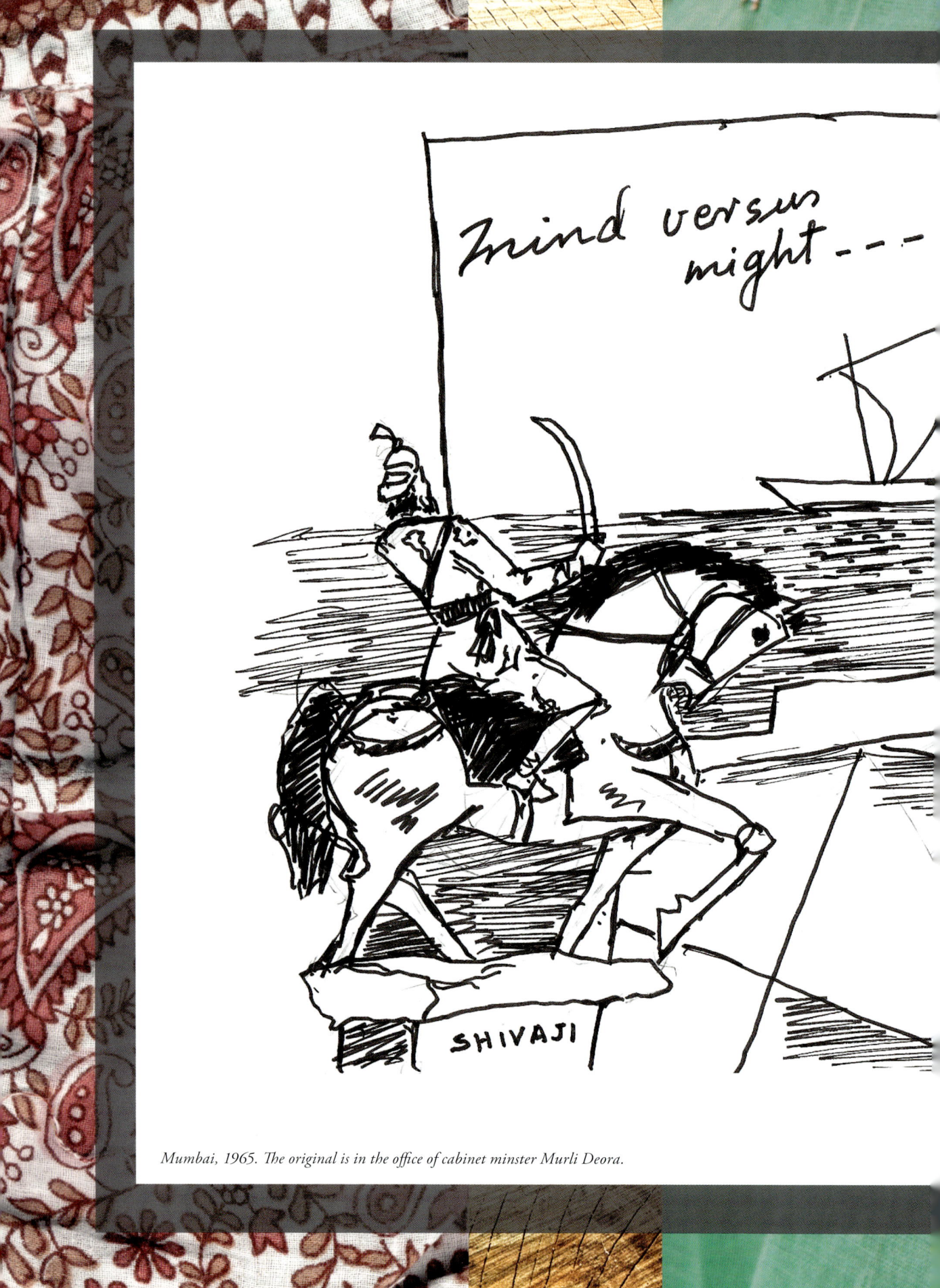

*Mumbai, 1965. The original is in the office of cabinet minster Murli Deora.*

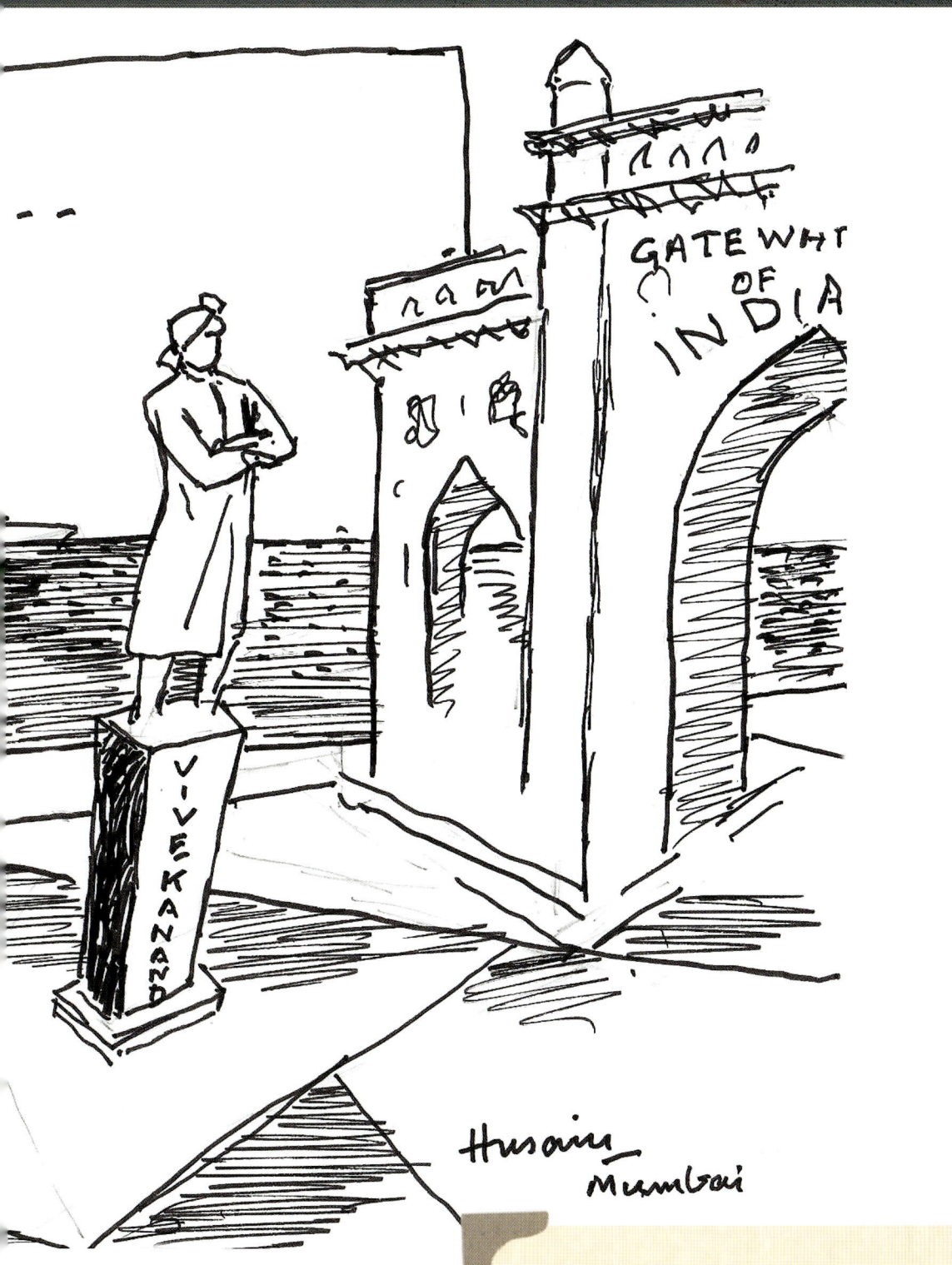

## M. F. Husain

*Artist*

# Pier Luigi Loro Piana
*President and CEO, Loro Piana*

India! The country of contradictions, where elegance, tradition, and beauty overshadow everything else; where past, present, and future live together in harmony; and where fears walk side by side with dreams.

During my many trips to India—my first was to Mumbai in 1978—I have learned to appreciate the only people and the only country where everything seems to be a contradiction in terms. In India, you feel lost, often perplexed, at times confused, but constantly drawn in: India, the country of endless possibilities!

This photograph from my collection, taken by Sebastiano Moschini, says so much: the country looks inside you like this child looks through the window of the car. India leaves you naked, defenseless, yet always intrigued.

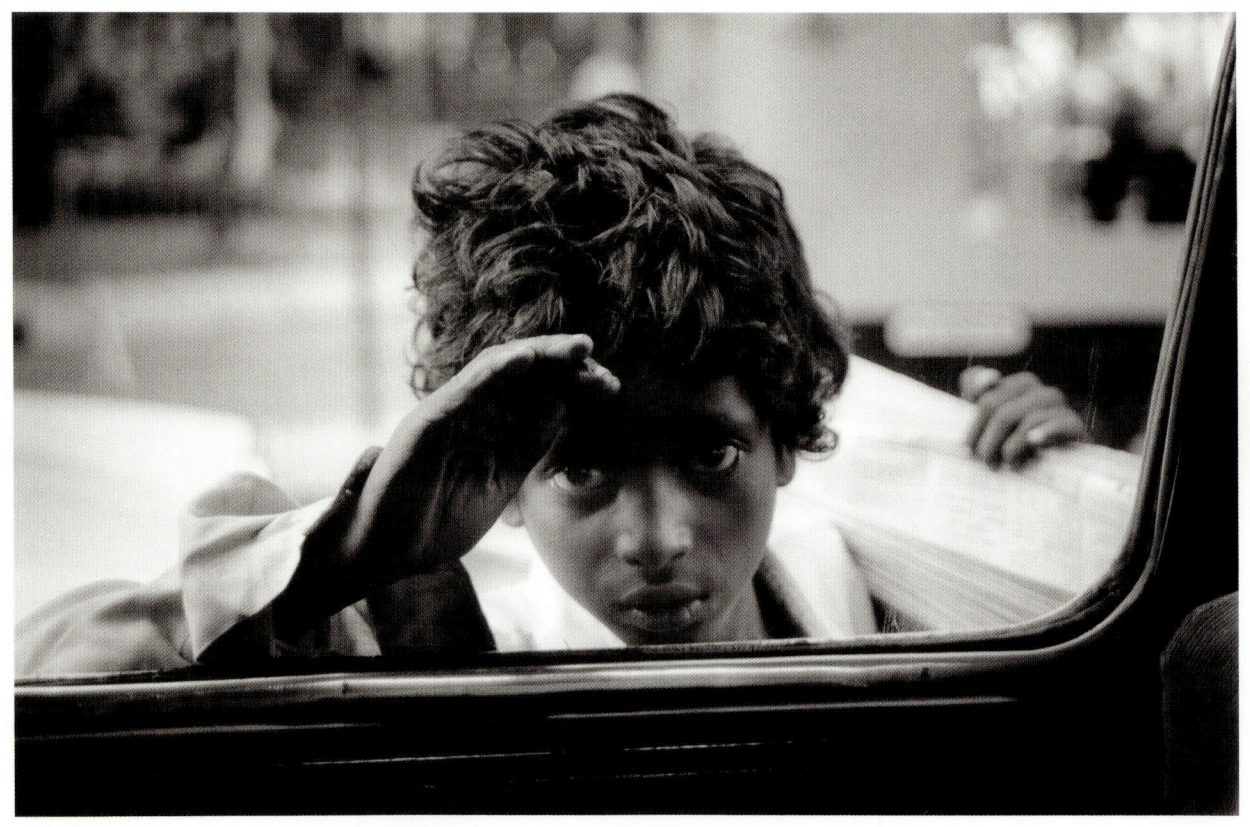

*New Delhi, 1998. Photograph by Sebastiano Moschini.*

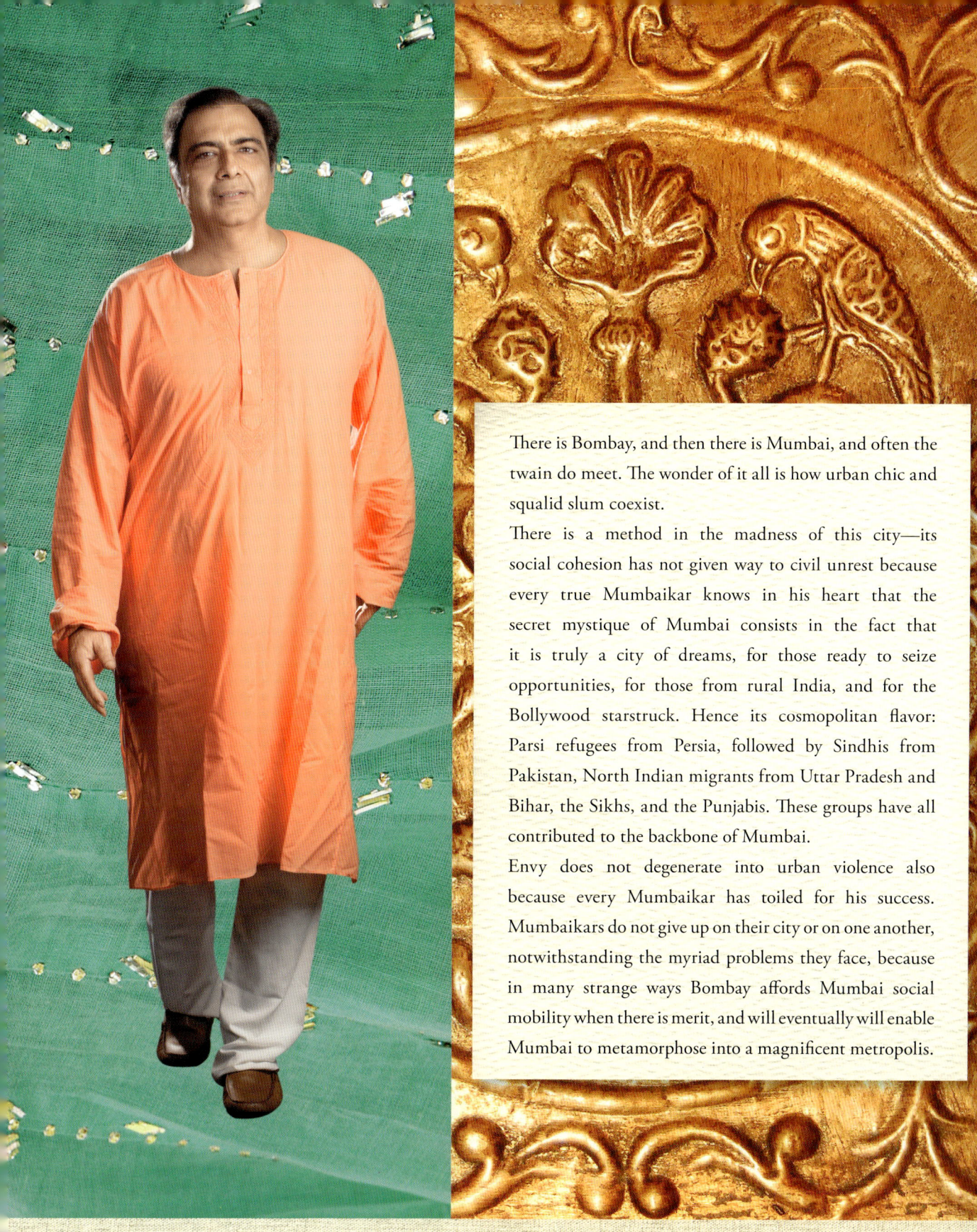

There is Bombay, and then there is Mumbai, and often the twain do meet. The wonder of it all is how urban chic and squalid slum coexist.

There is a method in the madness of this city—its social cohesion has not given way to civil unrest because every true Mumbaikar knows in his heart that the secret mystique of Mumbai consists in the fact that it is truly a city of dreams, for those ready to seize opportunities, for those from rural India, and for the Bollywood starstruck. Hence its cosmopolitan flavor: Parsi refugees from Persia, followed by Sindhis from Pakistan, North Indian migrants from Uttar Pradesh and Bihar, the Sikhs, and the Punjabis. These groups have all contributed to the backbone of Mumbai.

Envy does not degenerate into urban violence also because every Mumbaikar has toiled for his success. Mumbaikars do not give up on their city or on one another, notwithstanding the myriad problems they face, because in many strange ways Bombay affords Mumbai social mobility when there is merit, and will eventually will enable Mumbai to metamorphose into a magnificent metropolis.

# Mahesh Jethmalani
*Politician and Lawyer*

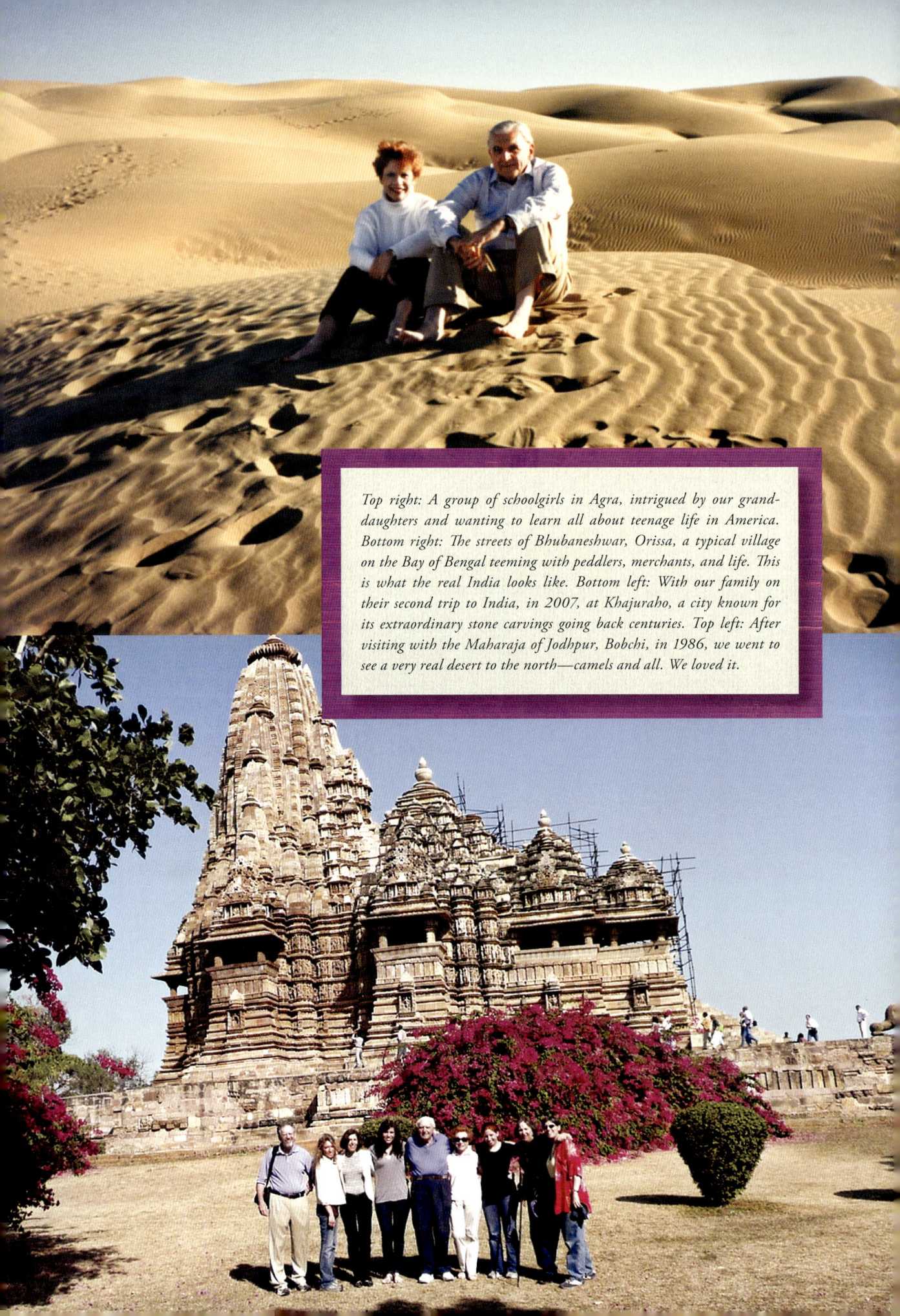

*Top right: A group of schoolgirls in Agra, intrigued by our granddaughters and wanting to learn all about teenage life in America. Bottom right: The streets of Bhubaneshwar, Orissa, a typical village on the Bay of Bengal teeming with peddlers, merchants, and life. This is what the real India looks like. Bottom left: With our family on their second trip to India, in 2007, at Khajuraho, a city known for its extraordinary stone carvings going back centuries. Top left: After visiting with the Maharaja of Jodhpur, Bobchi, in 1986, we went to see a very real desert to the north—camels and all. We loved it.*

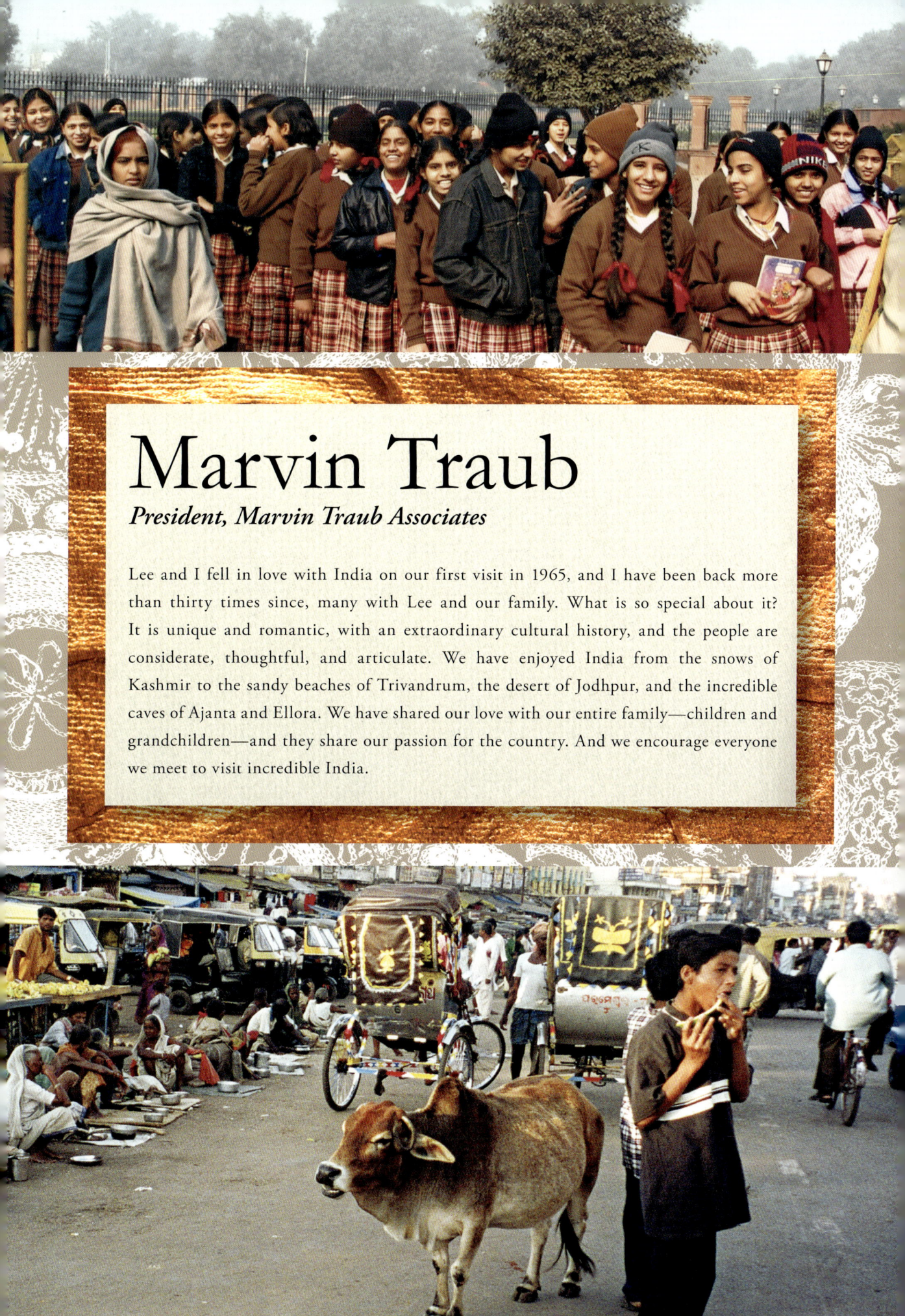

# Marvin Traub
*President, Marvin Traub Associates*

Lee and I fell in love with India on our first visit in 1965, and I have been back more than thirty times since, many with Lee and our family. What is so special about it? It is unique and romantic, with an extraordinary cultural history, and the people are considerate, thoughtful, and articulate. We have enjoyed India from the snows of Kashmir to the sandy beaches of Trivandrum, the desert of Jodhpur, and the incredible caves of Ajanta and Ellora. We have shared our love with our entire family—children and grandchildren—and they share our passion for the country. And we encourage everyone we meet to visit incredible India.

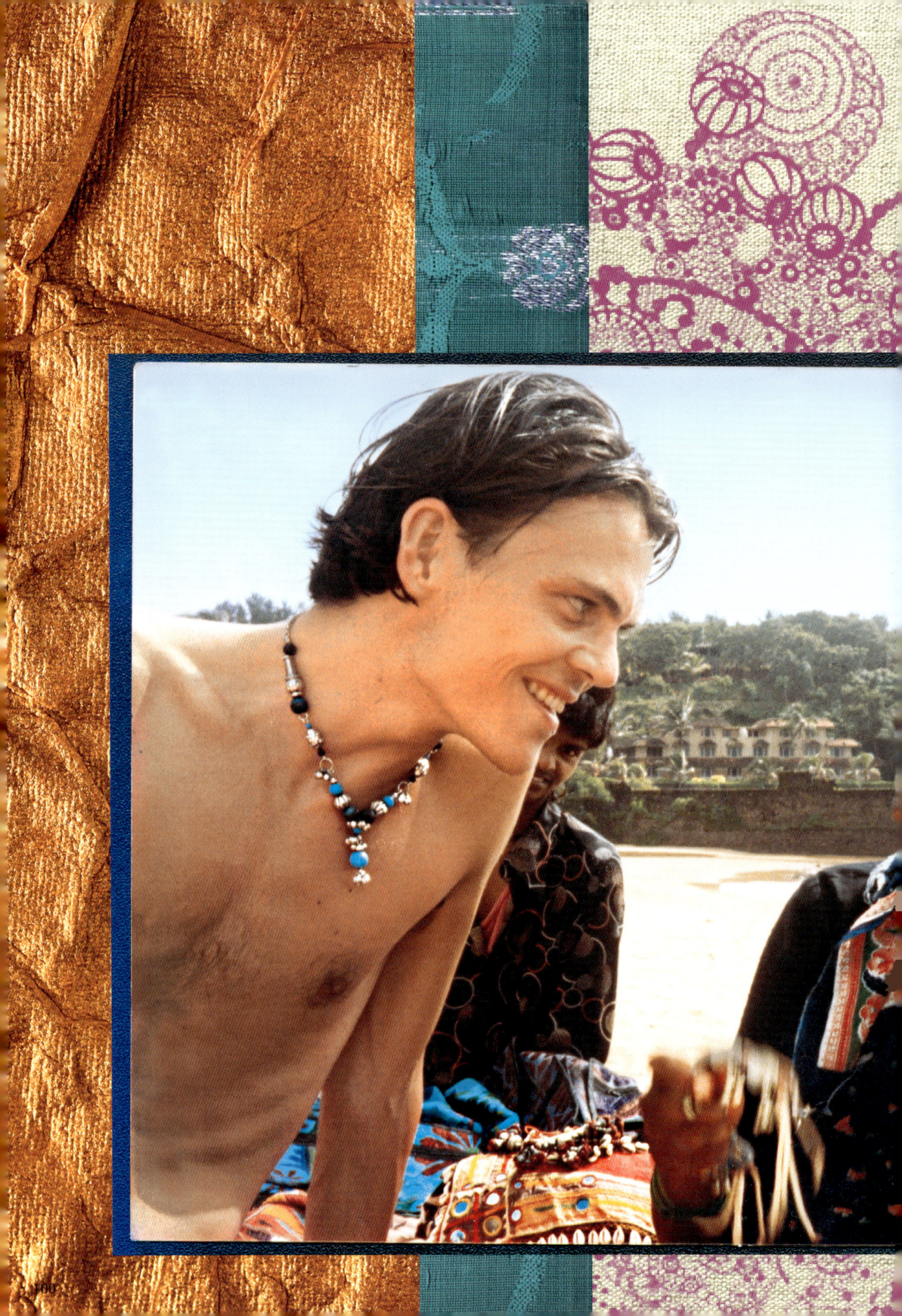

# Matthew Williamson
*Fashion Designer*

This was taken on my first trip to India. I was enthralled and amazed by the vibrancy of how everyone looked. I have been back many times since and love experiencing the different cultures in different areas. India has played a large part in influencing my work; it continues to inspire my color palette, beading, and embroidery.

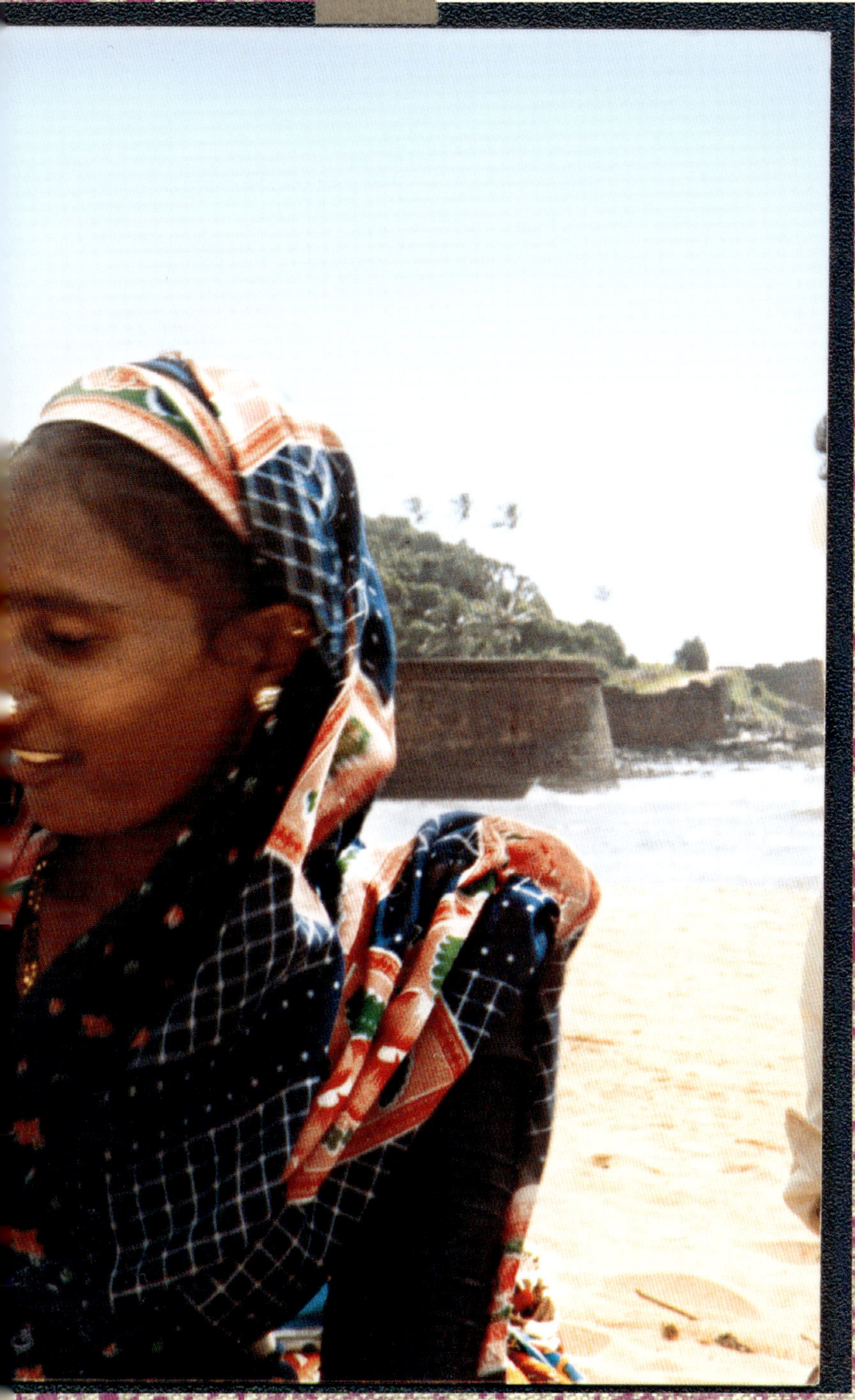

# Mickey Boardman
*Editorial Director,* **Paper** *Magazine*

When I think of Mumbai, I think of fabulousness. Mumbai is one of the glamour capitals of the world. Sure, I also think of culture and urban chaos, beauty and history, but we're talking about the movie capital of all time. Mumbai is like New York, Hollywood, and London combined and dropped on a gorgeous strip of Indian Ocean.

Mumbaikars know the meaning of hospitality, and rarely have I been more lavishly and lovingly entertained than in their homes. My first trip to India was for Lakme Fashion Week in Mumbai, and ooh, what parties! Queenie Dhody, supermodel-turned-gossip-columnist, threw a shindig for the chicest fashion people in town—Mohan Murjani, Suzy Menkes (on her eighteenth trip to India), Priya Tanna, Kalyani Chawla, Lalit Tehlan, and Rohit Bal.

I've never felt luxury like I've felt in India, and yet it was welcoming and warm. And that's what the people of Mumbai are: the kindest, warmest, most welcoming people in the world. That's what keeps me coming back, and that's what has made Mumbai my favorite destination.

*All photographs Mumbai, May 2008*

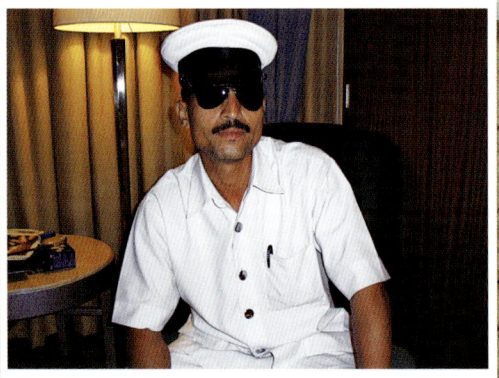
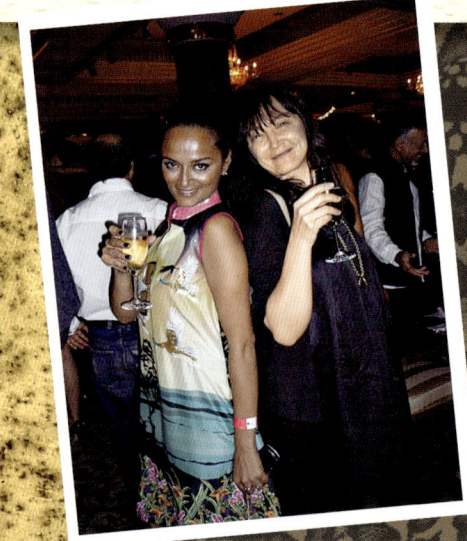
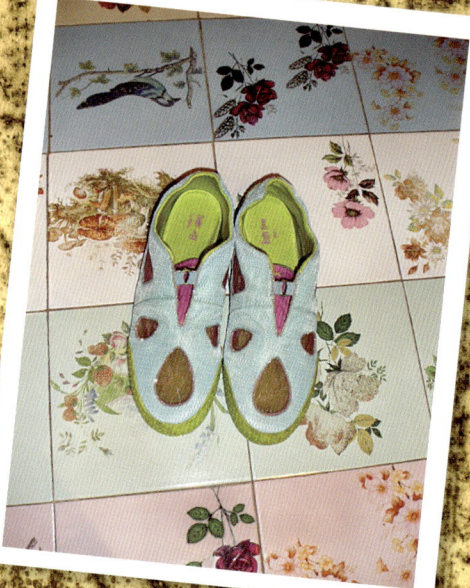
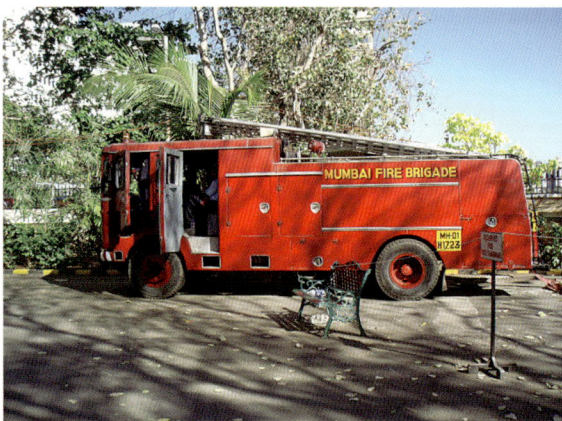

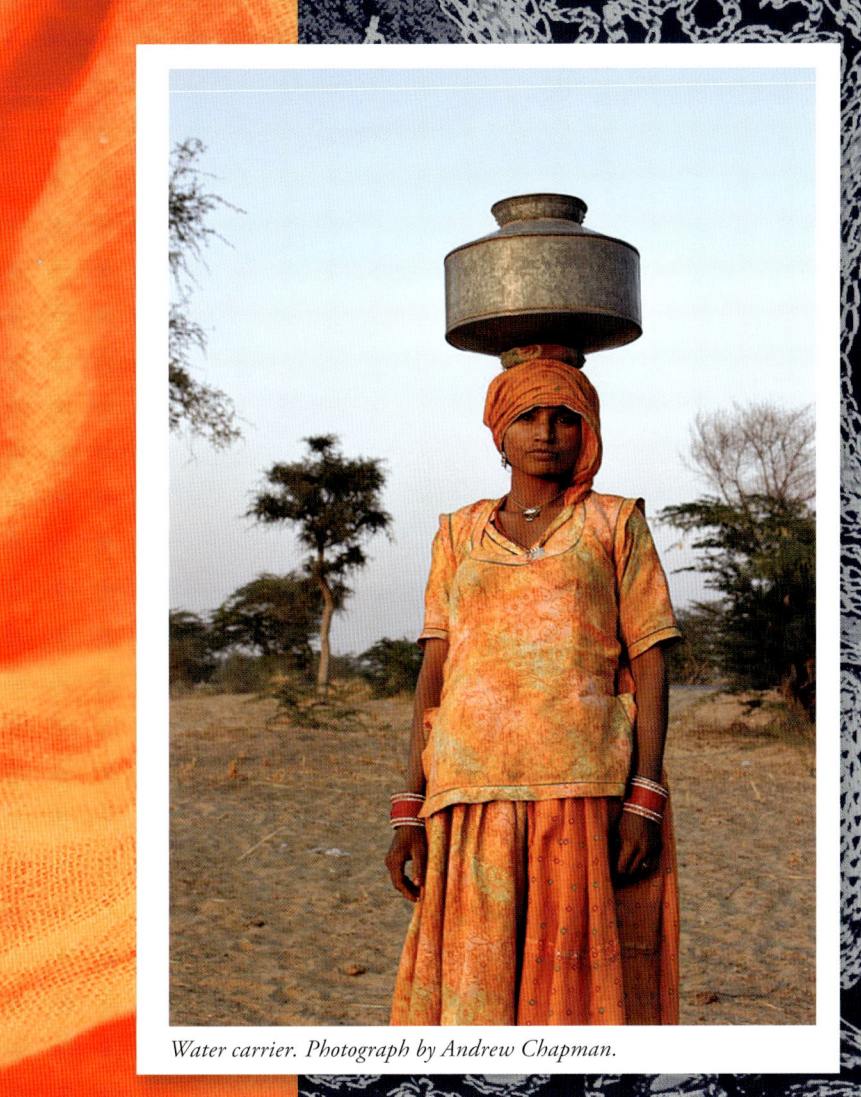

Water carrier. Photograph by Andrew Chapman.

# Mickey Drexler
*Chairman, J. Crew*

"*I was inspired by the architecture, the landscape, and the vibrant colors, but what struck me most about this country's dynamic culture was the people—welcoming, full of spirit, and incredibly resilient.*"

# Milena Canonero
*Costume Designer*

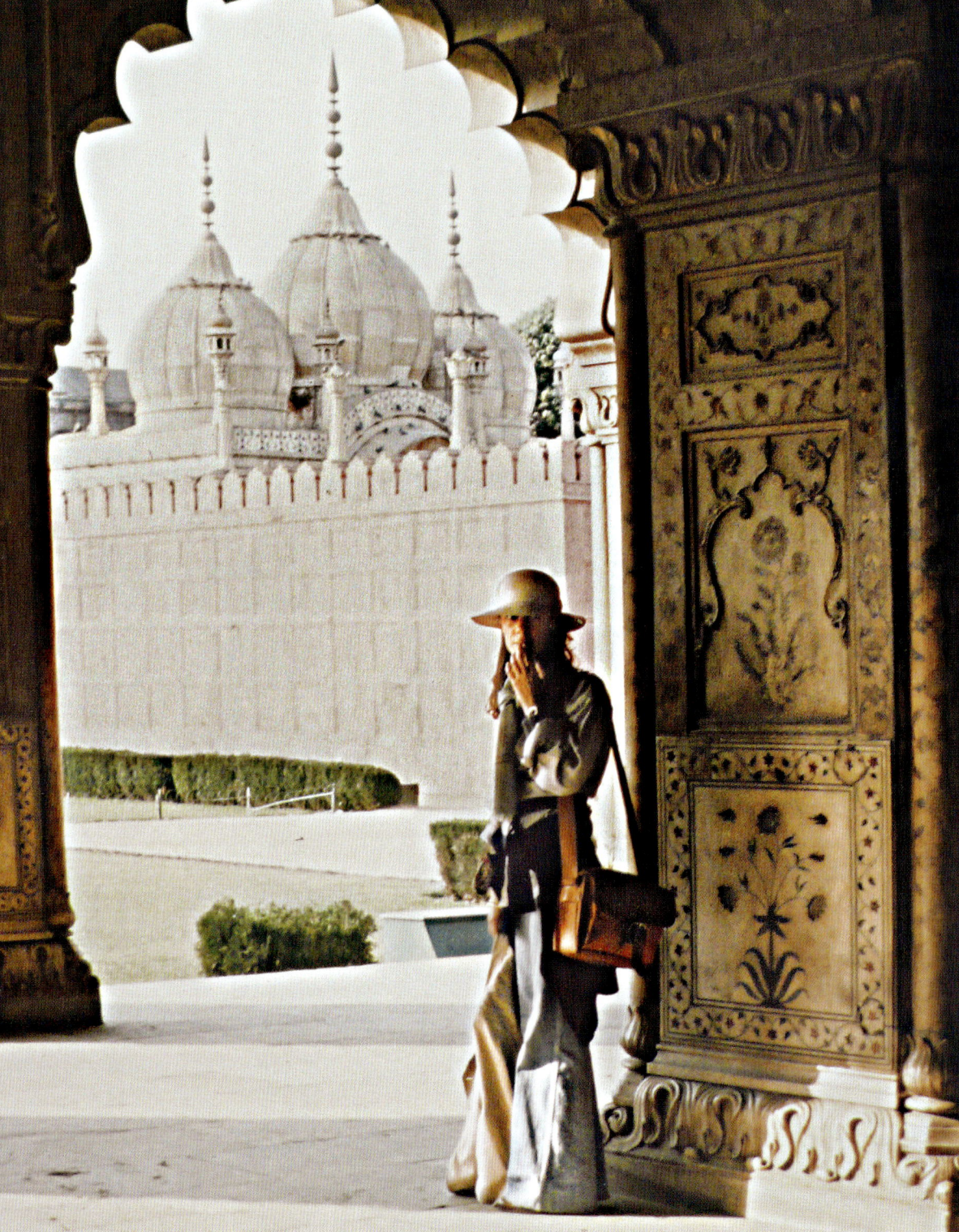

*Agra, 1976*

Namaste.

This photo is from Agra, from the first time I went to India, in 1976. Studying and working in England in the 1970s, I had my head and my imagination full of Indian culture and food and spices: George Harrison, V. S. Naipul, Rudyard Kipling, Satyajit Ray, Louis Malle documentaries. And I loved going to Indian restaurants, so I was familiar with Indian cuisine. Or so I thought.

Nothing prepared me for the first impact of India: when, after arriving in in Calcutta, I was driven at high speed in a very old taxi to my hotel, a young boy next to the driver dangerously stretching out the window to wipe away, with a rag, the dust that would immediately settle back onto it. The dust everywhere. I could faintly see the outlines of strange buildings where still figures sat wrapped up in off-white or grayish sheets, then suddenly millions of people coming toward us, then people lying in the streets among cows. In this first drive in India, toward my nice old Imperial Hotel, I saw an unexpected world; it shocked me. For three days I didn't leave my hotel, staying in instead and wondering about my life. When at last I went out, with my boyfriend, a writer who was working on a project there, we went all over. North, south, east, and west.

I was here in Agra when I got the invitation to go to Los Angeles for the Oscar ceremony. Stanley Kubrick's *Barry Lyndon* had been nominated for best costumes, which I had codesigned. It was a movie I had lovingly worked on for a very long time, but I didn't want to leave India. By that time I was totally in love with it and afraid I would never be able to come back again. My partner went, but I preferred to stay on where I was. I wasn't a hippie, but I was into India, from my Indian breakfast to my Indian sandals. I was never sick, and I never tired of the smells and colors and people and places I was discovering.

India brought me good karma. We won the Oscar for the costumes.

It was a very long time before I could go back. Then a few years ago I was asked by Wes Anderson to work on his movie *The Darjeeling Limited*. I jumped at it. But then my mother "left" us, and I was very low and swamped by the funeral arrangements. Wes was very kind and generous to me; he waited for me to come over as soon as I could.

We shot in Jodhpur and Udaipur mainly, and working in India with an Indian crew, you get to go into territories that as a foreigner and a tourist you would never have access to. Marshall, my husband, joined me. He walked everywhere, making friends with local people, but he is special. He is good at languages, so he could communicate more easily than I could. Usually I am an observer, but even I made friends this time. My fondest image of India? The children, the poor children always smiling, those incredible white teeth. Smiling no matter how hard it must be for them. India makes you feel alive and grateful.

I hope to go back soon.

# Mitter and Preeti Bedi
*Photographers*

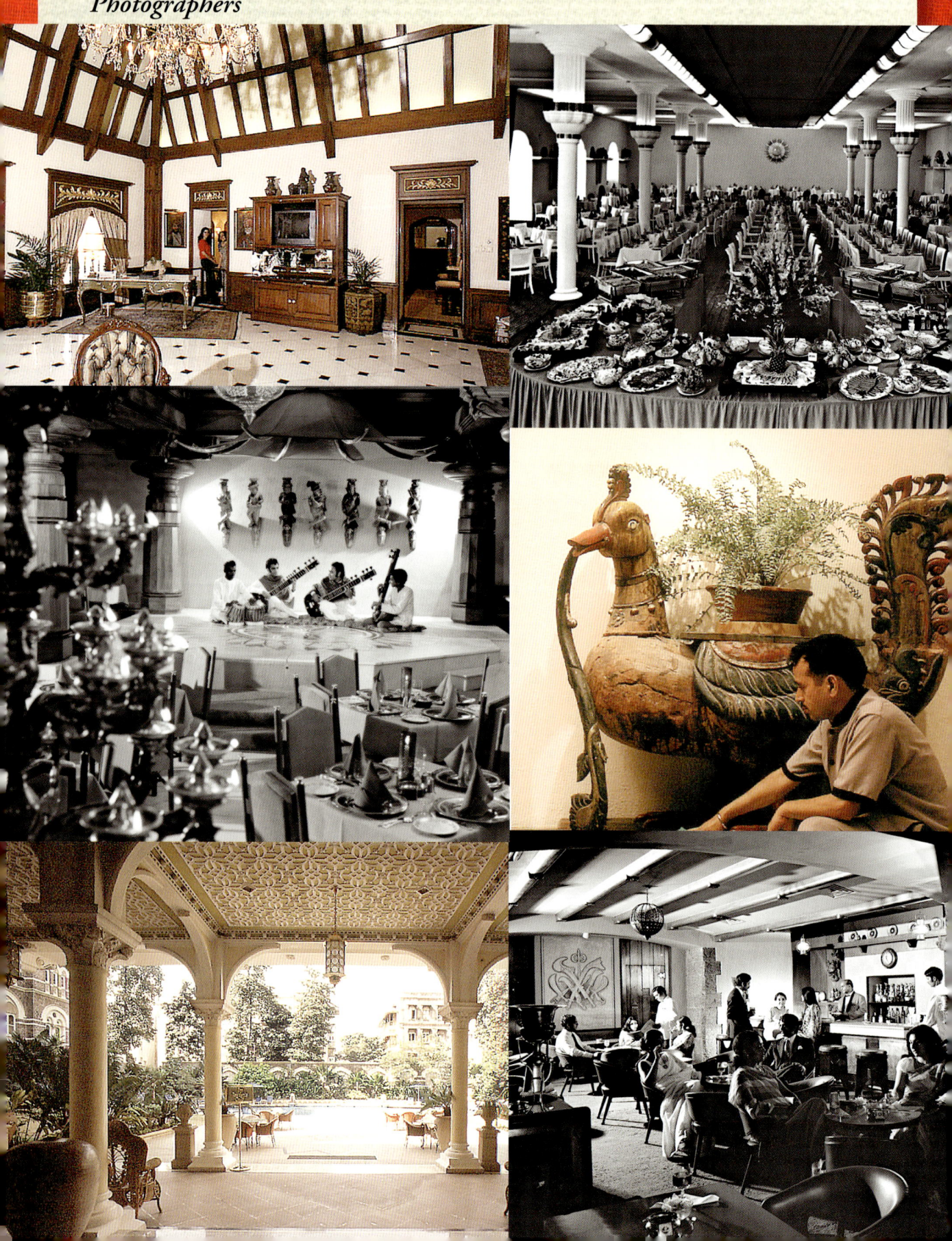

I have grown up in the munificent shadow of a legend, the Taj hotel, that has woven itself into the fiber of so many lives. Homes, businesses, and people have existed in and around it for more than a century, and for most of us, the Taj is an integral part of who we are.

My five-decade-long existence is rife with memories connected to the Taj, sweet and bittersweet, a plethora of human emotions. Delving into them, some truly lovely, simple moments come to mind. Growing up in its shadow, I see the Tower replacing Green's Hotel. I remember the conical, canopied Shamiana, the ultimate coffee shop, where bhelpuri and dosas got upgraded. In the 1970s, teenagers would sit there for hours to chat and daydream. Many graduated to the "M.P.M."—matrimonial prospect meetings—at the Sea Lounge. We spent nights dancing at Blow Up, a discotheque after your wildest imagination.

Sneaking into Dad's photo shoots at the Taj had special moments. At the first Shamiana shoot, kids of senior management happily posed as restaurant guests; I was excited to be included but sulked when I was asked to fill a gap in the far corner. We hung around while our parents worked. The Taj commands your best professionally and gives you a very familylike atmosphere to work in. But sitting on the swing in the Rajput Suite, you can be forgiven for dreaming that you are a princess.

I particularly remember the candlelit grand-staircase shot, people rushing around lighting candles—the effect was pure magic. Sitting in the center of the stairwell, gazing upward, I was starry-eyed. The glee on the faces of everyone involved was infectious; guests stood spellbound, asking if it was for a royal wedding. No, the Taj is regal in itself.

The Taj's centenary in 2003 was poignant. As I set up my camera in the suites, photographed so long ago by my dad, memories of myself as a brat getting underfoot engulfed me. This time around it was my daughter watching me work. Life at the Taj had come full circle.

The Taj is a monument that has embodied celebration for millions… celebrations of births, marriages, anniversaries, aging parents, special days—setting eyes on a future life partner, bonding over quiet coffee and dinner. It has been there, holding us, nurturing us, putting us back together when we feel shattered and scattered.

I still walk through the Taj, right past the lobby, gazing at the store windows like treasure chests, stopping to browse at the bookstore. Today it feels even more like a caring friend welcoming me yet again. The images of long ago come rushing back. My daughter in her infancy, laughing by the pool, her wide-eyed gaze as she noticed pigeons on the opposite sidewalk, her fascination with the panoramic view of the city from the rooftop restaurants, her growing up and discovering the myriad exquisite nooks and crannies, and just strolling with her, soaking up the beautiful, comforting atmosphere so unique to the Taj. Even today you may chance upon a person in an alcove, diligently polishing an artifact. He has been doing it for decades. He will greet you, for he has watched you grow up, just as the Taj has seen the neighborhood and this city grow.

The Taj has changed appearance time and again, but its spirit and soul are timeless.

—*Preeti Bedi*

*Clockwise from top left: the Presidential Suite, photographed by Preeti Bedi; ballroom buffet, photographed by Mitter Bedi; dedication, Preeti Bedi; Harbour Bar, Mitter Bedi; pool deck, Preeti Bedi; and Tanjore, Mitter Bedi.*

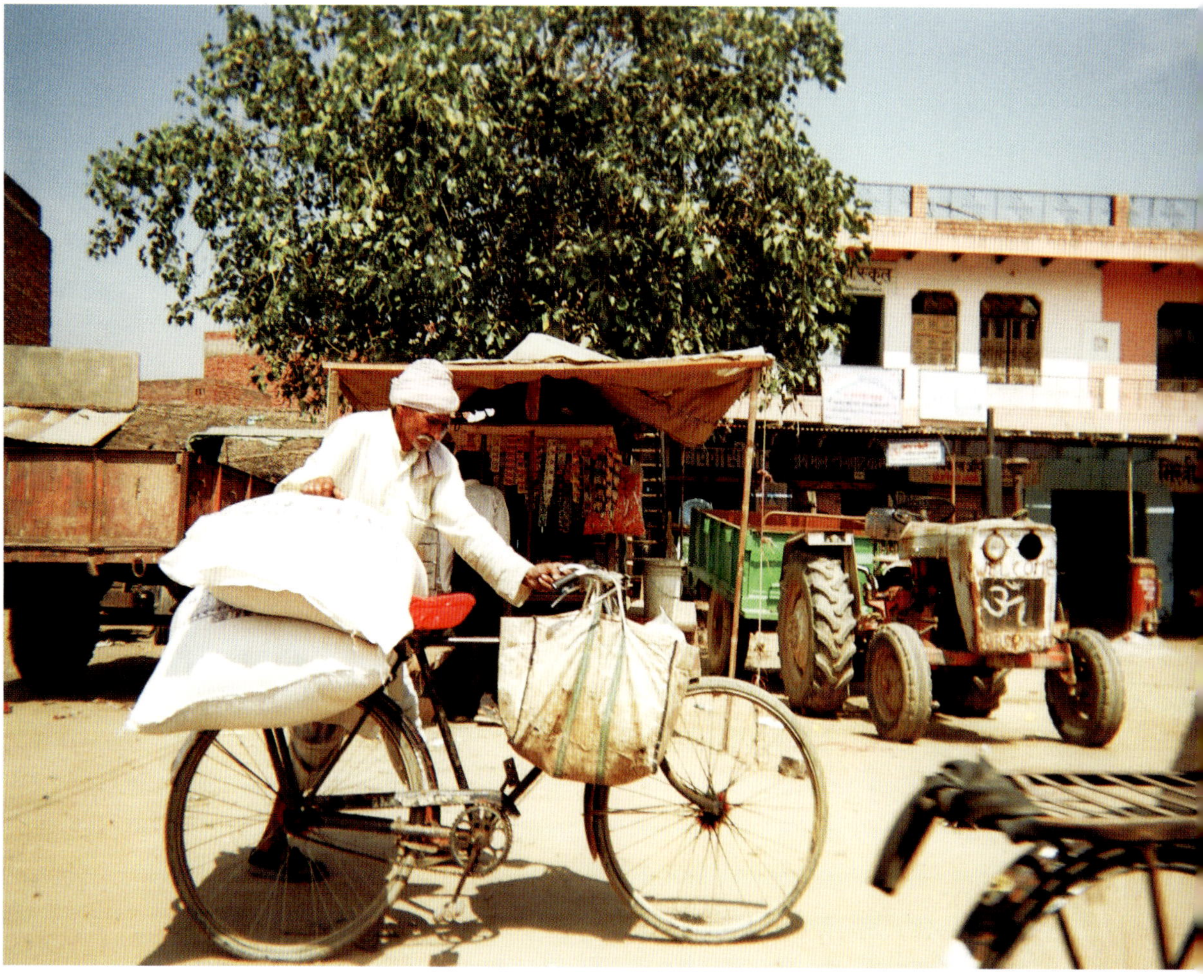

On the road to Fatehpur Sikri from Agra, May 2006

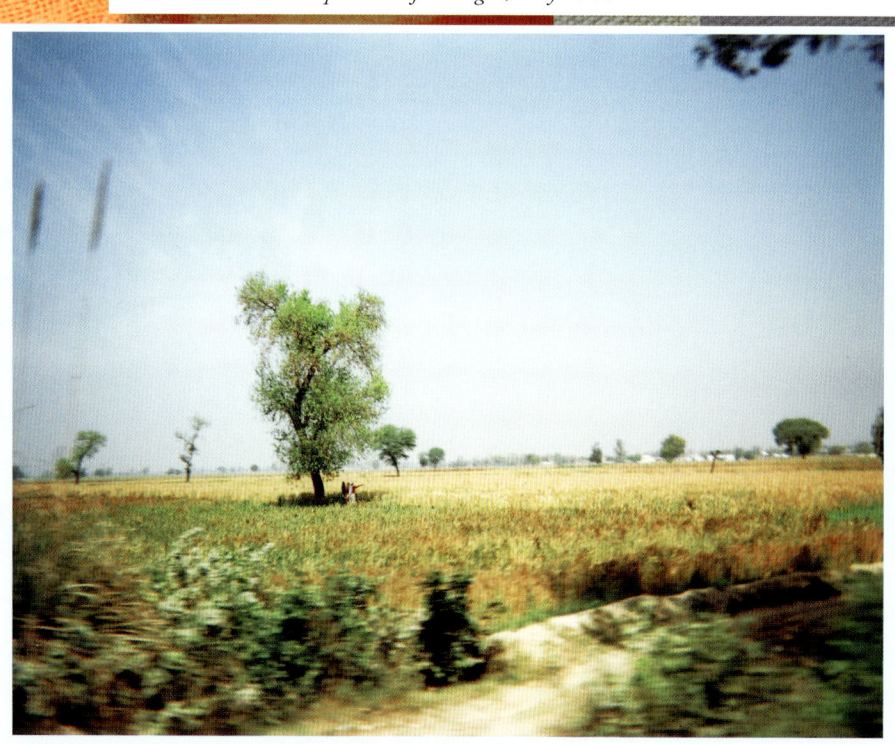

On the road to Agra from New Delhi, May 2006

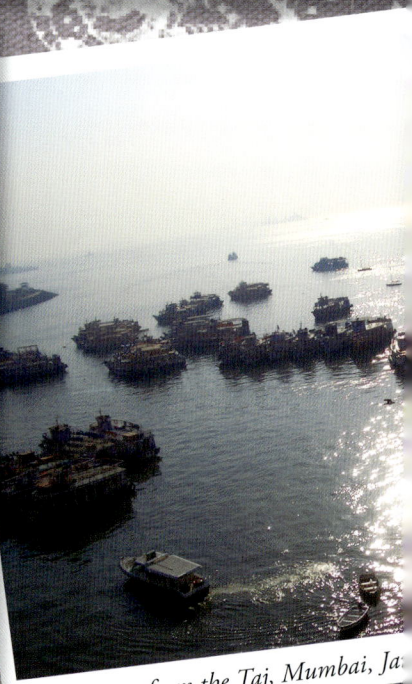

Looking out from the Taj, Mumbai, Ja

# Mortimer Singer

*Senior Vice President, Marvin Traub Associates (Cofounder, Mumbai: We Got Your Back)*

I woke up early on this, my first-ever morning in India. The sun was lifting itself slowly over the Arabian Sea and was starting to bring it to a slow simmer, not unlike countless chai teapots all over Mumbai. I walked outside the Taj hotel. The porter smiled a butterfly smile from beneath an elegant cream feathered turban and from behind a perfectly manicured princely beard.

The air was sweet and sour, heavy with floral scents, burnt wood, rickshaw exhaust, and people. The smell is well known to me now. You can get off an airplane blindfolded and know you are in India. It hugs you. A welcome by smothering. It is the kind of familiar and pleasant smell that reminds you of your childhood, but when you think about it, you realize it not to be such a pleasant smell, just a comforting one.

I crossed the street and walked along the shoreline away from the India Gate. I stopped when an old man offered to give me a shoeshine. I didn't think I needed one, but he sold me on his real estate more than his services, gesturing with an open hand at the view of the bay over his shoulder. As I stood there lulled by the bobbing of the dozens of boats, I was approached by a tour guide, then two flower-bearing young girls wearing technicolor saris, and finally a holy man. Each was peddling something. The shoe-shiner chuckled. The holy man put a dot on my forehead, tied an orange ribbon around my wrist, and forced a sugary substance into my mouth and a coral carnation into my pocket. He urged me to throw it into the ocean in three days with a wish. Not before or it would bring bad luck.

So there I was. I hadn't left the Taj but four minutes earlier and I was already entered into four-way negotiations with the holy man, the flower girls, the tour guide, and the shoeshine man. This five-minute walk will always be with me. For me it is India in a bottle: color, unexpected and breathtaking views, curious smiles, confusion, and spirited discussion. This is why the Taj will always hold a large place in my heart. All I can wish upon anyone who reads this is for them to experience their very own first Indian morning.

*Following page: The view over the shoeshine man's shoulder, Mumbai, January 2005*

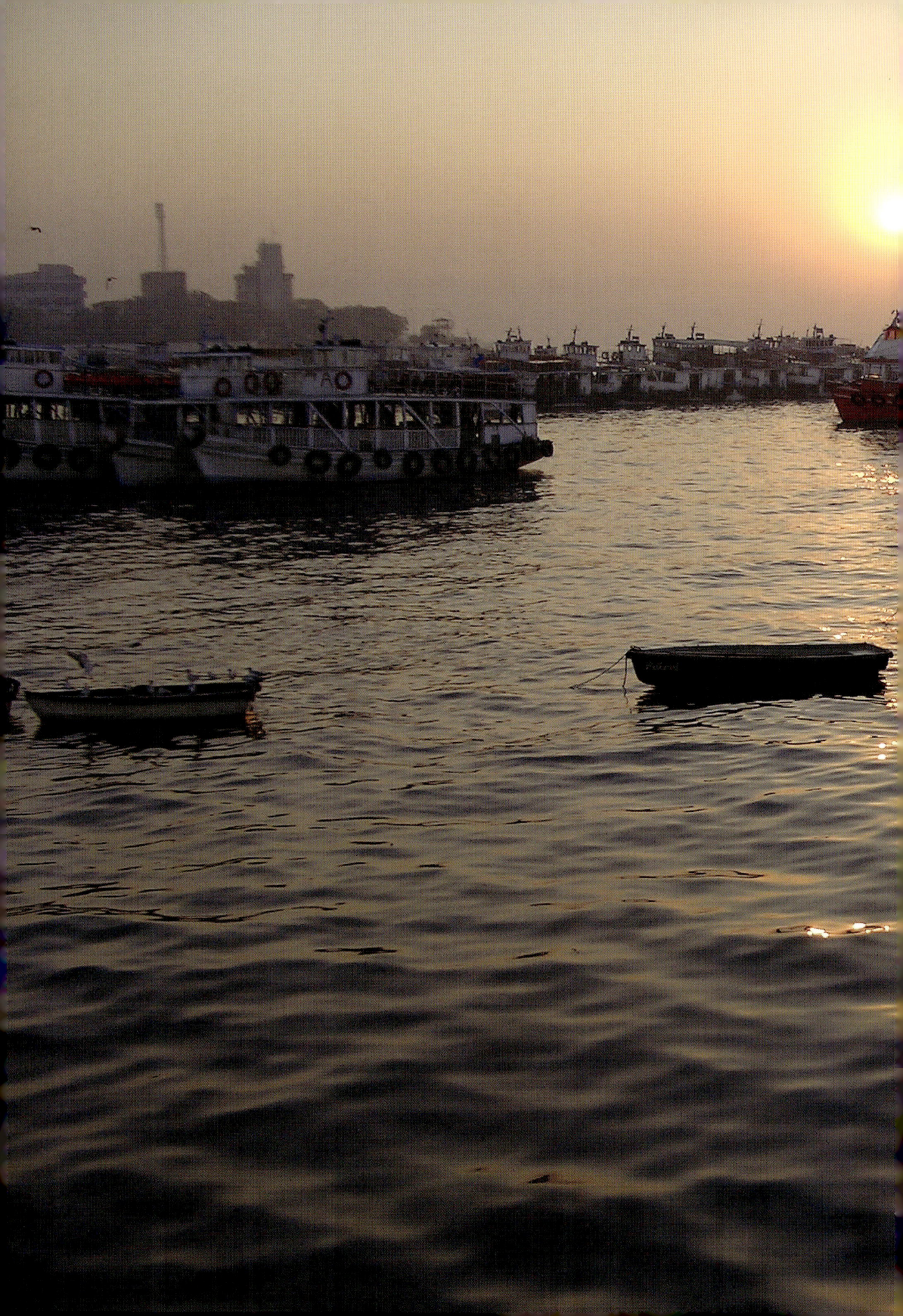

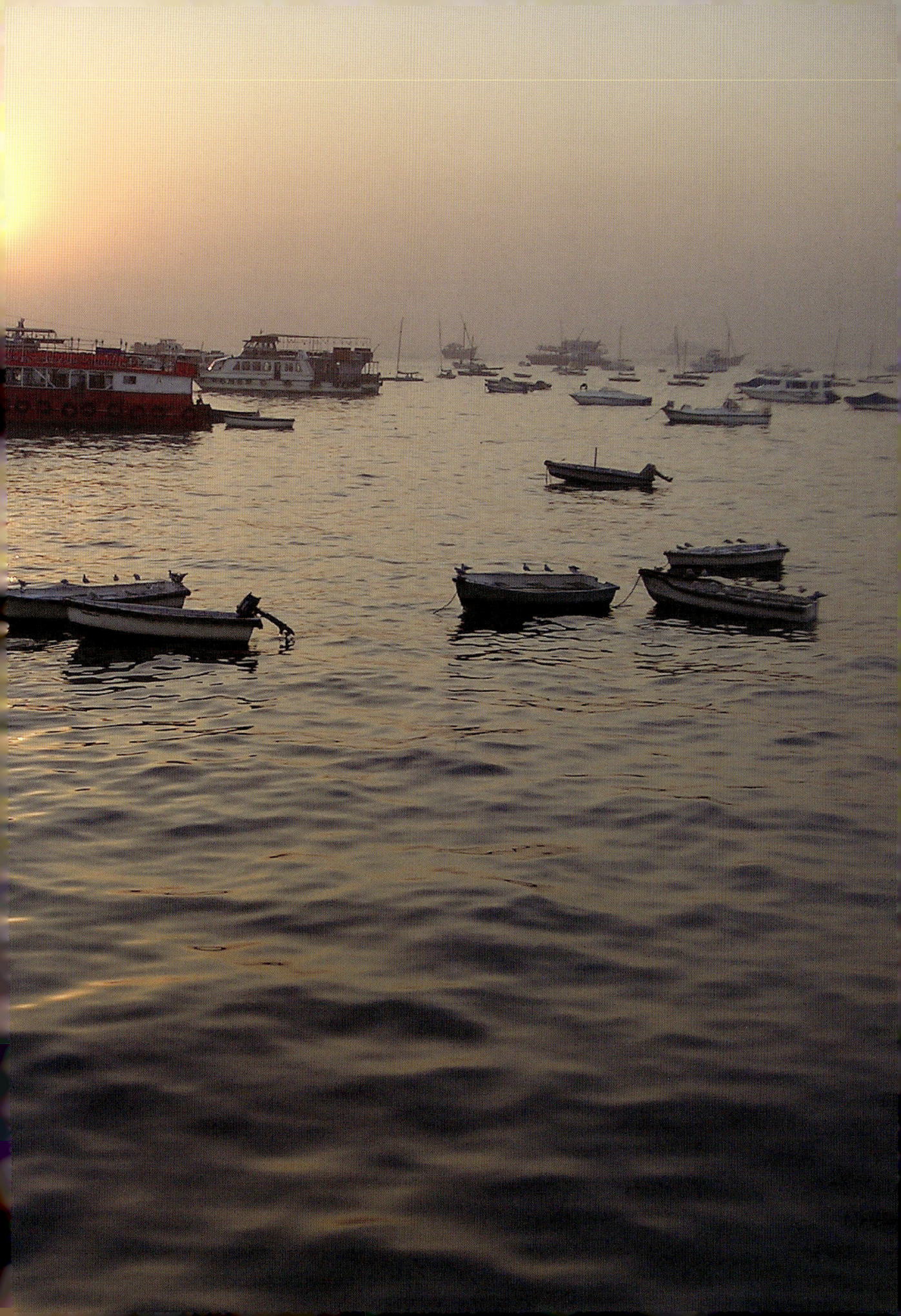

# Mukesh Ambani

*Chairman and Managing Director, Reliance Industries Limited*

I am a Mumbai boy. I grew up in this fishing village that's grown up to become the cradle of Indian entrepreneurship.

While my father struggled to make a name for himself in the textile business after returning to India from Aden, we used to play in the streets below our house in Bhuleshwar under the watchful gaze of my mother.

My memories of the faces, smells, and events of those times remain some of my fondest: rusty Vespas and Fiats, lumbering BEST buses, overladen trucks, hathgaris, and cyclists all competing for progress as pedestrians skillfully checkmated them. Mumbai began changing in earnest just as I was growing up. Suddenly "Chinese" noodles were as common on the streets as bhelpuri, dosas, and ragda pattice. The university's soaring Rajabhai tower, the stern-looking High Court skirting the Oval Maidan, and the gently derelict Colonial-era buildings were suddenly seeing new structures mushroom around them. But even as the new Mumbai Stock Exchange soared over the Colonial Indo-Saracenic buildings around Flora Fountain, and skyscrapers gave the city a new skyline, Mumbai somehow managed to retain its charm.

In the older quarters of the city, many cultures and generations coexisted side by side. Mosques, temples, synagogues, fire temples, gurdwaras, and churches stood just paces from one another. Apart from migrants, the port brought in all manner of visitors. When you passed people in the streets you could hear languages and accents from all over the world. There could have been no more stimulating place to grow up.

If our environments mold us, then Mumbai has made me much of who I am. On its streets, I learned to stand up for myself; in its roadside stalls, I learned to bargain; in its commercial centers, I learned business; and in its cinemas, I learned to dream. But more than all this, this city of contradictions has taught me how to navigate a world that is increasingly complex and global, while always retaining the best of our collective heritage. For no single thing has ever defined Mumbai, and while it welcomes every new influence and immigrant, space is always left for the old.

As kids, when we could get together enough money, we would take the 123 bus to Navy Nagar, where walking abround gave an idea of Mumbai was like a century ago—leafy roads lined with garden residences and elegant stone buildings. Even today, while driving home from work I'll often watch in wonder as the Koli fisherfolk sail their Arabian-style dhows from their village, crammed between the office complexes at Nariman Point and the residential towers at Cuffe Parade, seemingly unperturbed by the world that has risen around them.

And what a world it is. Financial capital, home to Bollywood, military base, fashion hub, and cultural center, Mumbai is a multitude of things to a multitude of people—twenty-five million at last count. Many of them never seem to sleep, for this city radiates an energy that perfectly captures the inner drive of Indians to create a nation that is one of the foremost in the world. Already, many Mumbai-based companies are renowned across the globe, and are serving as the accelerators speeding India toward entry into the developed world. True, when passing through (or by, as many of us do) the sprawling

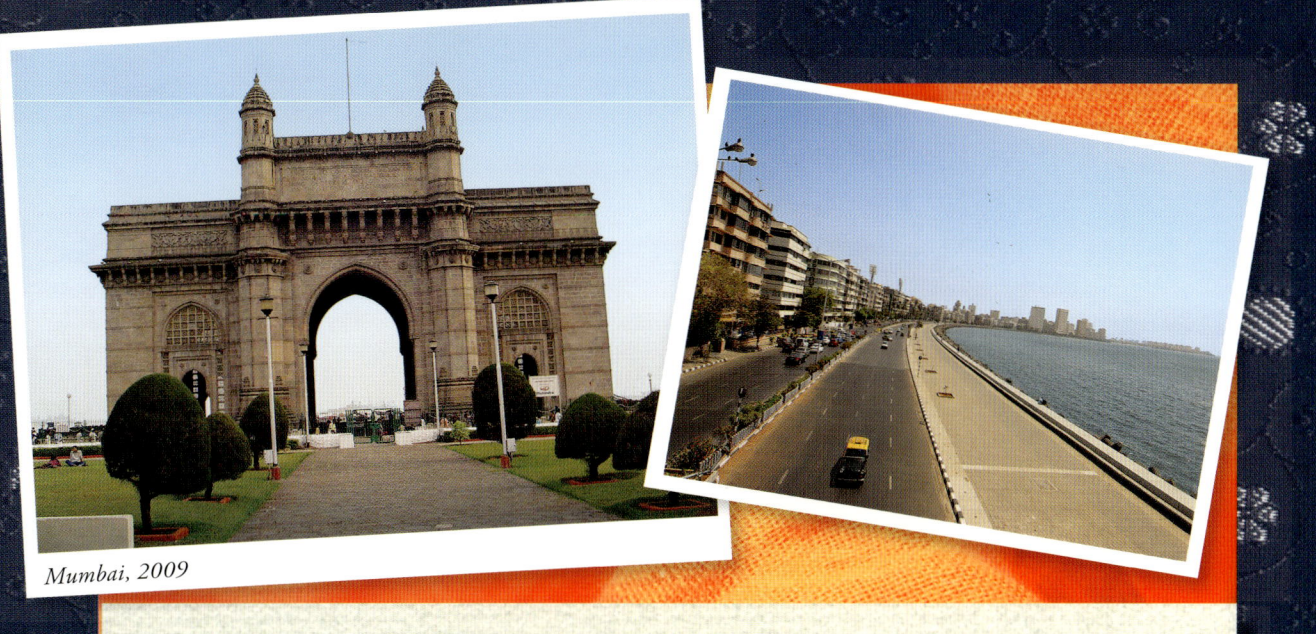

*Mumbai, 2009*

shanties of Dharavi, the sight of naked children playing in gutters is enough to tear at the hardest hearts and hold up as invalid our dream of a great India. But the promise of change is everywhere in Mumbai, and what I love and admire about this city is the manner in which it overcomes all the naysayers and obstacles that try to constrain its ambition. Riots, cyclones, protests, floods… this city has seen it all and always comes through stronger, wearing its scars with dignity.

Its history of successful struggle against defying odds is etched into every corner. Mani Bhavan on Laburnum Road, Mahatma Gandhi's Mumbai residence, reminds us of the great man and that the call for Britain to "Quit India" was made at the August Kranti Maidan. On Marine Drive we can enjoy one of the world's finest collections of Art Deco buildings only because of a land reclamation project once thought impossible. And India's most iconic landmarks, the Gateway of India and the grand Taj Mahal hotel behind it, were funded and built by Indians during a period of Colonial rule.

When terrorists made the Taj the center of their vendetta against this country and its ideal of secularism on November 26, 2008, they hit us where it hurt. As flames licked the hotel's dome, and as the Chhatrapati Shivaji station, Leopold Cafe, and Oberoi hotel also bled, I felt personally wounded. Mumbai is the place where people come to forget their narrow differences of caste, creed, and culture and become part of something bigger, something better. In fact, the Taj was built to transcend human differences, as an "all races" hotel, after its founder, Jamsetji Tata, was denied entry into one of the city's "whites only" hotels. For a moment, I worried whether the fabric of the city would be soiled by the random violence of 26/11. But in the days following the attack, my faith in Mumbai was only reinforced as its citizens came out onto the streets—sometimes in common protest against politicians, sometimes in quiet remembrance of those who perished, but always together. This is what gives me faith in our city and our country, which I feel certain is on the cusp of a great new destiny. This is why I love Mumbai.

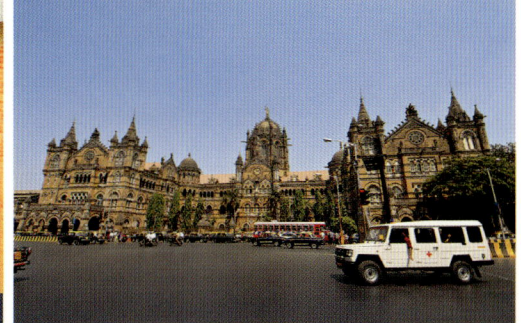

# Natalie Portman
*Actor*

I was in a local beauty shop with a friend who needed grooming while we were in Udaipur. It was one room with a floor-to-ceiling darkened window as the street-side wall. My friend had her legs perched on a table as the beautician curled hot wax around a popsicle stick and readied a ripped denim square to remove the unwanted hair. She spread the wax and patted down the cloth to adhere to it.

As she was about to pull, we heard devastated shrieks of pain outside the shop.

A dog had been hit by a car and was crying loudly, nauseatingly, dyingly in the road just outside. We watched as it lay on its side, crying on the pavement.

As if they were police responding to an alarm, the other dogs in the neighborhood came out from their repose in the shade, running toward the suffering one, a small black-and-white mutt. The dogs that ran toward its cries were larger, wolfish-looking ones.

"Don't look," my friend told me, even as she could not look away herself. "They're going to eat it."

I shut my eyes, wondering, Do dogs cannibalize one another? I didn't think so. But then, I reminded myself, there was that saying: dog-eat-dog world. It must come from somewhere.

I opened my eyes just in time to see one of the larger dogs open its mouth and bite into the injured dog's leg. The poor sufferer still whimpered as the larger dog dragged it out of the street and into the shadow of a parked car. The other dogs swarmed around them, and my friend and I half-shielded our eyes, unable to look away from how the dog's fate might unravel.

But the larger dog simply licked the injured dog's leg until it stood up. He limped, but had by now stopped crying. The larger dog nudged the injured dog's sagging tail until it perked up, signaling well-being. Then the larger dog walked away, leaving the limping dog to its independence. He walked past the car and out of sight from the beauty shop window.

The beautician ripped off the denim that had still been adhered to my friend's leg, which was still perched on the table.

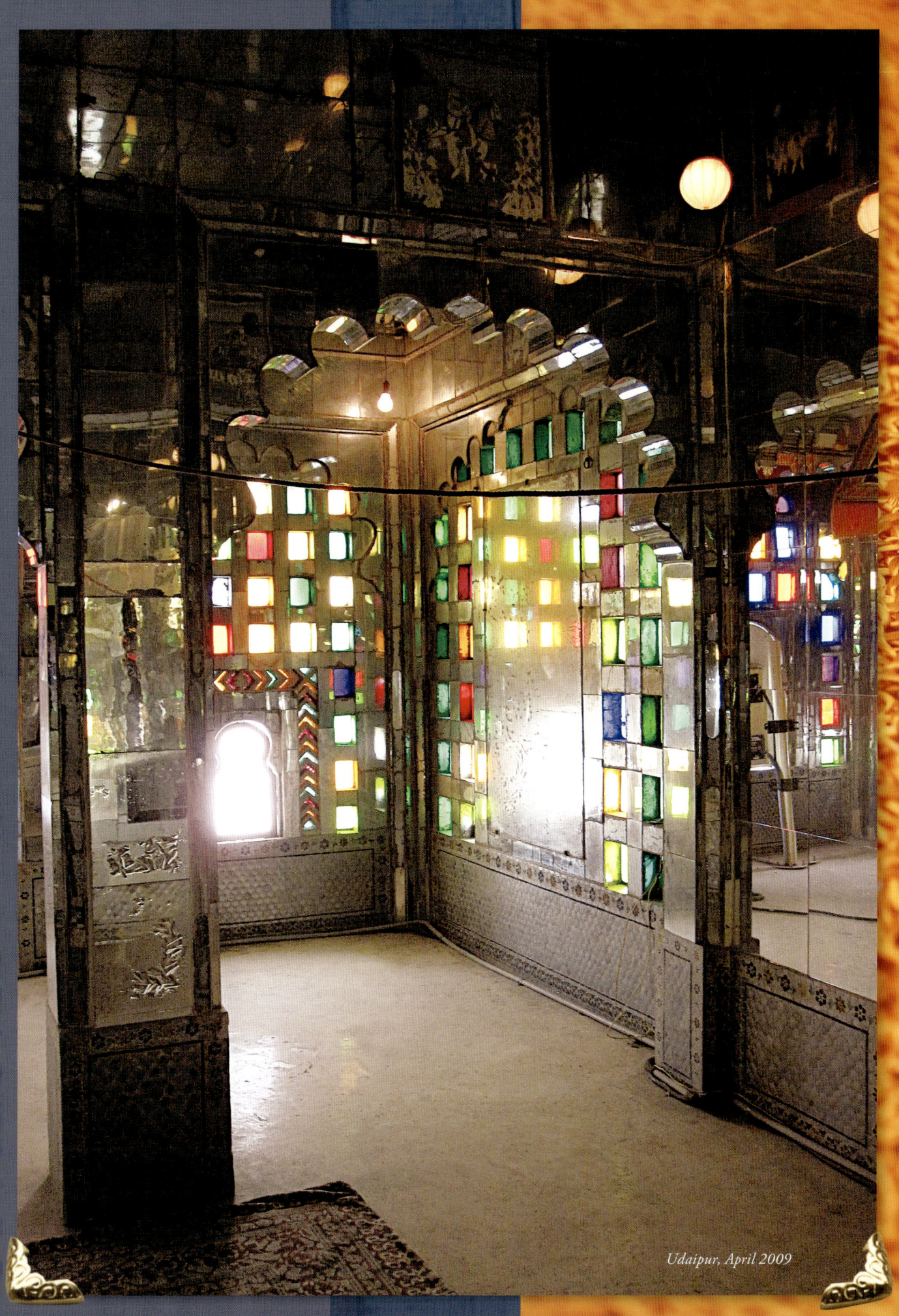

Udaipur, April 2009

# Naveen and Shallu Jindal

*Member of Indian Parliament (Naveen) and Cultural Activist and Kuchipudi Dancer (Shallu)*

Even when I was just a boy, I was fascinated by the colors of our national flag—saffron, white, and green. And that passion has stayed with me all my life. When I went to the U.S. to study for my MBA, one of the first things I noticed was how the American flag was used all over the country, in people's homes and on their clothes, as a proud symbol and a constant reminder in everyday life. Following that example, I proudly displayed the tricolor in the student union building.

On returning home, I found that there were all kinds of taboos with regard to the use of the national flag. Working now as a director of Jindal Strips, I hoisted the flag at our Raigad factory on Republic Day. A show of patriotism? Not according to the local authorities. I was summarily ordered to remove it, and told that the Flag Code of India does not permit private institutions to fly the flag.

I couldn't accept this. Why should I, a citizen of India, not be allowed to fly the flag? And so started my battle with the courts. I petitioned the Delhi High Court and won my case. I could now fly the national flag on my premises. It was a historic judgment—a reaffirmation of a fundamental right. However, the government appealed and the matter went to the Supreme Court. Finally, on January 23, 2004, nearly nine years after I had started my crusade, the Supreme Court decreed that flying the national flag was every Indian's fundamental right.

But the battle was not over. There were still restrictions on the use of the flag on clothing. I wanted our sports teams to display it on their uniforms, so I took the issue to parliament, and finally, on July 5, 2005, they allowed the use of the flag on clothes as well.

What India means to me—and to a billion people—is symbolized by the national flag. I am happy that I have won the right to display it with pride as an individual, a citizen of India.

My wife, Shallu, is a kuchipudi dancer. She echoes my love for the country in her own special way: in her dance for democracy.

People all over the world have lived and died for their national flags. And that's what I will do for our Tiranga.

—*Naveen Jindal*

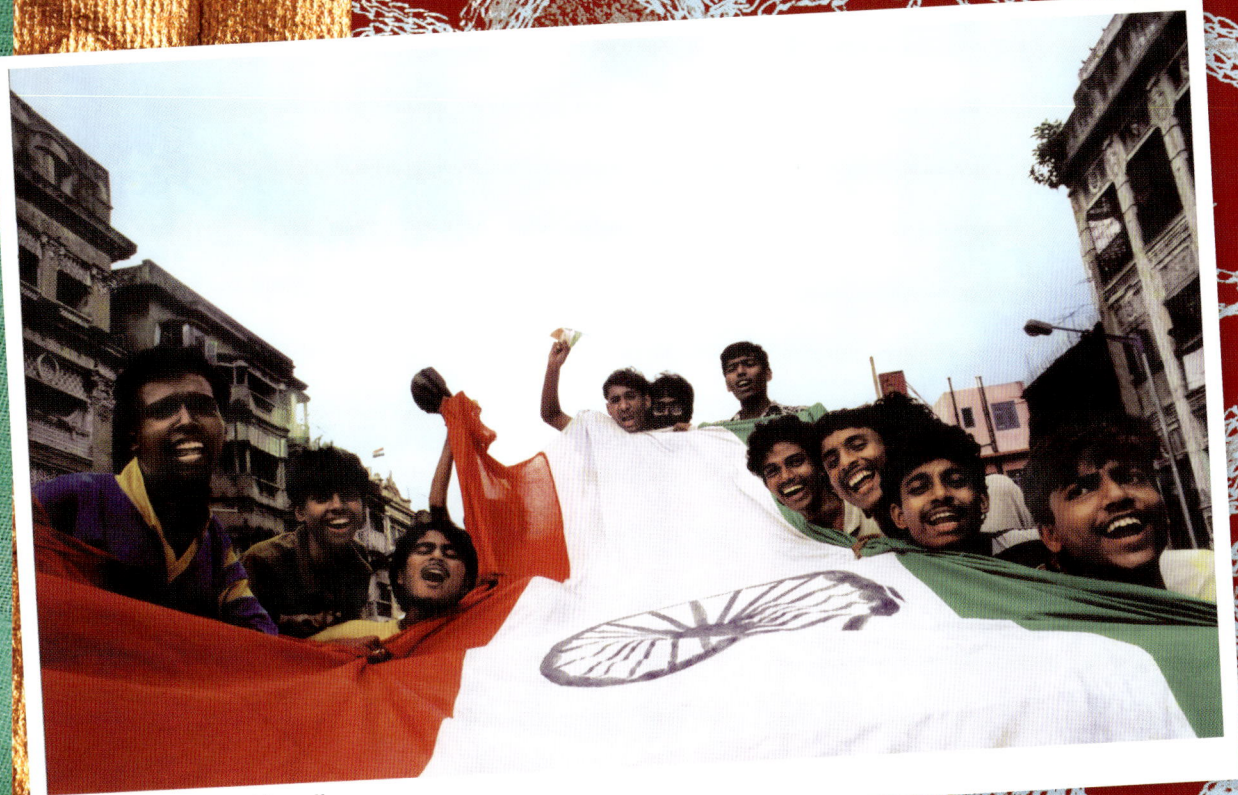

Photograph by Joy Mukhopadhyay

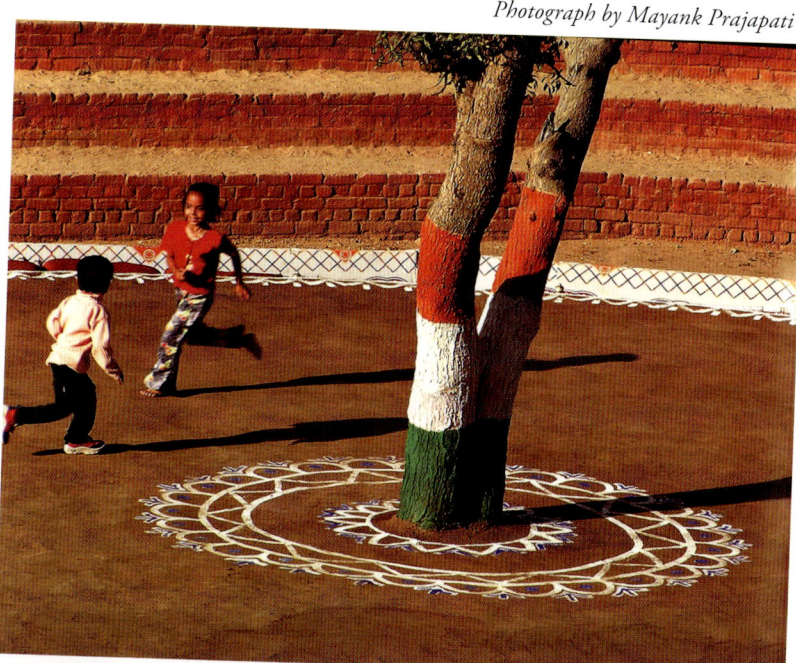

Photograph by Mayank Prajapati

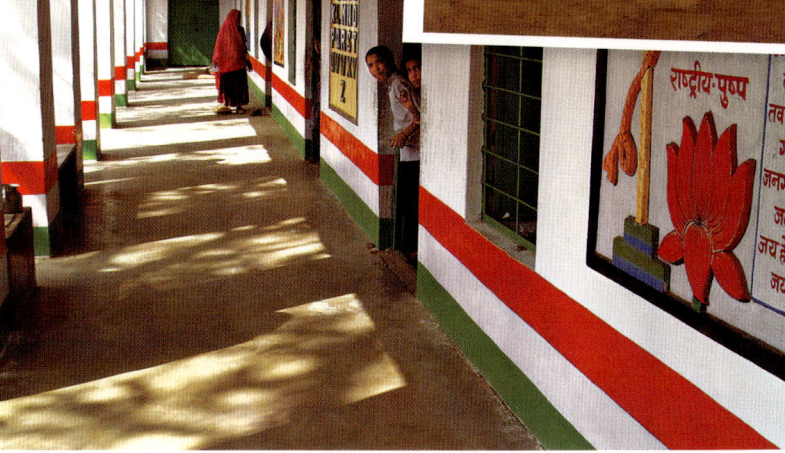

Photograph by Vijay S. Jodha

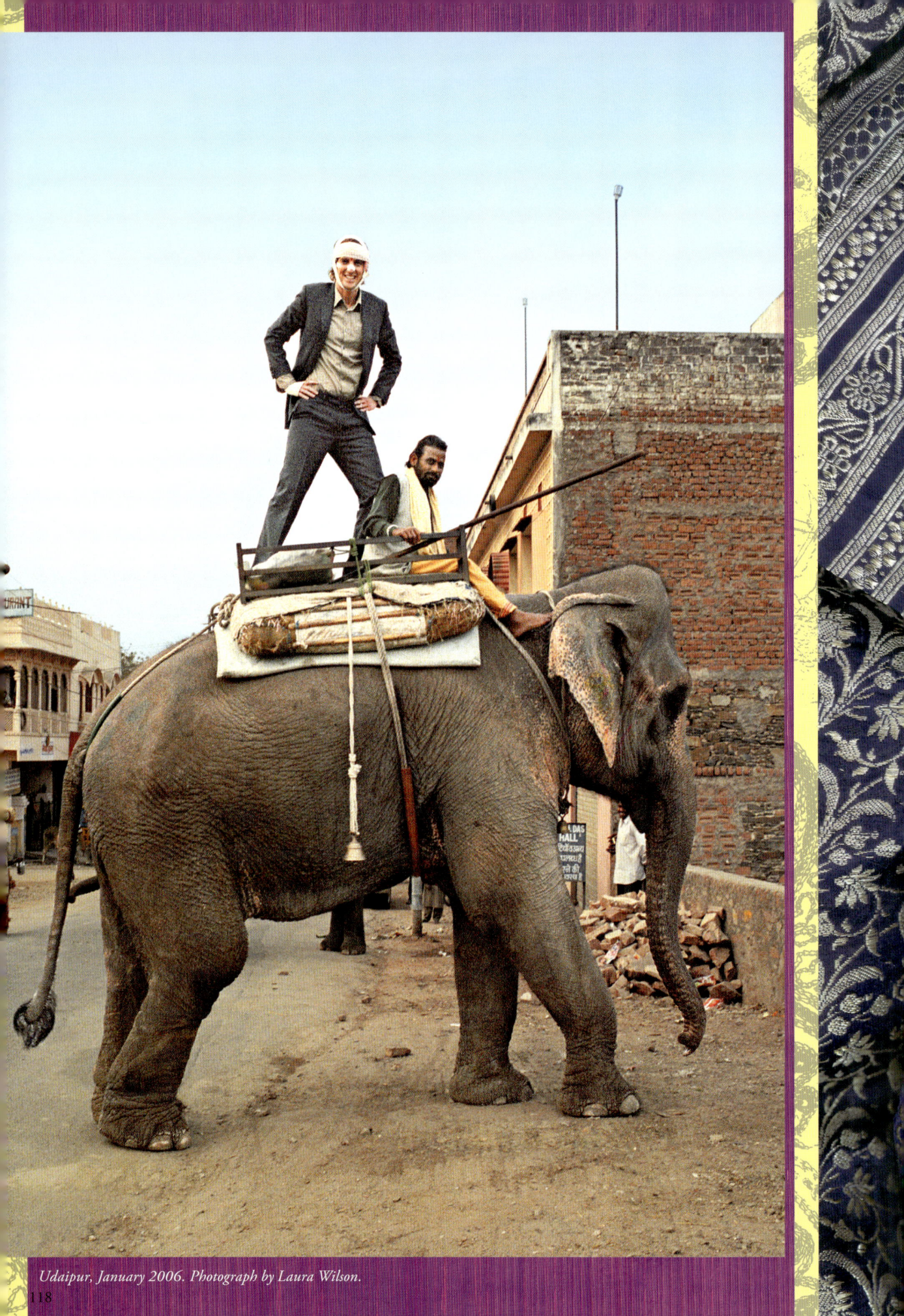

*Udaipur, January 2006. Photograph by Laura Wilson.*

# Owen Wilson
*Actor*

"*This was in Udaipur, in the western desert. We spent our last shooting days on* The Darjeeling Limited *there, and my mother came for a visit. She's a photographer, and we took this on the way home from set one day. Come to think of it, the whole country seemed like a movie set, where you could see something new and unexpected at any time or place. I'll never forget it, and if what they say about elephants is true, I guess he won't, either.*"

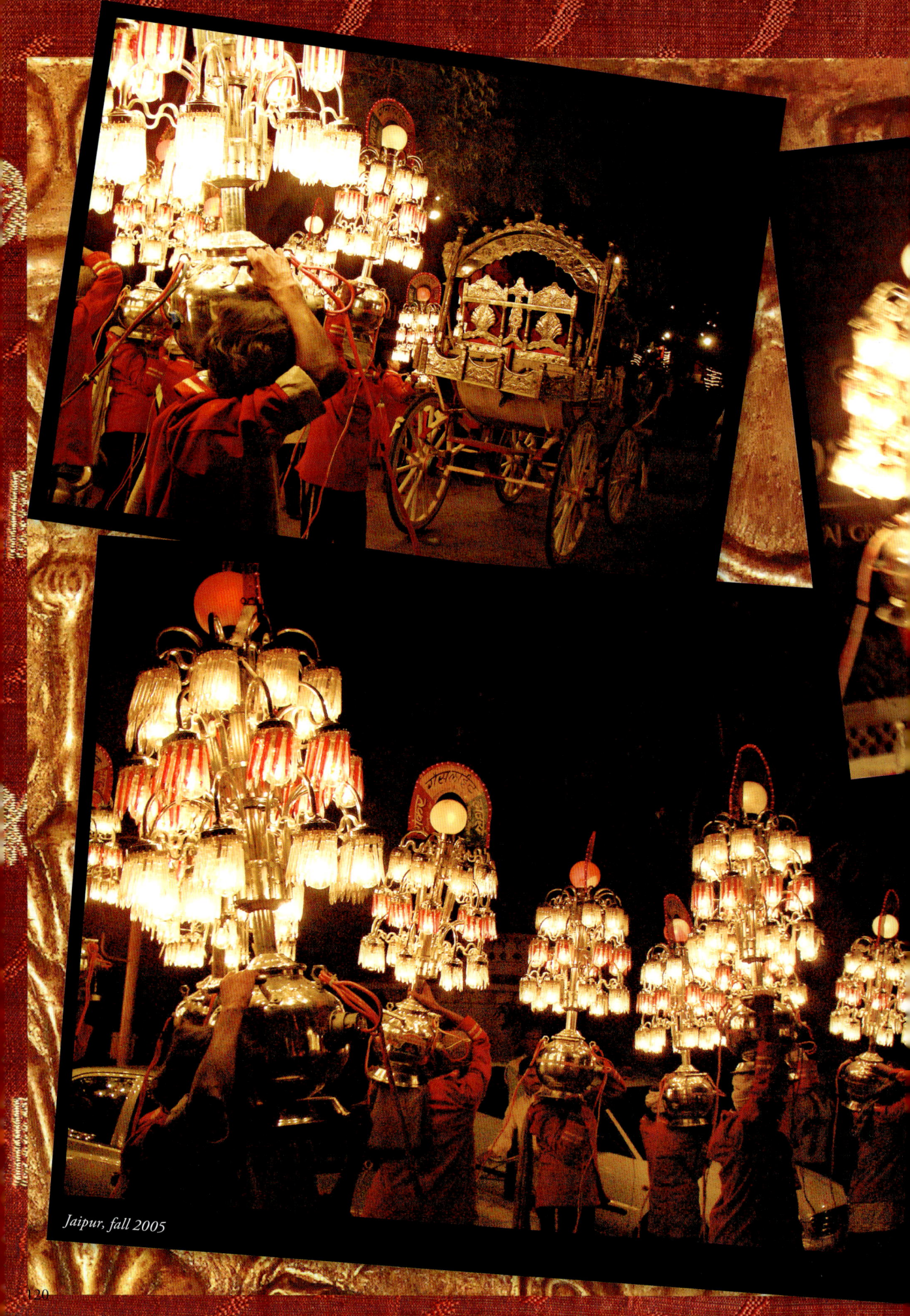
Jaipur, fall 2005

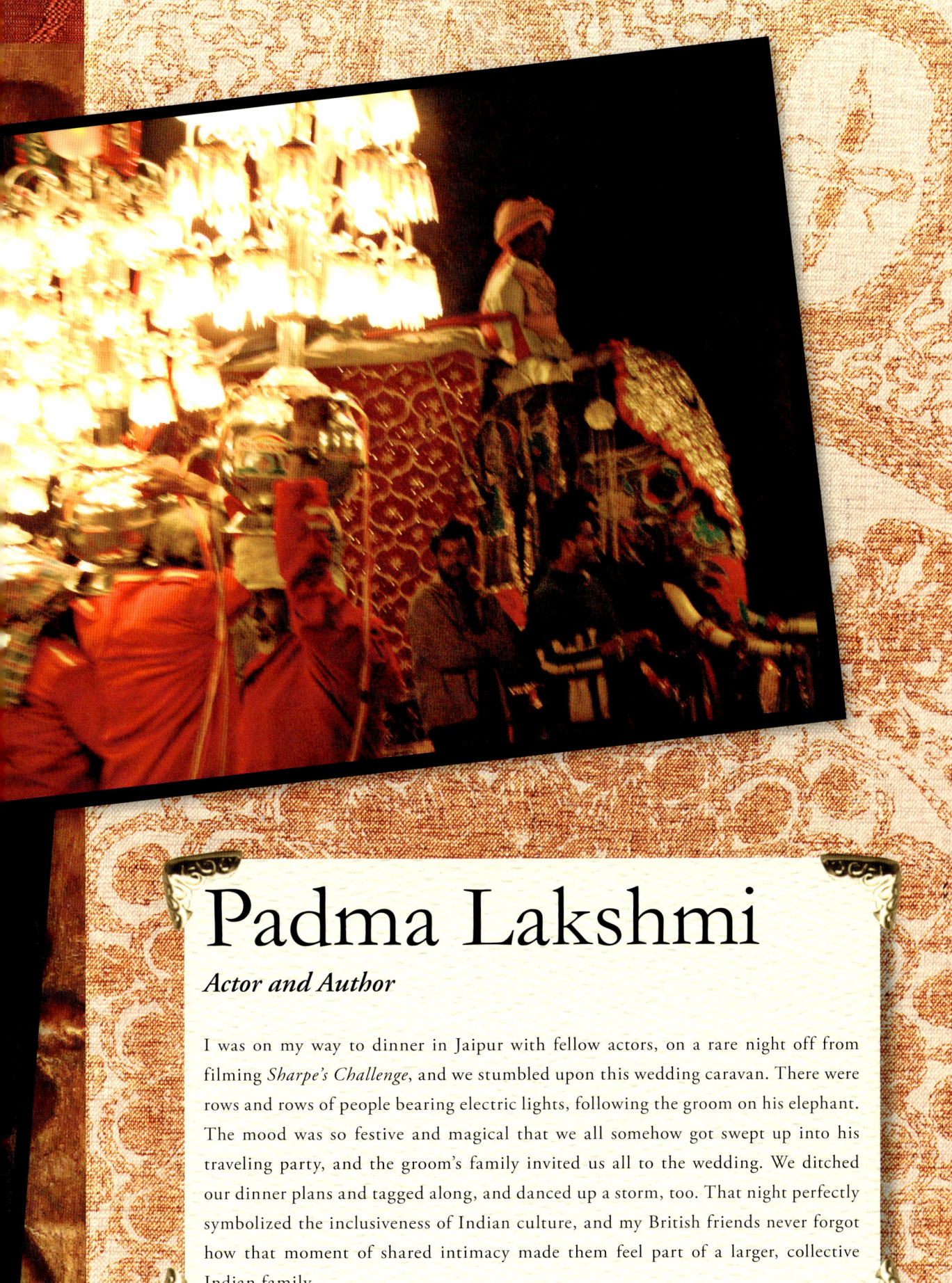

# Padma Lakshmi
*Actor and Author*

I was on my way to dinner in Jaipur with fellow actors, on a rare night off from filming *Sharpe's Challenge*, and we stumbled upon this wedding caravan. There were rows and rows of people bearing electric lights, following the groom on his elephant. The mood was so festive and magical that we all somehow got swept up into his traveling party, and the groom's family invited us all to the wedding. We ditched our dinner plans and tagged along, and danced up a storm, too. That night perfectly symbolized the inclusiveness of Indian culture, and my British friends never forgot how that moment of shared intimacy made them feel part of a larger, collective Indian family.

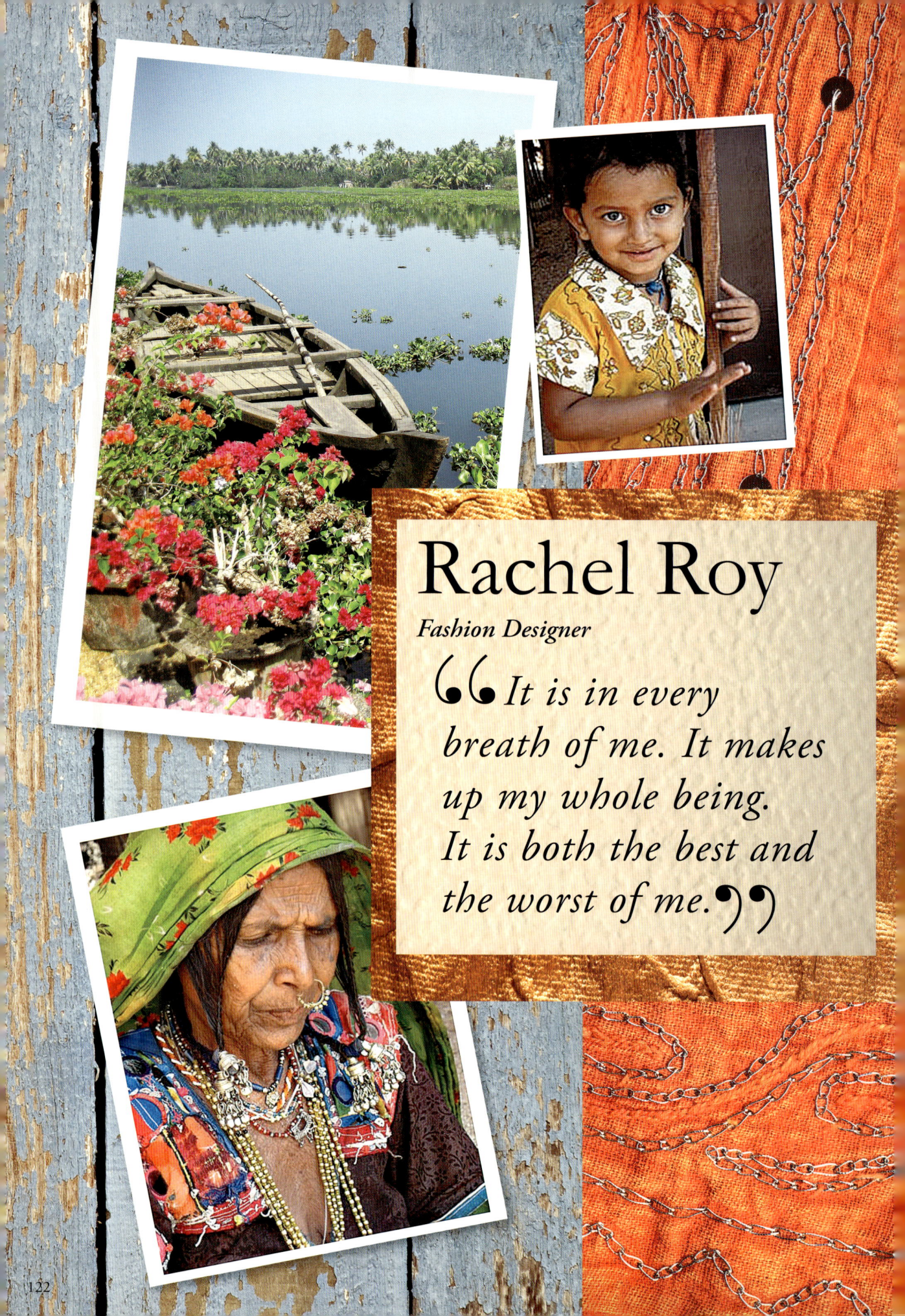

# Rachel Roy
*Fashion Designer*

❝ *It is in every breath of me. It makes up my whole being. It is both the best and the worst of me.* ❞

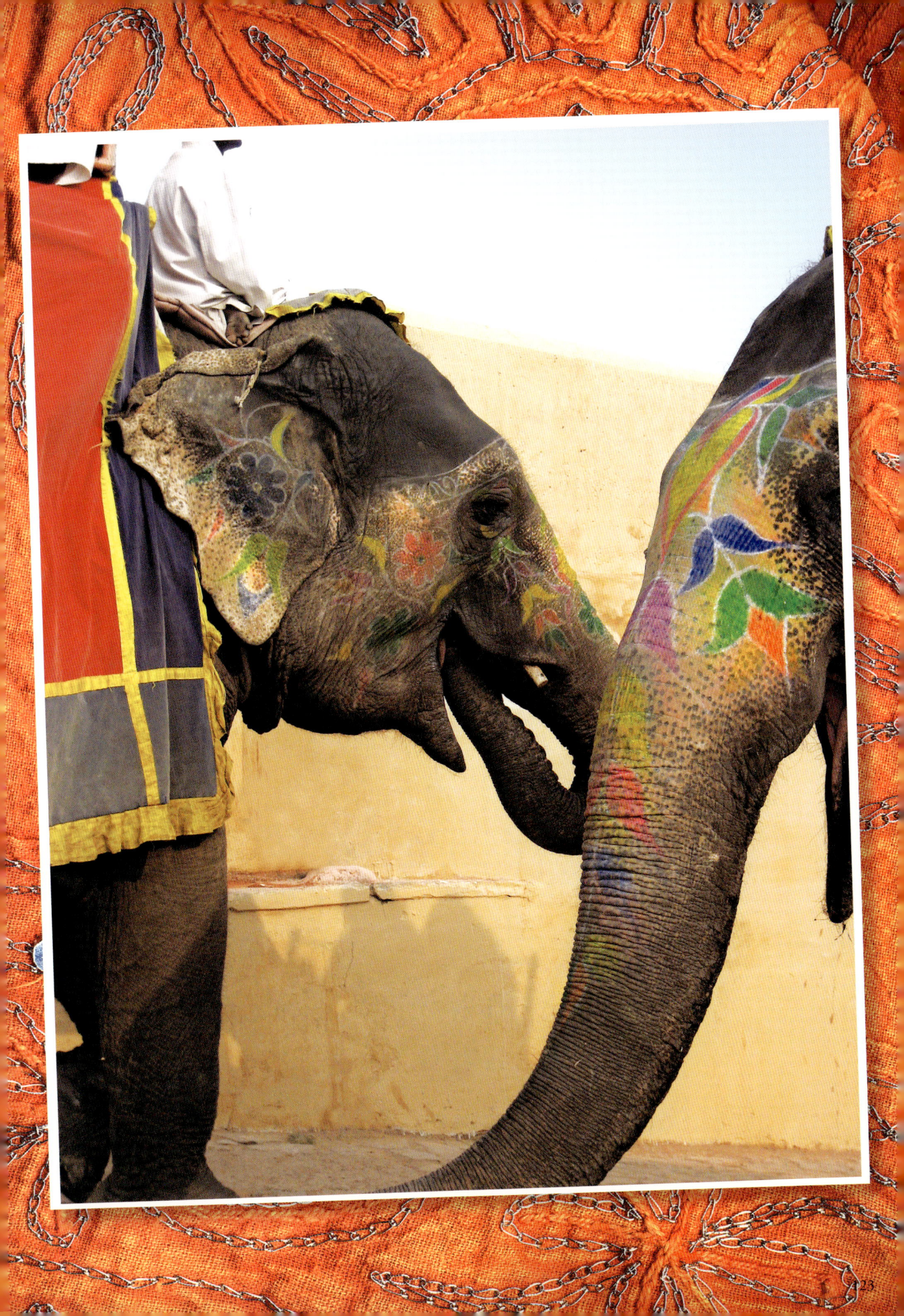

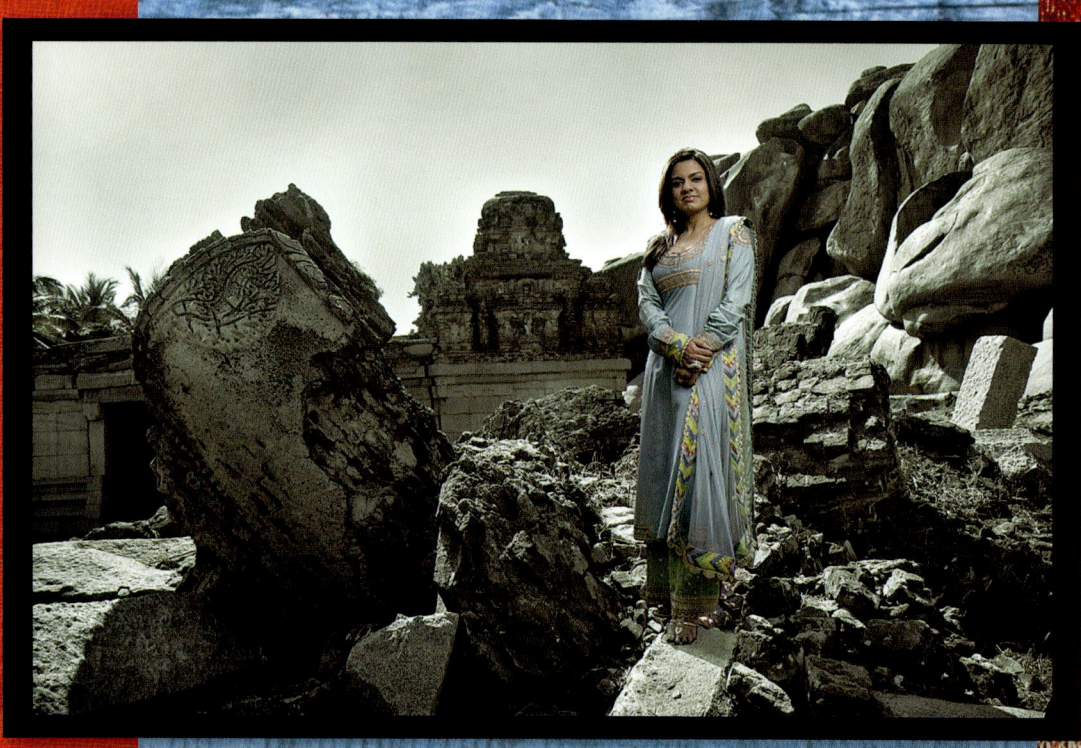

# Sangita Jindal

*Chairperson, Jindal Steel Works Foundation, and Publisher, ARTIndia Magazine*

*❝Being a Mumbaikar is so important to me! I live among the myriad hues of a cosmopolitan city, where people who want to try their luck, who want to dream, who want to make it big— who want to make a difference—come. As a Mumbaikar, I want to and I will make a difference. And we Mumbaikars are not afraid of storms: we are learning how to sail our ships.❞*

*Hampi, Karnataka, 2008*

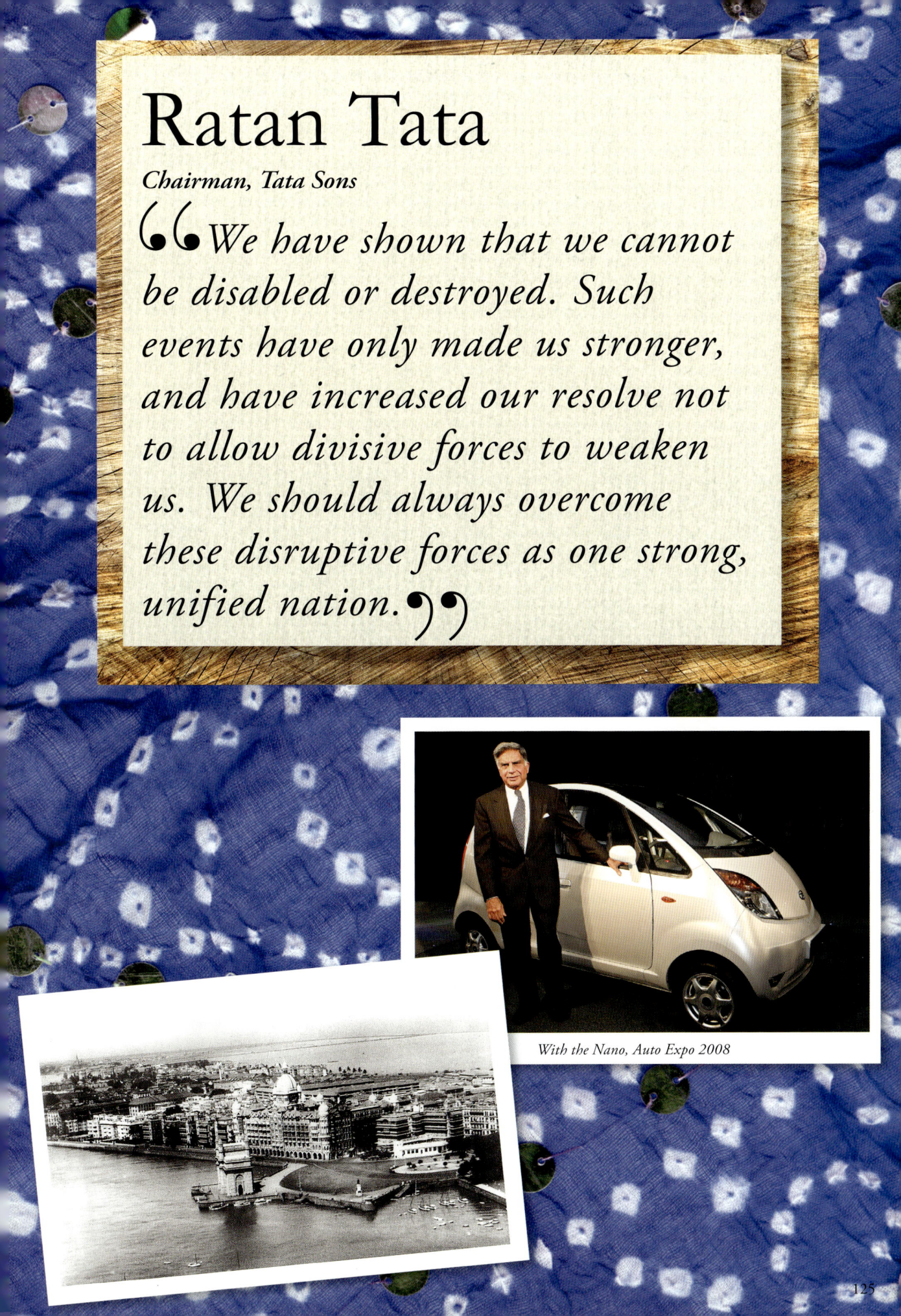

# Ratan Tata

*Chairman, Tata Sons*

"We have shown that we cannot be disabled or destroyed. Such events have only made us stronger, and have increased our resolve not to allow divisive forces to weaken us. We should always overcome these disruptive forces as one strong, unified nation."

*With the Nano, Auto Expo 2008*

# Robert Rabensteiner
*Stylist,* L'Uomo Vogue

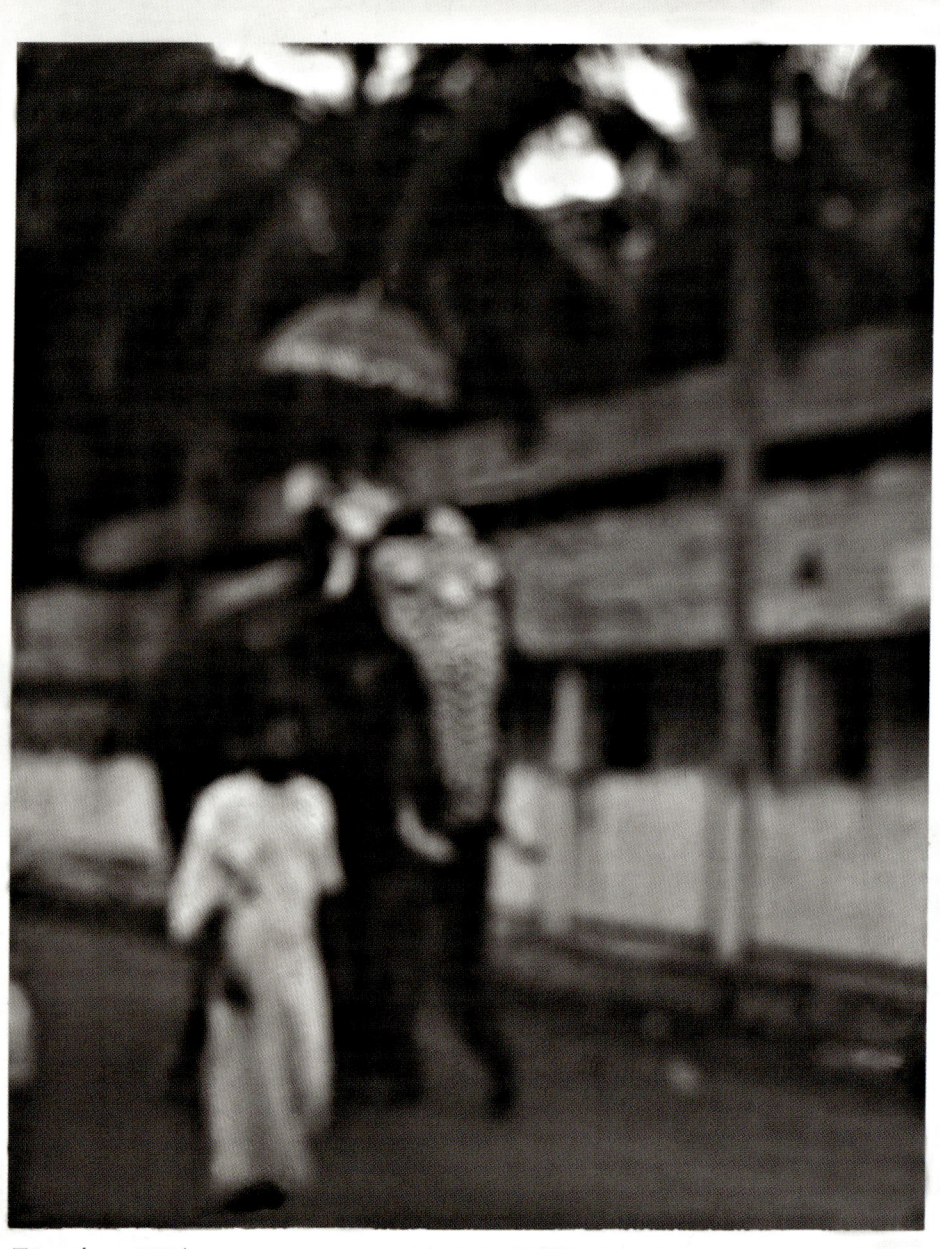

*Trivandrum, 2004*

# Saif Ali Khan

*Actor*

It's a day of leisure for me. A day with no shoot—I wake up late and sip coffee on the balcony, looking at the not-so-sprawling concrete jungle, engulfed in the bursting glory of green mango trees and gulmohar. That's the endearing view of Bombay that I see.

Bombay, the financial capital of India, offers you the adrenaline rush of a fast-paced life. At the same time, in one of the most laid-back suburbs of the city, Bandra, you can live a life in which you can read at a coffee shop, undisturbed by your stardom. You can walk in shorts, an old T-shirt, and kolhapuri chappals, go to a local multiplex, and guzzle a cold beer at one of many quaint hangouts.

Cuisines from all over the world are out there for you on a platter. Music, bars, and women, if they be your fancy, or churches and seaside, if that's more your pace—Bombay has all of this and more.

Of all the cities I have seen in the world—and apart from a handful, I have shot in most—Bombay stands out as exceptional, and Bandra even more.

I may go anywhere in the world, but it is this corner of it, this city of grit and gumption, with an almost phoenixlike spirit, ready to rise above adversity, that remains the center of my being.

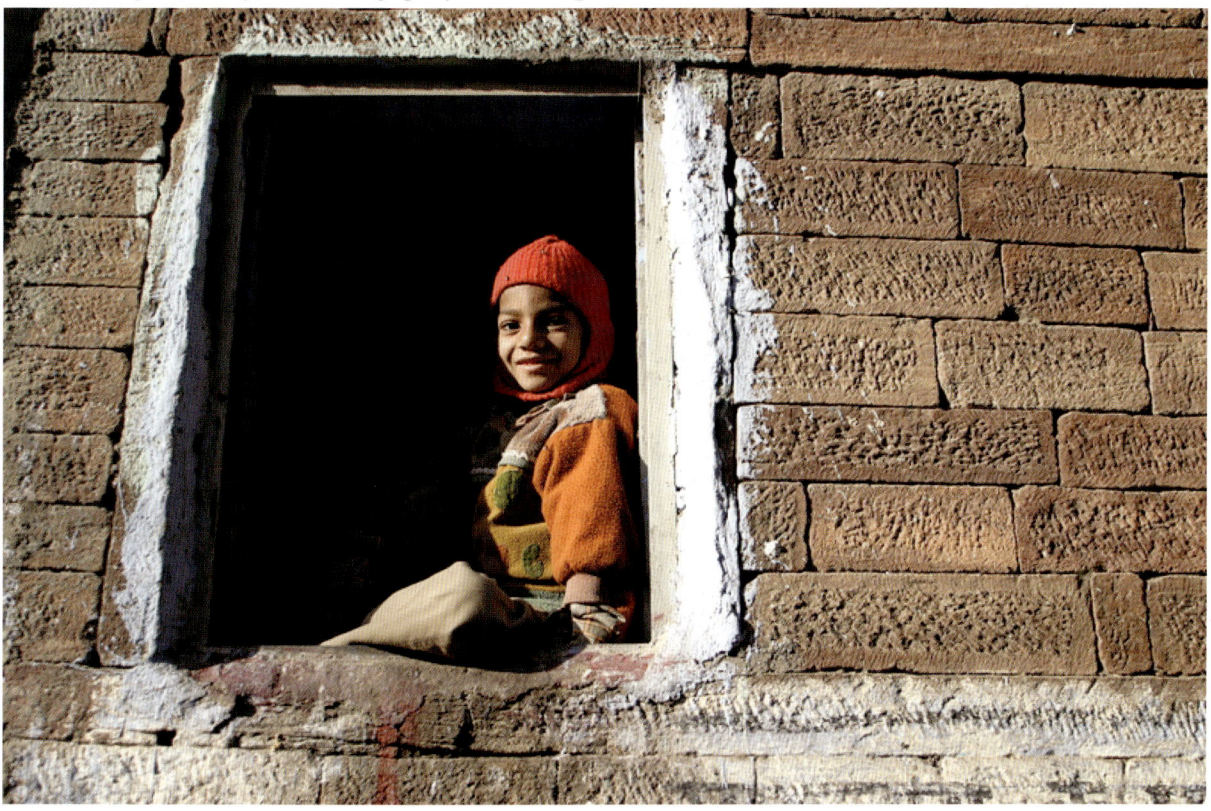

*Window, Jodhpur, January 2003. Photograph by Andrew Chapman.*

# Tarun Tahiliani
*Fashion Designer*

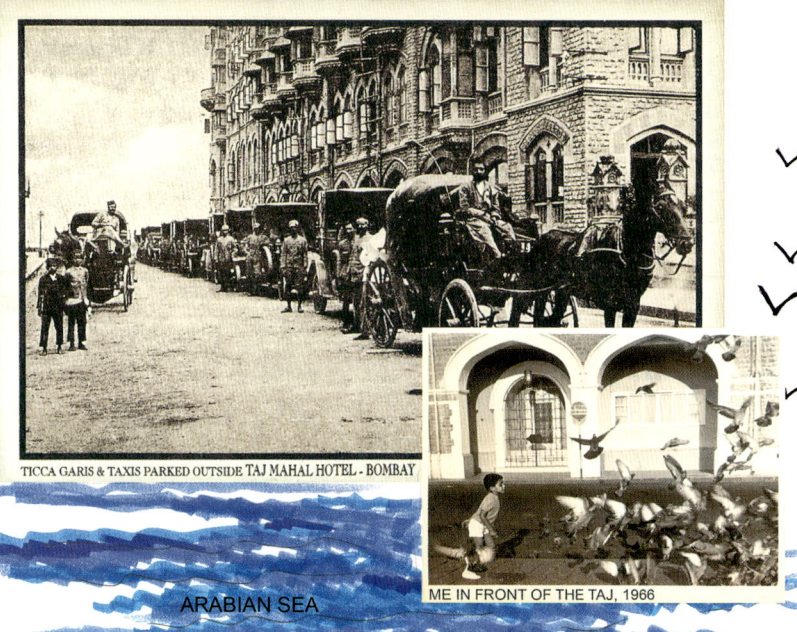

ARABIAN SEA

ME IN FRONT OF THE TAJ, 1966

This is the world I grew up in and done there levers that try and change that! Somewhere the need to go back in time! I abhor the delusional cowardice of the attackers for that's what it was. This is home. That's how it should stay!

*Tarun Tahiliani*

*May 2009*

# Sheikh Majed Al-Sabah
*Founder, Villa Moda*

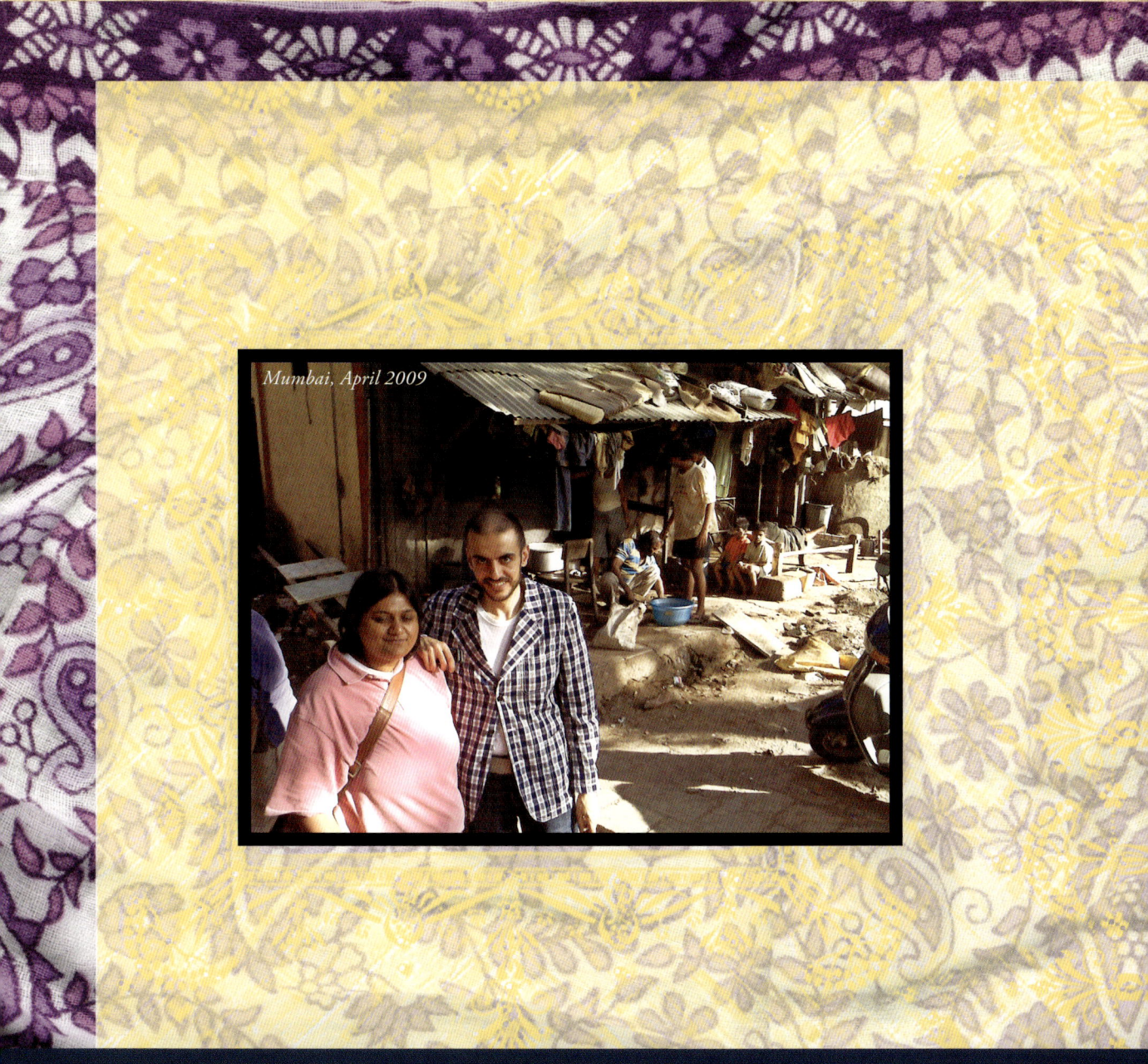

Mumbai, April 2009

"*I guess the words* peace, humble, colorful, *and* smile *were all created by the people of India. May God bless India and its wonderful people.*"

# Sanjay Kapoor and the Genesis Colors team
*Luxury Retailers*

## Jyoti Narula

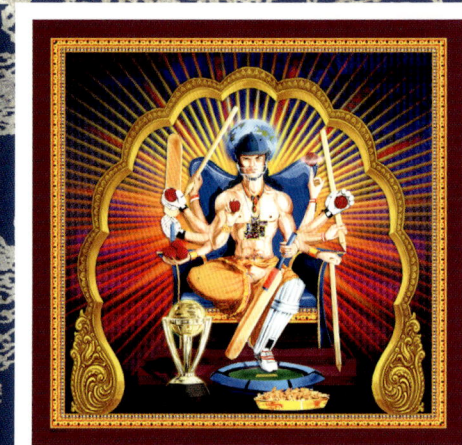

This is a Satya Paul scarf called "The Cricket God." I thought of it one day when an India-Pakistan final was on. I had a few friends over to watch the match with me, and as we sat there, I noticed people's reactions. The whole time, they kept saying "Sachin is God," and "Look at Dada play, his strokes are divine," and all I could think of was how we deify our cricketers, and how they are like gods to us. This picture represents the madness for the game in this country, and our tendency to make our sportsmen gods.

*March 2007*

## Sanjay Kapoor

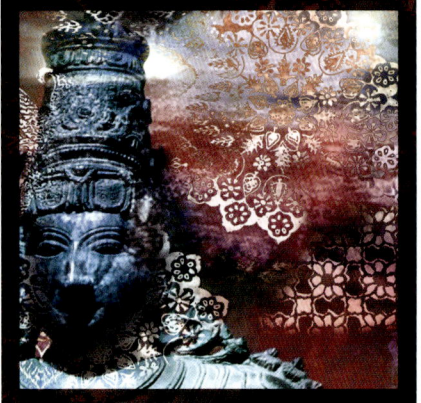

This is a scarf we thought of when we came across these figurines at a friend's place. They belong to the Chola period, which is one of our oldest dynasties. They represent ancient India in one of its most glorious times; a time of peace and harmony, with next to no religious divides; a time when our society was more open-minded and free-spirited. Chola figurines are known to be free-spirited ones.

*April 2008*

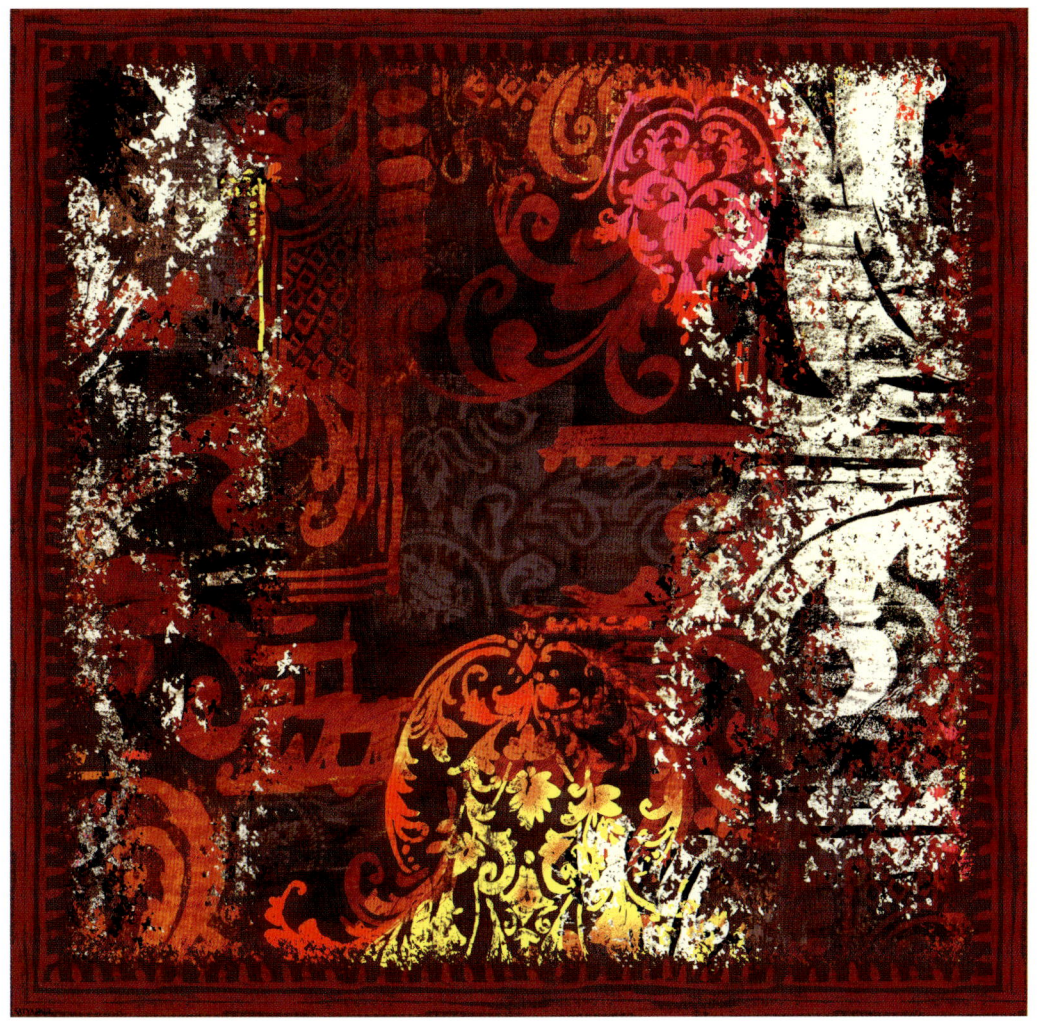

# Puneet Nanda

This scarf I call the "Cultures of India." I got the idea for it watching this heated argument on one of the news channels, listening to politicians fight over whose country India was, and who belonged to which region, and other such things. I started thinking about what India really is, and this is the design that came to mind. India is a mix of many cultures—each stands apart, maintaining its identity, and yet when they come together they stand for the essence of our country. Each pattern in this scarf represents one of the many traditions we have here, and though they stand out against one another, the picture is incomplete without all of the patterns. This is just how our country is. If one of our many religions or cultures went missing, we would be incomplete as a nation.

*December 2008*

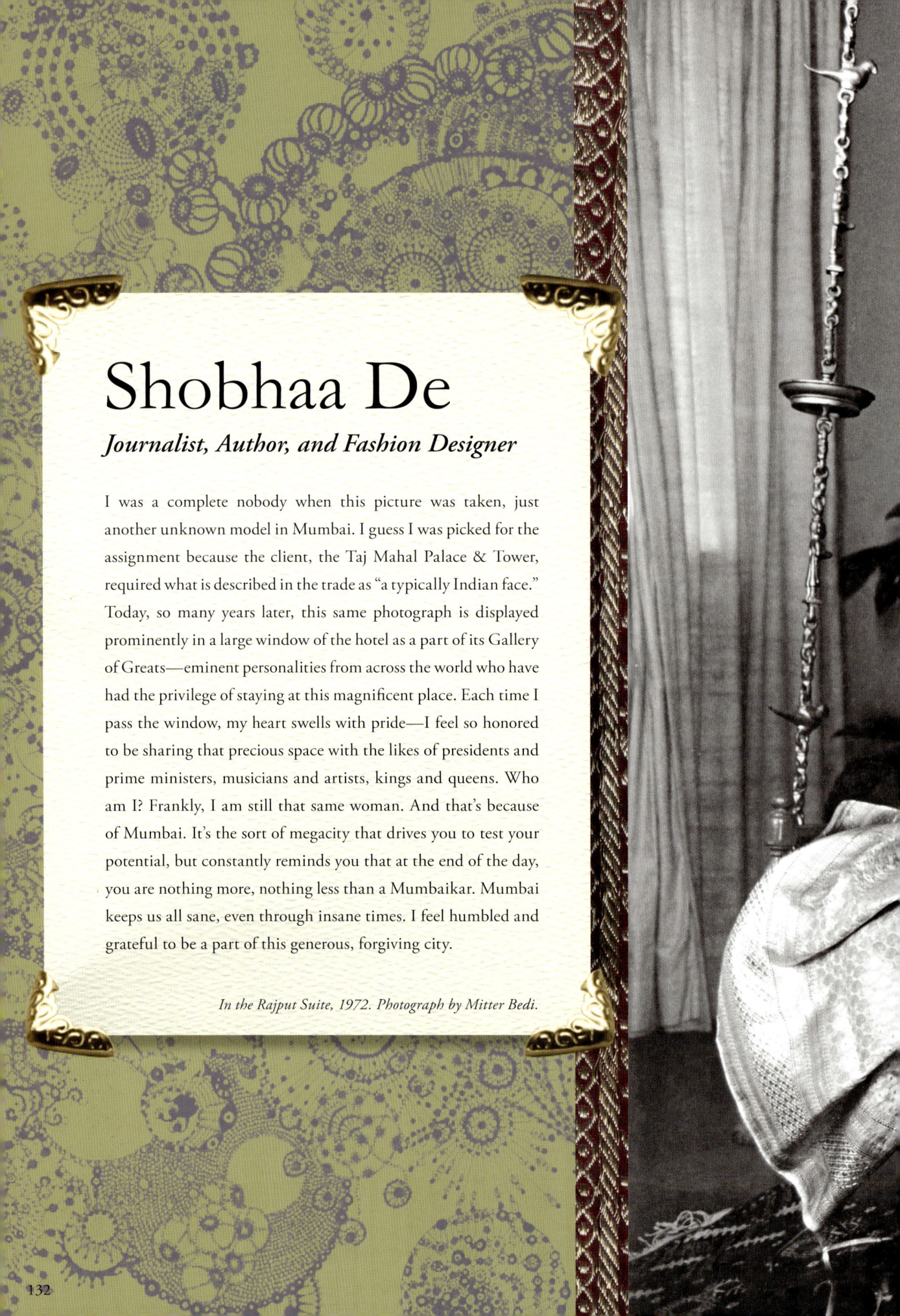

# Shobhaa De
*Journalist, Author, and Fashion Designer*

I was a complete nobody when this picture was taken, just another unknown model in Mumbai. I guess I was picked for the assignment because the client, the Taj Mahal Palace & Tower, required what is described in the trade as "a typically Indian face." Today, so many years later, this same photograph is displayed prominently in a large window of the hotel as a part of its Gallery of Greats—eminent personalities from across the world who have had the privilege of staying at this magnificent place. Each time I pass the window, my heart swells with pride—I feel so honored to be sharing that precious space with the likes of presidents and prime ministers, musicians and artists, kings and queens. Who am I? Frankly, I am still that same woman. And that's because of Mumbai. It's the sort of megacity that drives you to test your potential, but constantly reminds you that at the end of the day, you are nothing more, nothing less than a Mumbaikar. Mumbai keeps us all sane, even through insane times. I feel humbled and grateful to be a part of this generous, forgiving city.

*In the Rajput Suite, 1972. Photograph by Mitter Bedi.*

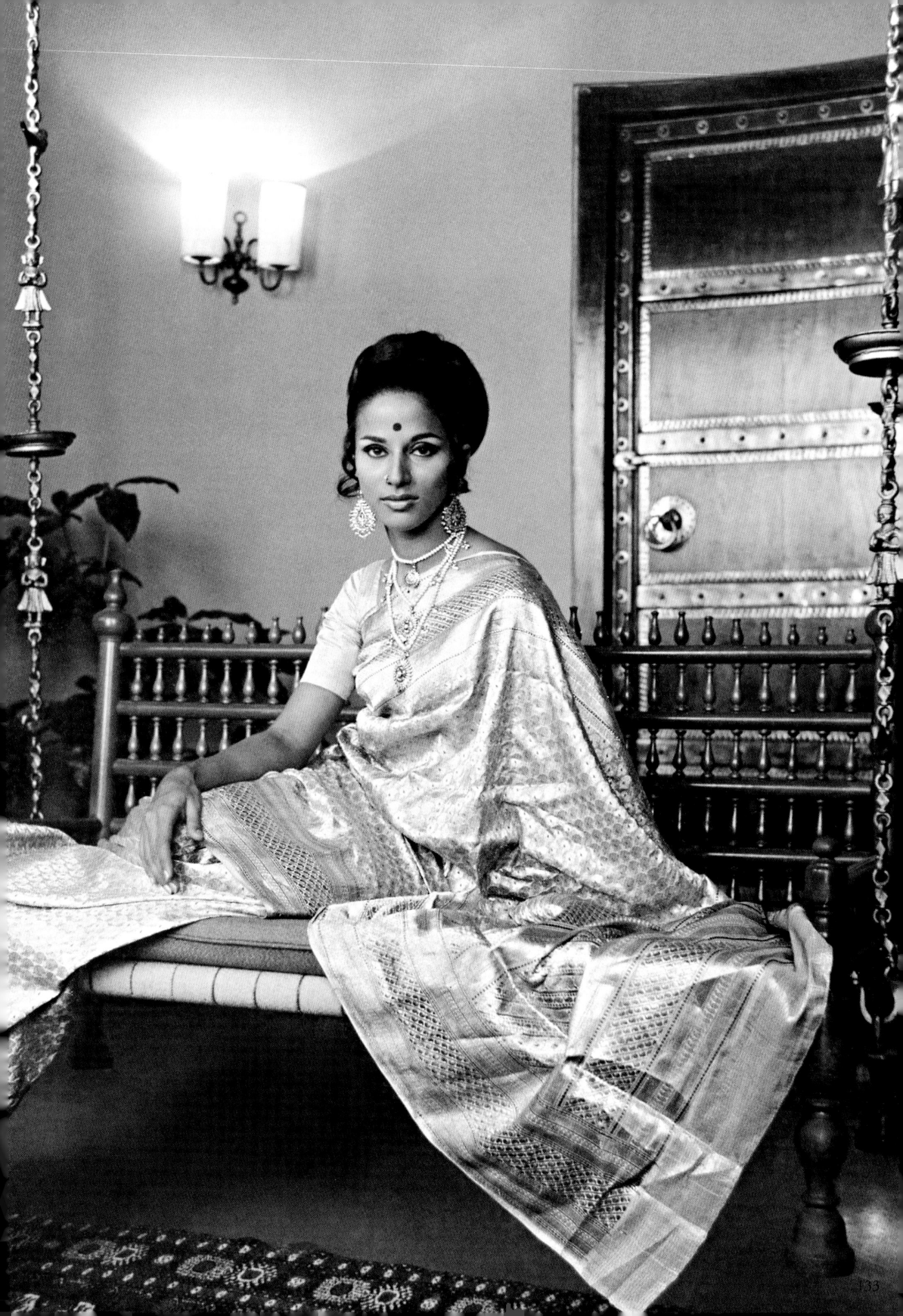

# Tina Bhojwani

*Senior Vice President, Theory*
*(Cofounder, Mumbai: We Got Your Back)*

An oasis of calm in the riotous urban jungle, the Taj will forever be one of my favorite spots in Bombay. Conceived of by Jamsetji Tata as a hotel worthy of this great city, it has stood as a symbol of fine Indian hospitality since 1903. Returning recently was like reuniting with an old friend; this icon still stands gracefully as ever by the sea, a powerful reminder that courage and spirit cannot be diminished by acts of violence.

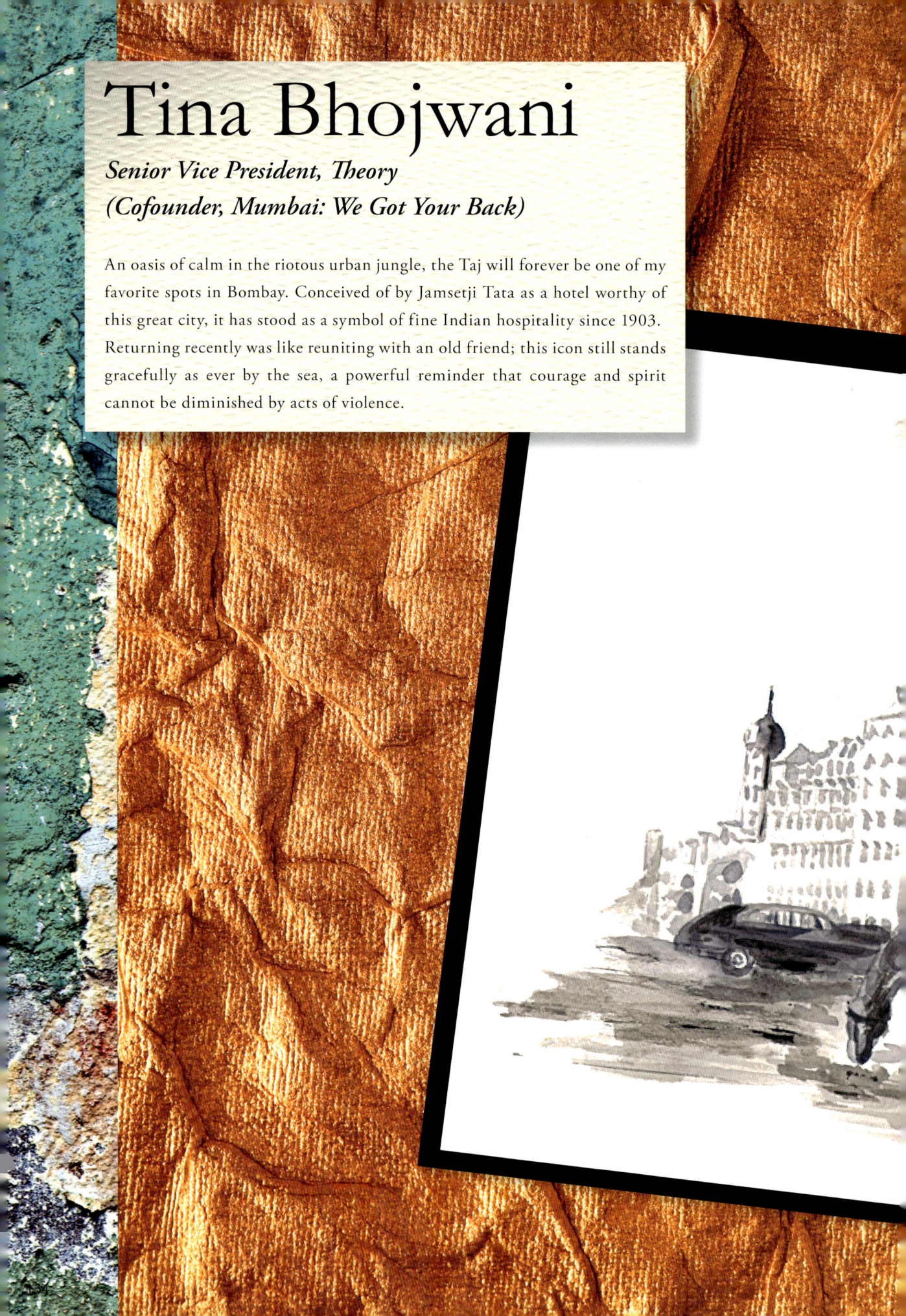

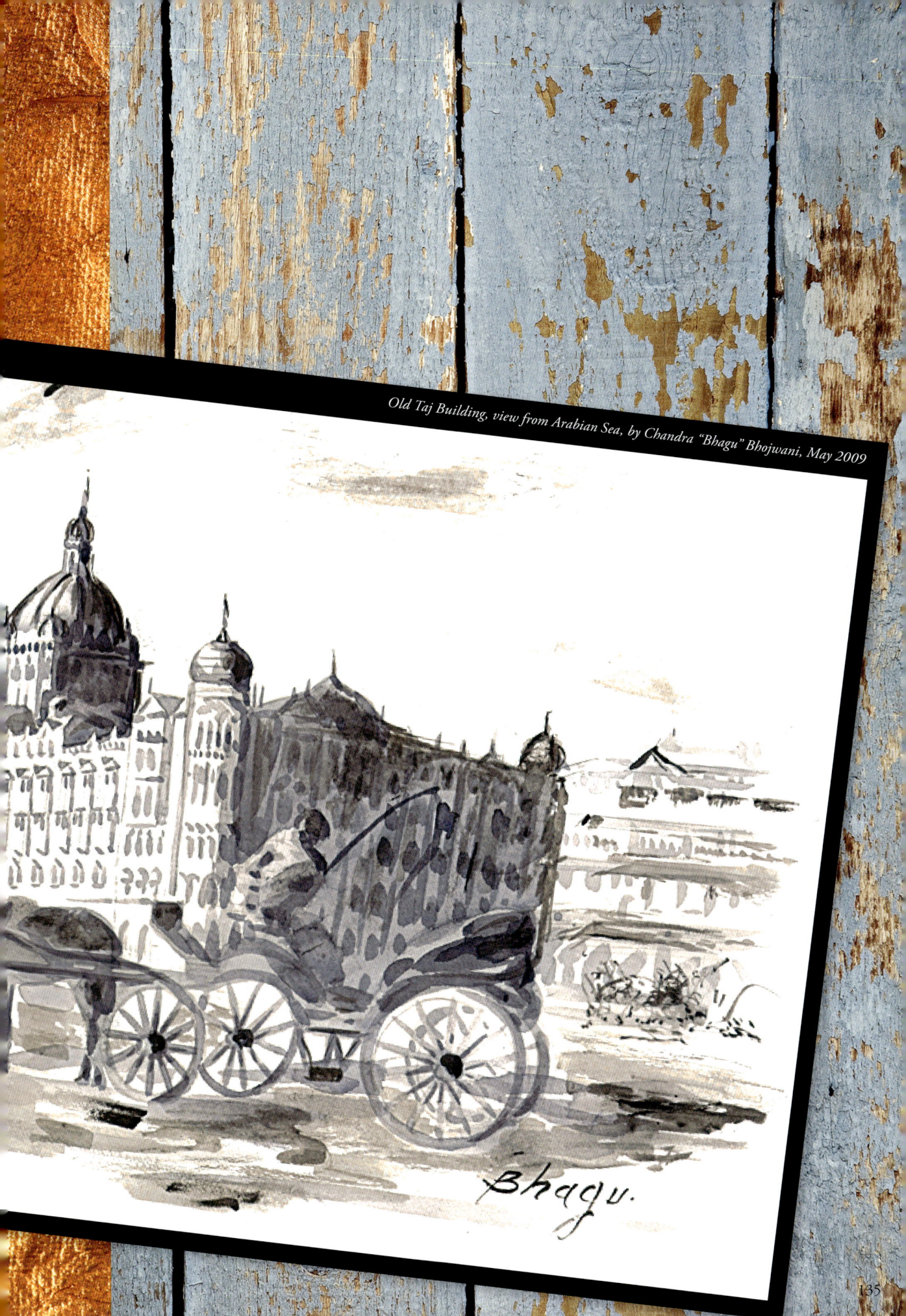

*Old Taj Building, view from Arabian Sea, by Chandra "Bhagu" Bhojwani, May 2009*

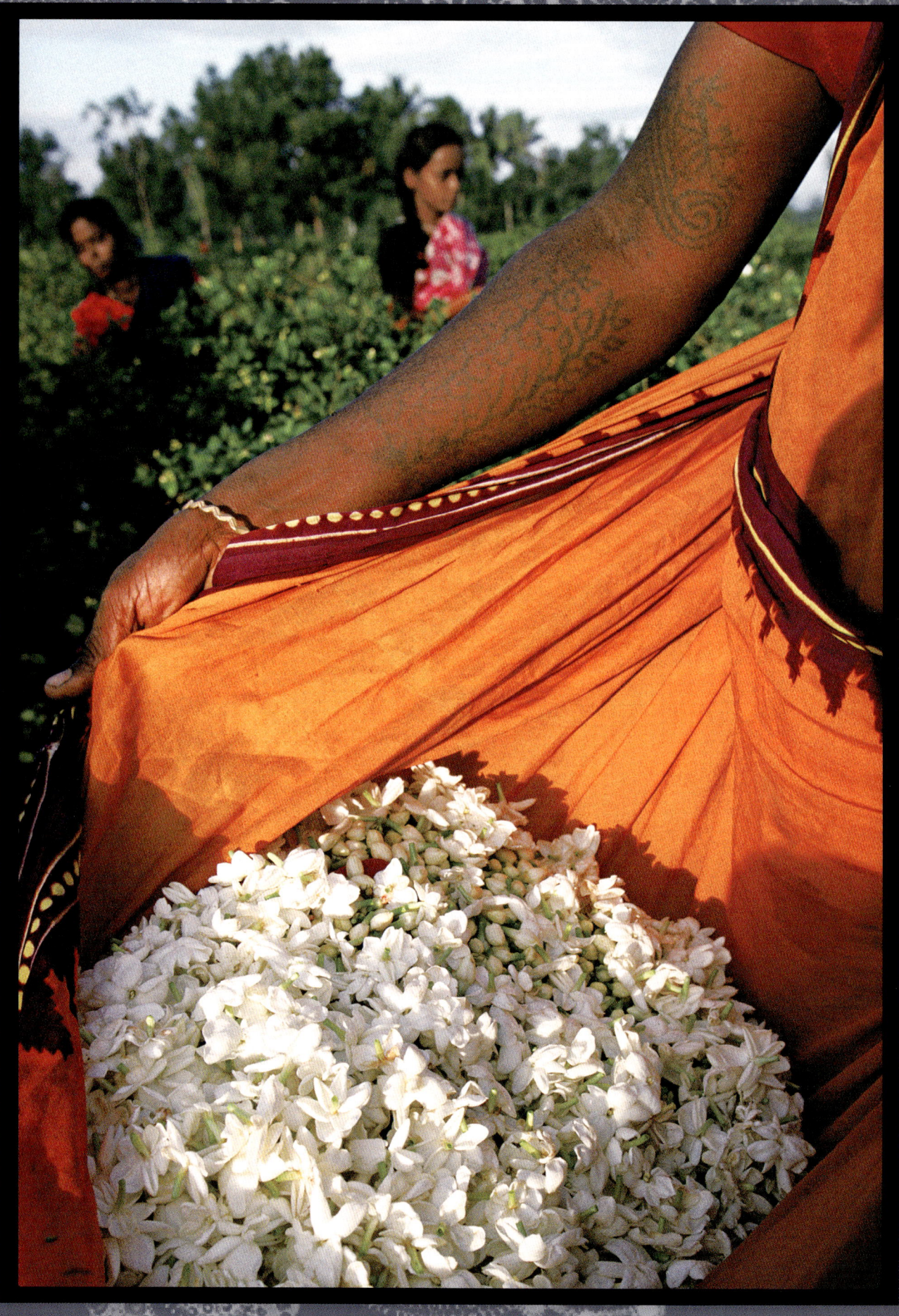

# Silvia Venturini Fendi

*Fashion Designer*

Gudia talks to me about the beauty of fundamental values....

Pureness, spirituality, simplicity......

Simple things full of meanings where anything can be everything.

Like the warm welcome of a bowl of Jasmine petals that scents the air.

Every time I come back from Gudia I want to be a better person!

*Silvia*

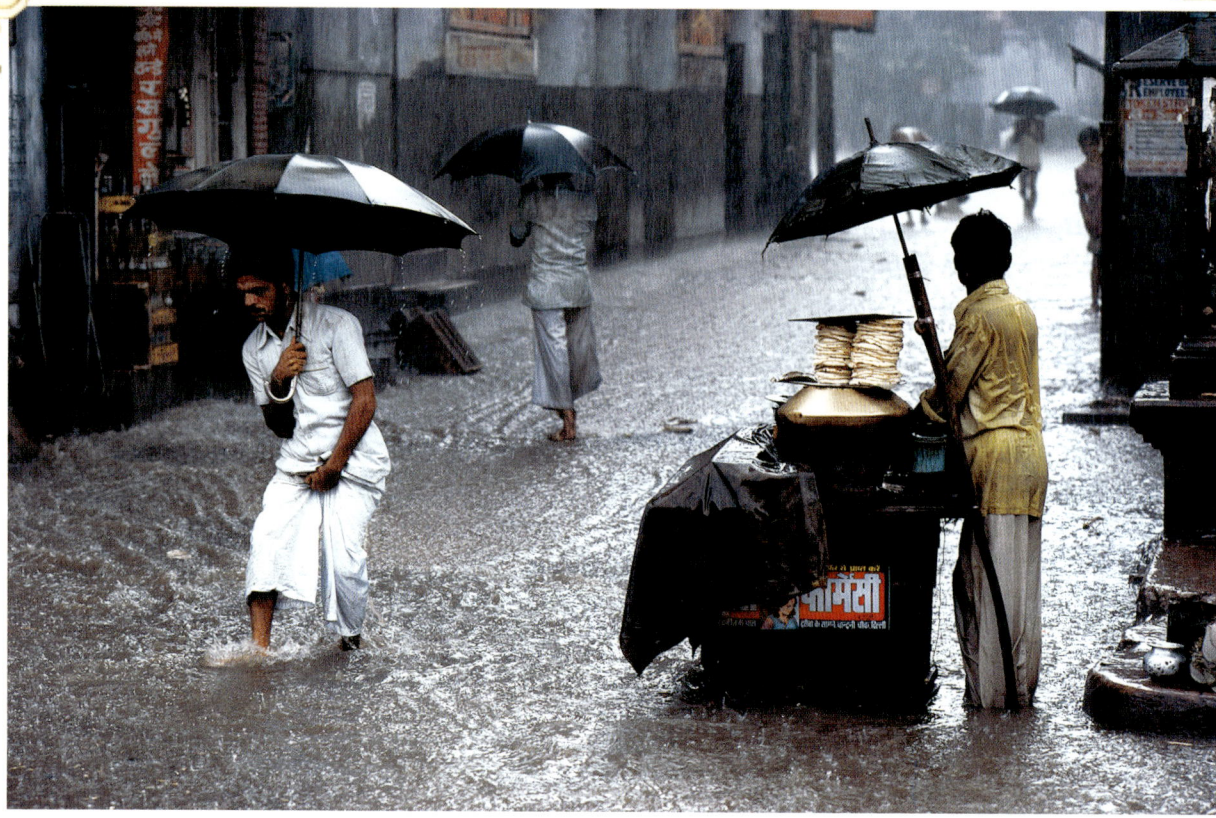

*Monsoon, Chandni Chowk, Old Delhi, 1983*

# Steve McCurry
## *Photographer*

The monsoon is the earth's most awesome climate event. It has spiritual weight in India, literally bringing resurrection as it turns brown earth green.

Monsoon weather is challenging for a photographer, but I am drawn to it. There are as many different kinds of rain-saturated light as there are storms. Writers can revise and rewrite their descriptions, but photographers' critical decisions are instant, and with monsoon light changing fast, the urgency of the photography can be intense.

The paradox of the monsoon is that there is usually too much or too little rain for the health and livelihoods of rural people, dependent on a force indifferent to them. It has little direct effect on the urban population, which grits its teeth and carries on.

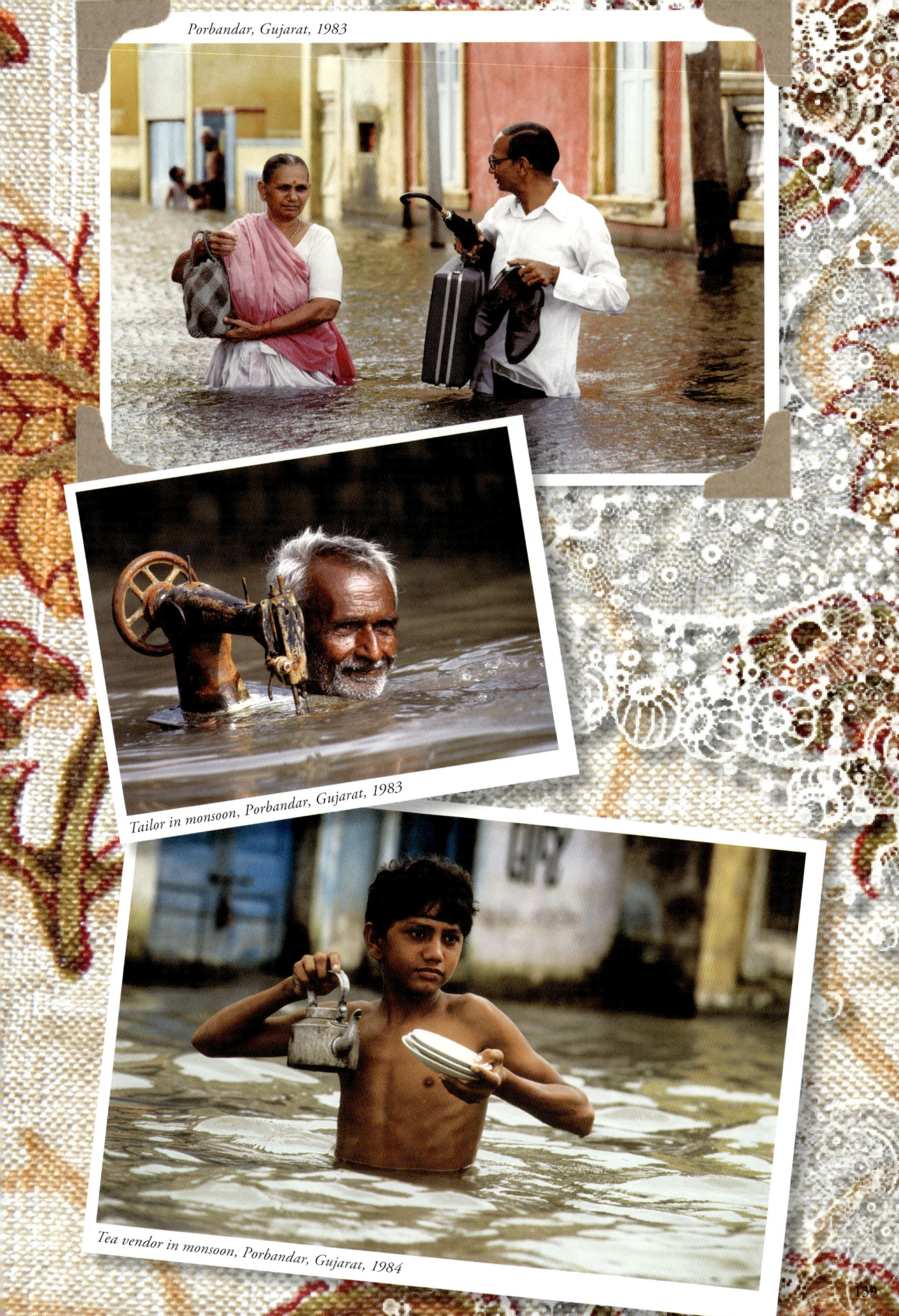

Porbandar, Gujarat, 1983

Tailor in monsoon, Porbandar, Gujarat, 1983

Tea vendor in monsoon, Porbandar, Gujarat, 1984

# Stuart Goldfarb

*President and CEO, Direct Brands, Inc.*

In the mid-1990s, I spent a significant amount of time in India. India was, and still feels like, my home away from home.

To me, India's welcoming graciousness, hospitality, playfulness, and deep-rooted traditions are perfectly revealed at weddings. My first Indian wedding was overwhelming in every way—a solid week of parties, events, celebrations, and rituals. Ten thousand people attended the wedding itself, which was held in a stadium in Mumbai. In India, a wedding does not just signify two individuals coming together, it marks the joining of two souls, two families, two cultures, and two communities.

I remember the beauty of the saptapadi ritual, in which the couple moves seven times around a fire together, each time exchanging a wedding vow, with the fire as witness. I remember the fun of being in my friend Tushar's barat, the grand procession from the groom's house to the bride's house. Following tradition, Tushar, dressed in his beautiful wedding attire, rode a decorated white horse through the streets of Mumbai, with his family, friends, and musicians dancing alongside him. I remember food and friends and stories and smiles. I remember the incredible adornments, the honor of the families, the great acceptance, the sacredness. I remember love and beauty and hope—everything India represents.

*May 2009*

# Tadashi Yanai

*Chairman, President, and CEO, Fast Retailing Company, Ltd.*

I am overcome with great grief when I think about not seeing Mourad-san and Loumia-san anymore. I sincerely pray that their souls rest in peace. Together with employees who are left behind at the company, I will make sure that Princesse tam.tam continues to grow and to blossom into a global brand.

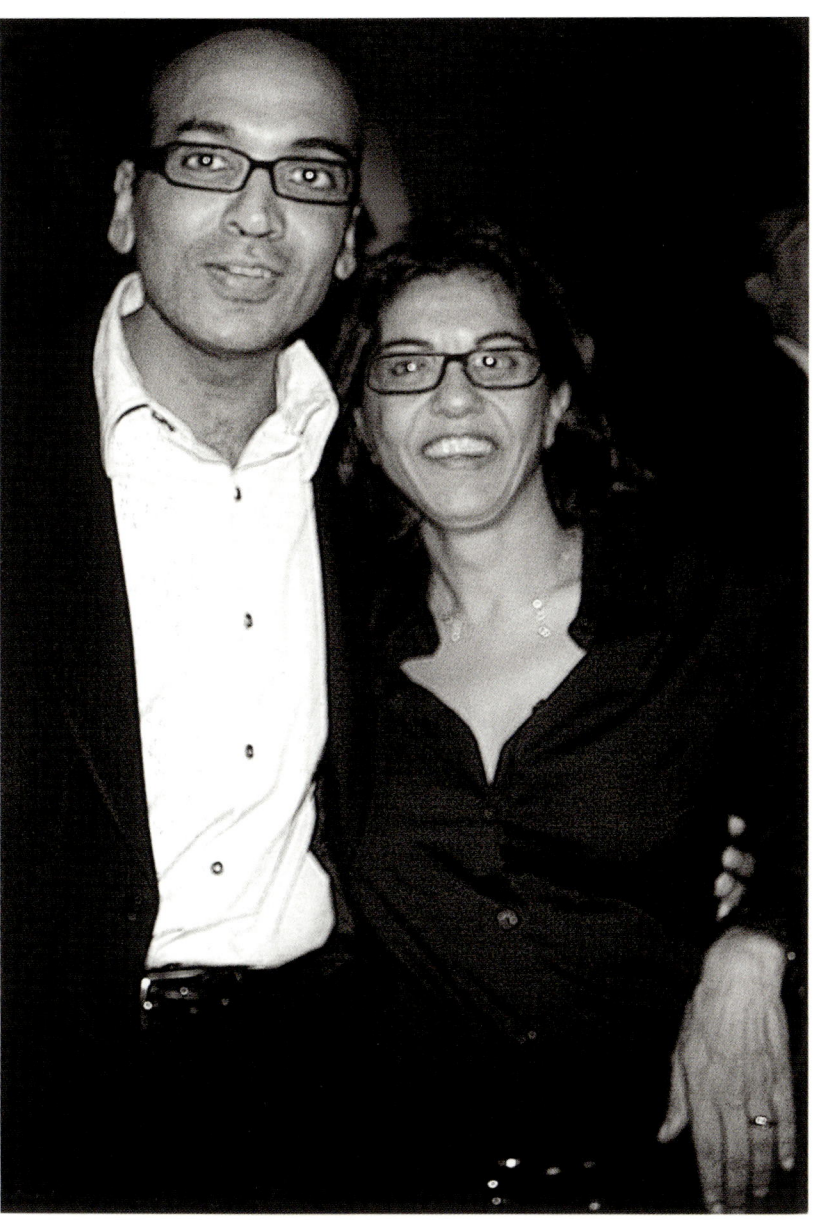

*Loumia Hiridjee and Mourad Amarsy, husband-and-wife founders of the French lingerie brand Princesse tam.tam, were killed in the attacks of November 26, 2008.*

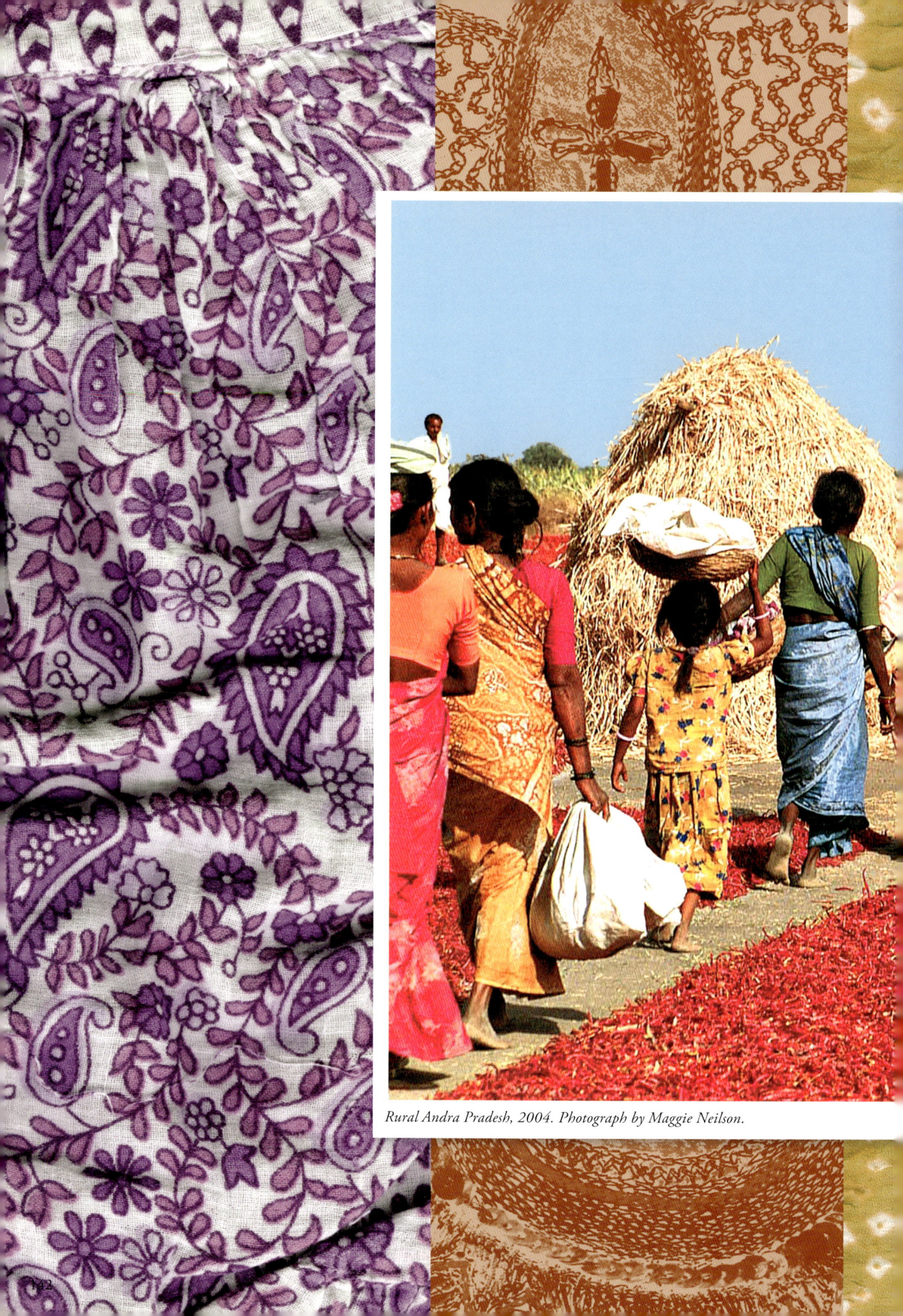

*Rural Andra Pradesh, 2004. Photograph by Maggie Neilson.*

# Tory Burch
*Fashion Designer*

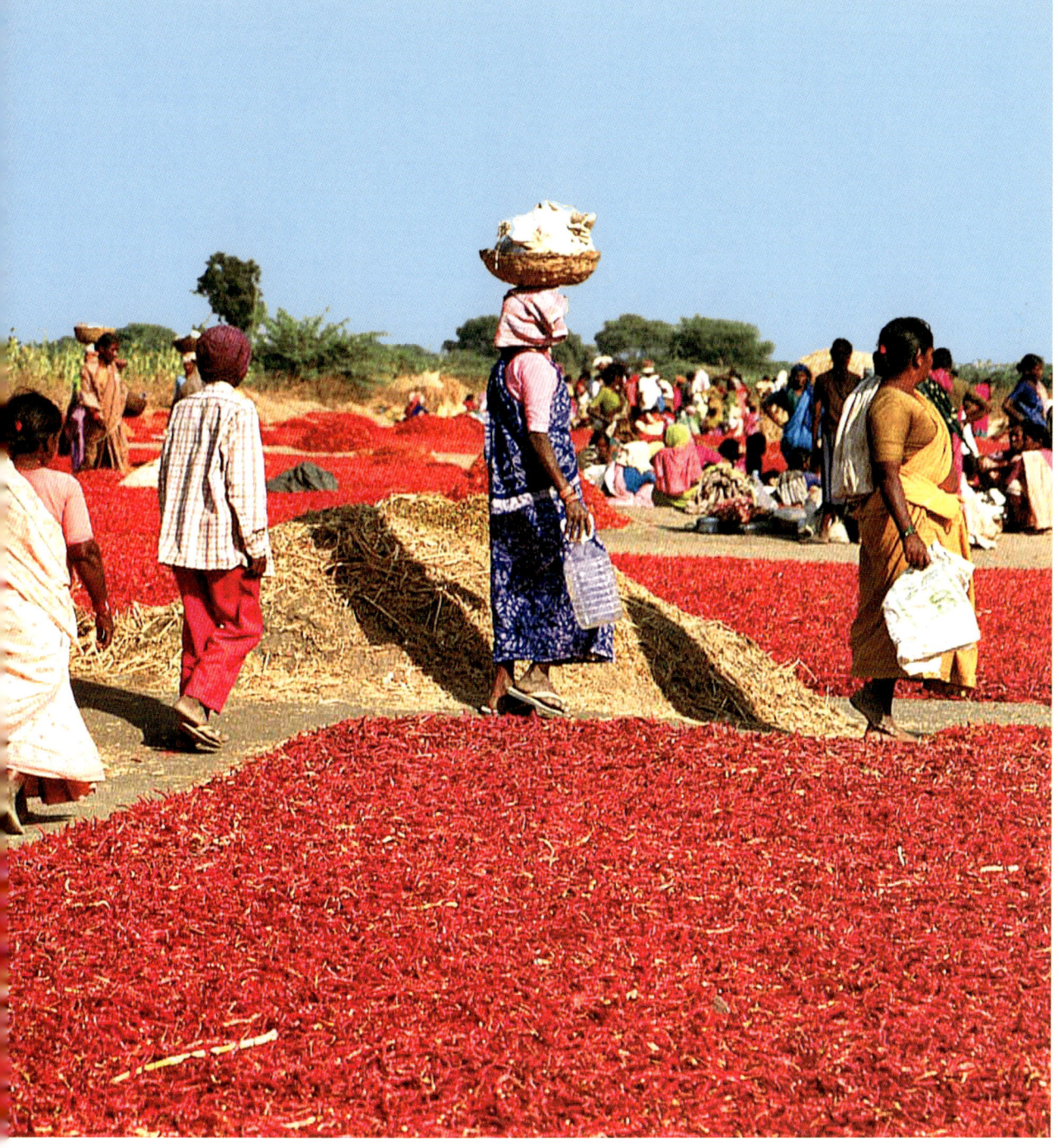

I went abroad during my junior year of college on Semester at Sea. Visiting India was one of the most life-changing experiences I have ever had. I waited in line for six hours to meet Mother Theresa, which was incredibly moving, and the vibrant colors and unique culture are so inspiring. I cannot wait to go back.

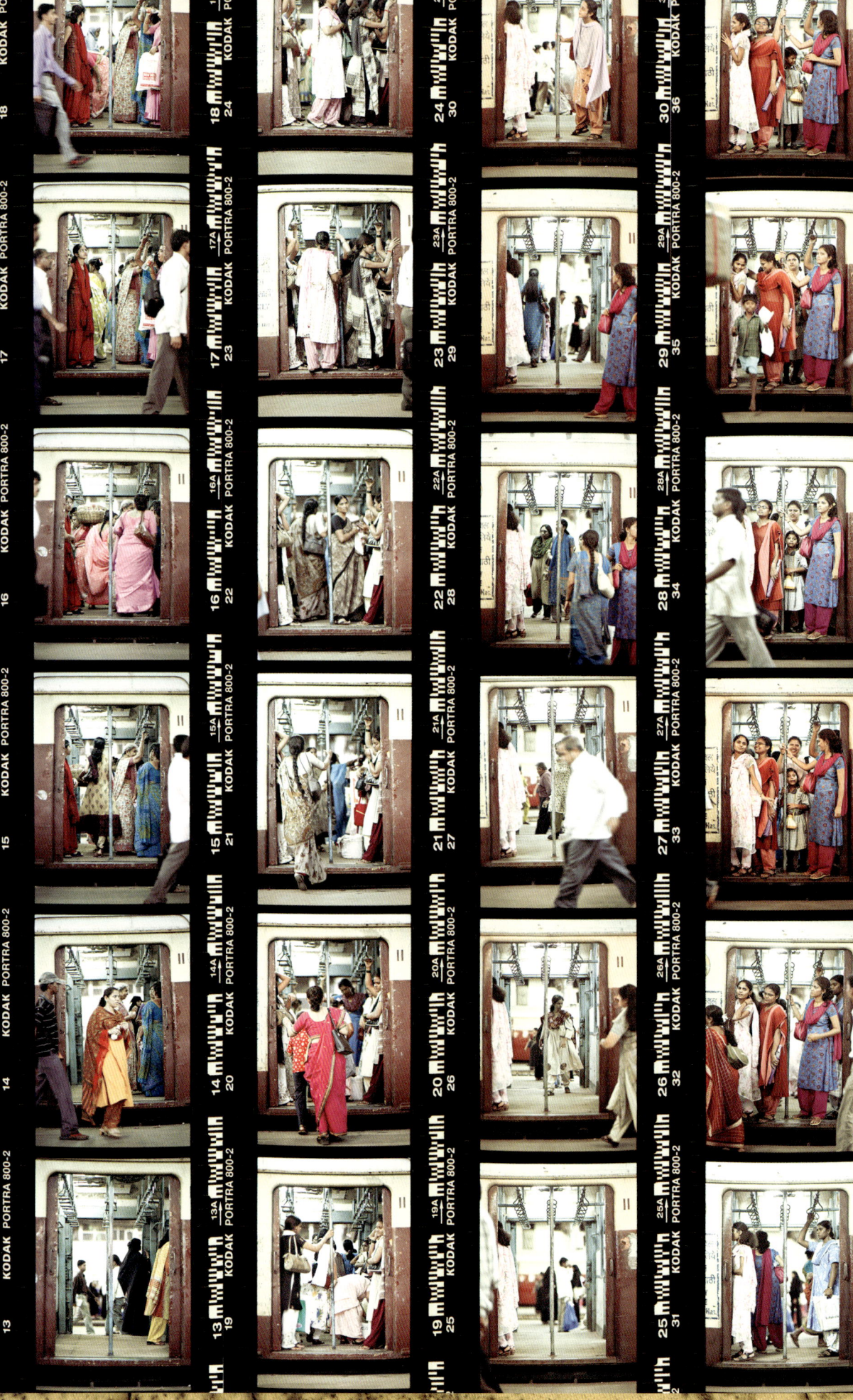

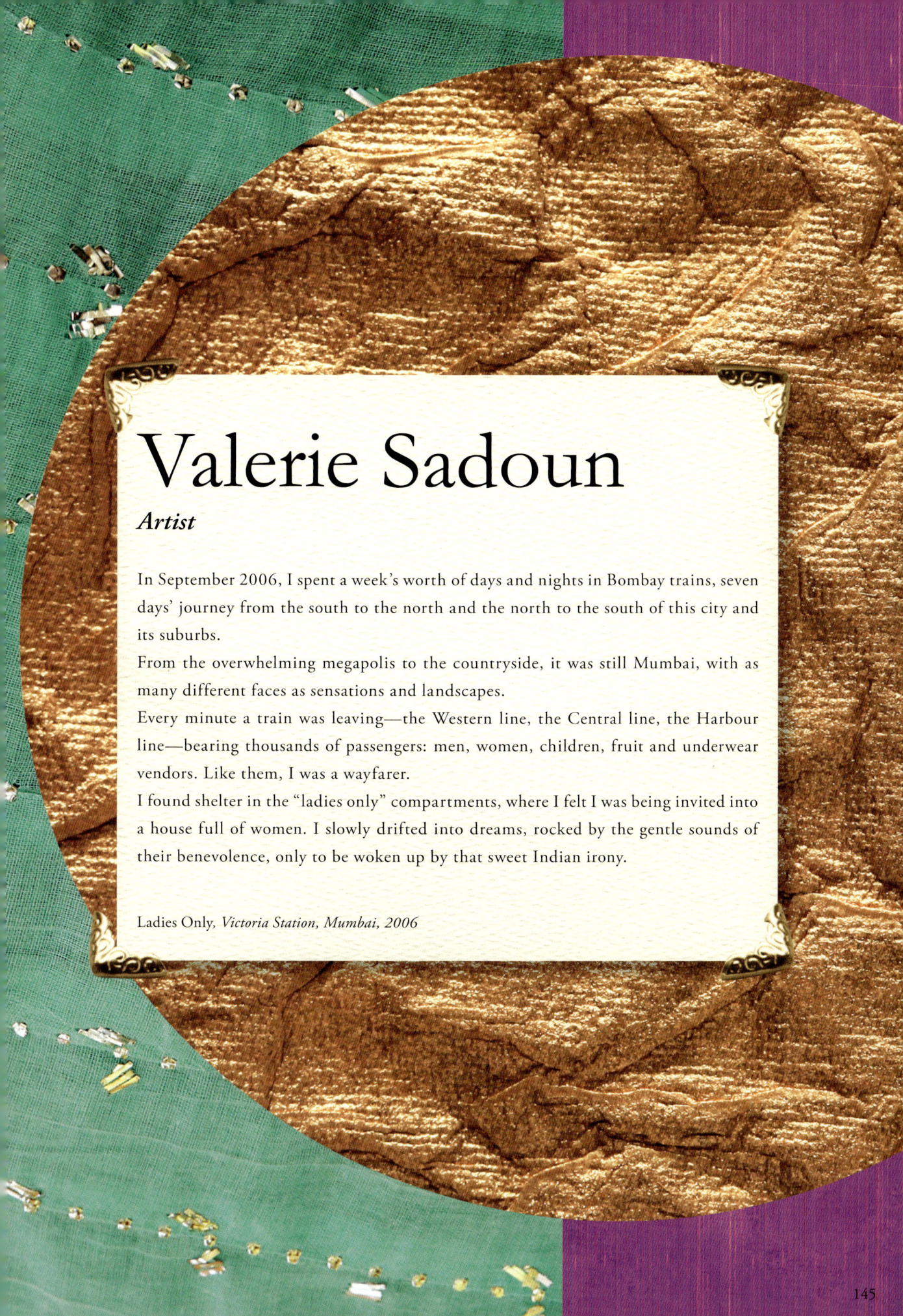

# Valerie Sadoun

*Artist*

In September 2006, I spent a week's worth of days and nights in Bombay trains, seven days' journey from the south to the north and the north to the south of this city and its suburbs.

From the overwhelming megapolis to the countryside, it was still Mumbai, with as many different faces as sensations and landscapes.

Every minute a train was leaving—the Western line, the Central line, the Harbour line—bearing thousands of passengers: men, women, children, fruit and underwear vendors. Like them, I was a wayfarer.

I found shelter in the "ladies only" compartments, where I felt I was being invited into a house full of women. I slowly drifted into dreams, rocked by the gentle sounds of their benevolence, only to be woken up by that sweet Indian irony.

Ladies Only, *Victoria Station, Mumbai, 2006*

# Vanessa von Bismarck
*Partner and Founder, Bismarck Phillips Communications & Media*

Arriving for a two-month trip to India in 1996, we stayed in Jodhpur, with the Maharaja's uncle in his hotel, which looked like a *Flintstones* village. One day he told us that we were invited to an annual event on the walls of the fort, and that we would have to buy something to wear. As we arrived in our new saris and jewelry, bought in Jaipur, we didn't know what to expect. Candles lit the way up the ramp and the stairs, and as we arrived on the terrace we saw a hundred and fifty maharajas, maharanis, and their children in full regalia, like something out of *The 1001 Nights*, high above the blue city of Jodhpur. I will never forget playing games on that rooftop and watching eight-year-old girls run around with ten-karat diamonds on their foreheads. We were welcomed like honored guests, and the warmth and sparkle of that night will always stay with me.

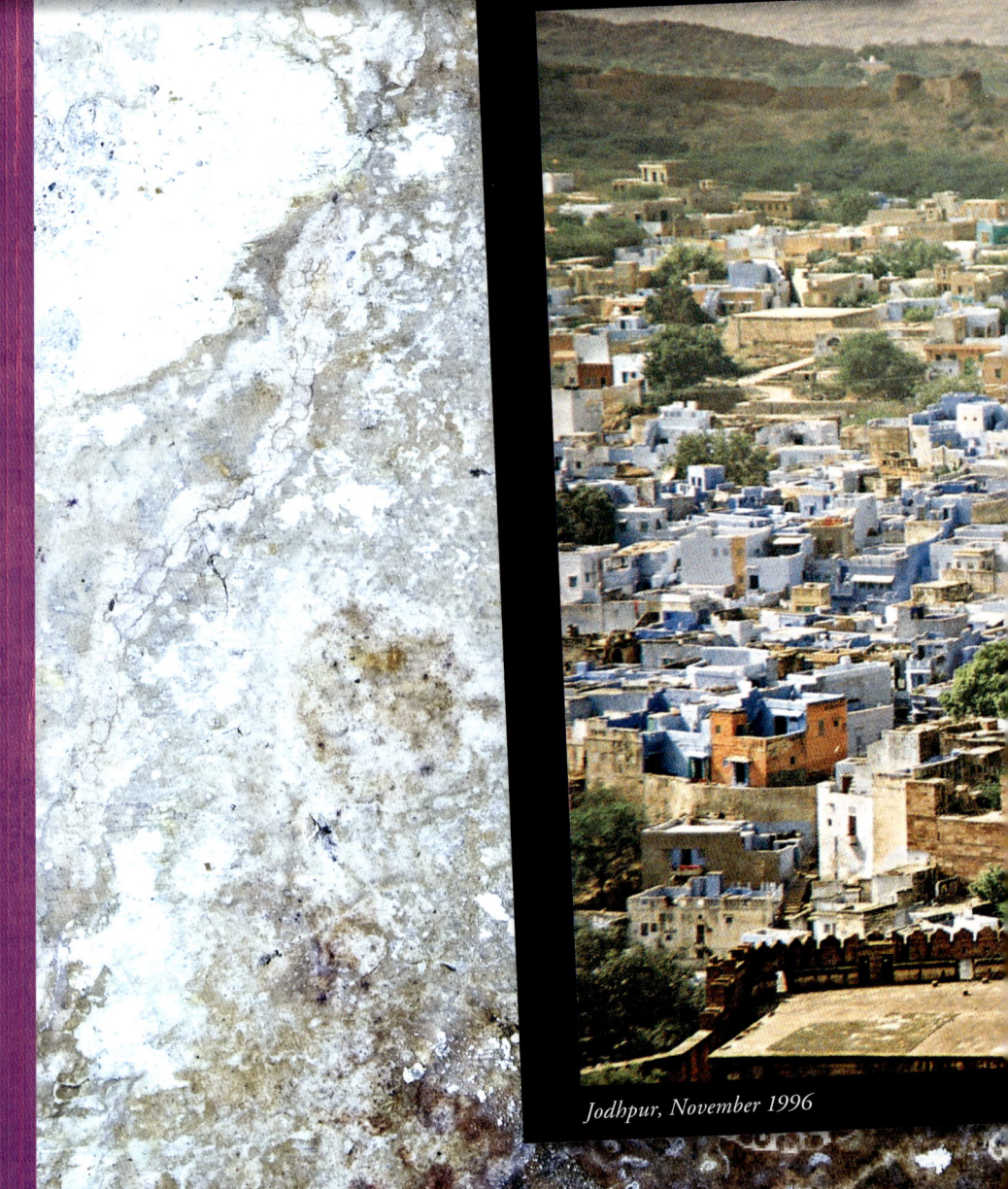

*Jodhpur, November 1996*

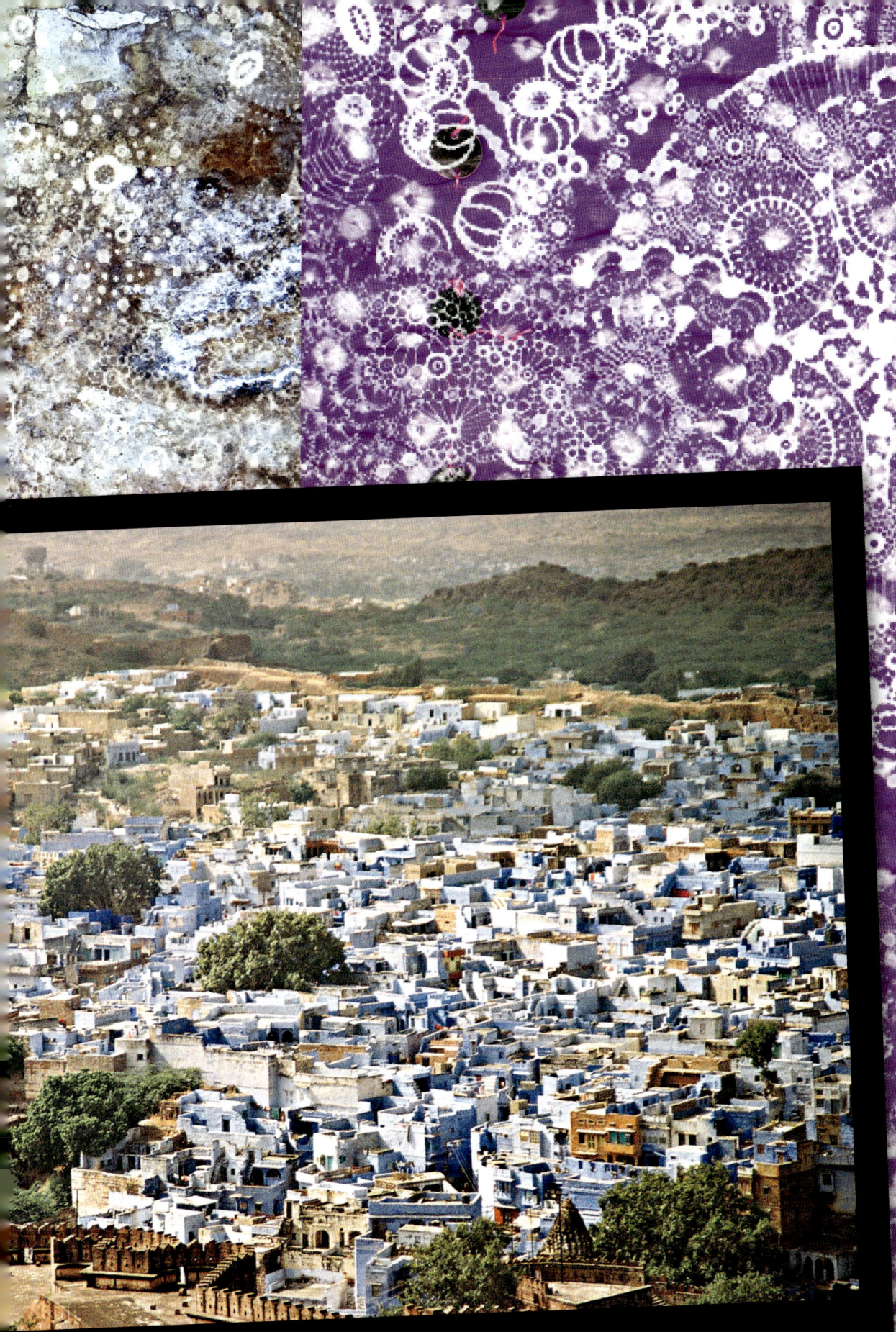

# Vishakha Desai
*President, the Asia Society*

"*I took this photograph more than thirty years ago, while I was traveling through Rajasthan for my dissertation research. To me it is an iconic image of India—even today, it is typical to see women carrying loads as they build roads in the countryside. Their colorful clothes and open smiles continue to provide an image of the Indian woman not as a weaker gender, but as a confident one participating in a wide variety of work. They inspire all of us who are proud to be Indian women in the public space.*"

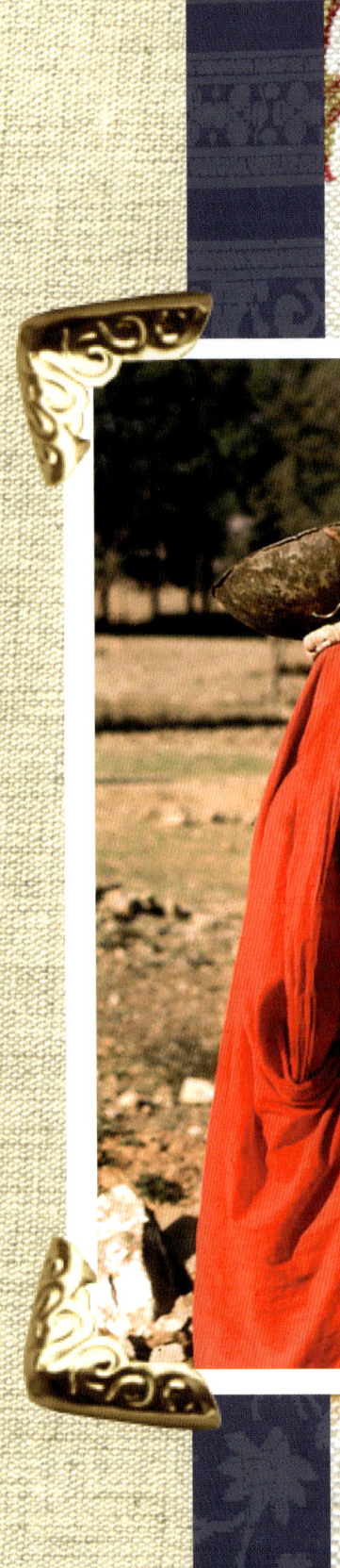

*Women workers by the roadside, Rajasthan, 1977*

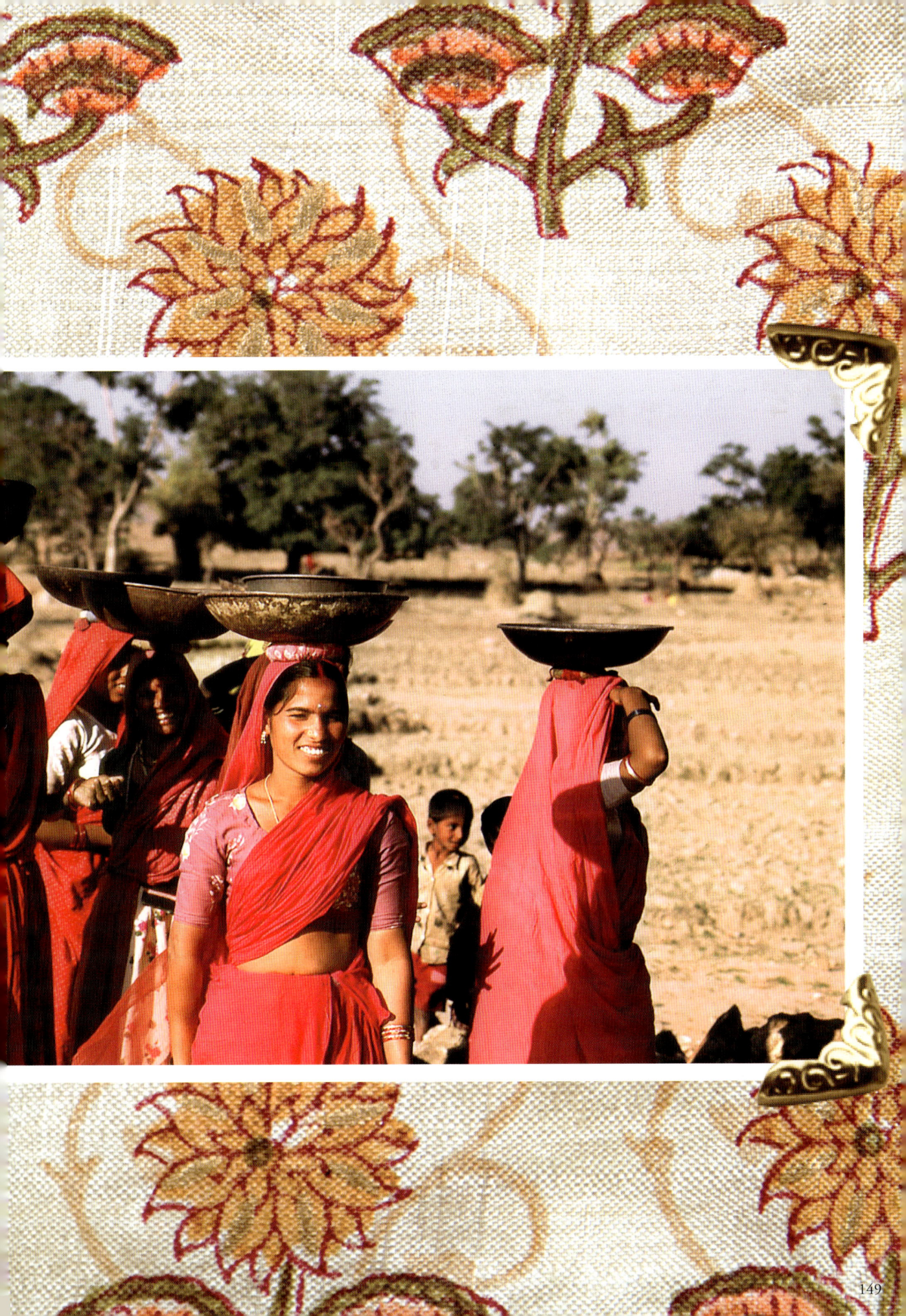

# Waris Ahluwalia

*Actor and Jewelry Designer (Cofounder, Mumbai: We Got Your Back)*

This is Abdull. He has a family farm, drives an auto-rickshaw in Jaipur, and speaks fluent English and Italian.

When I told him I didn't care much for winter, his response was simple and to the point, "We need winter to grow chickpeas."

He's worked with me since the day I landed in Jaipur and he's had my back since day one. This is the least I could do.

Grazie mille Abdull.
A presto.

2009

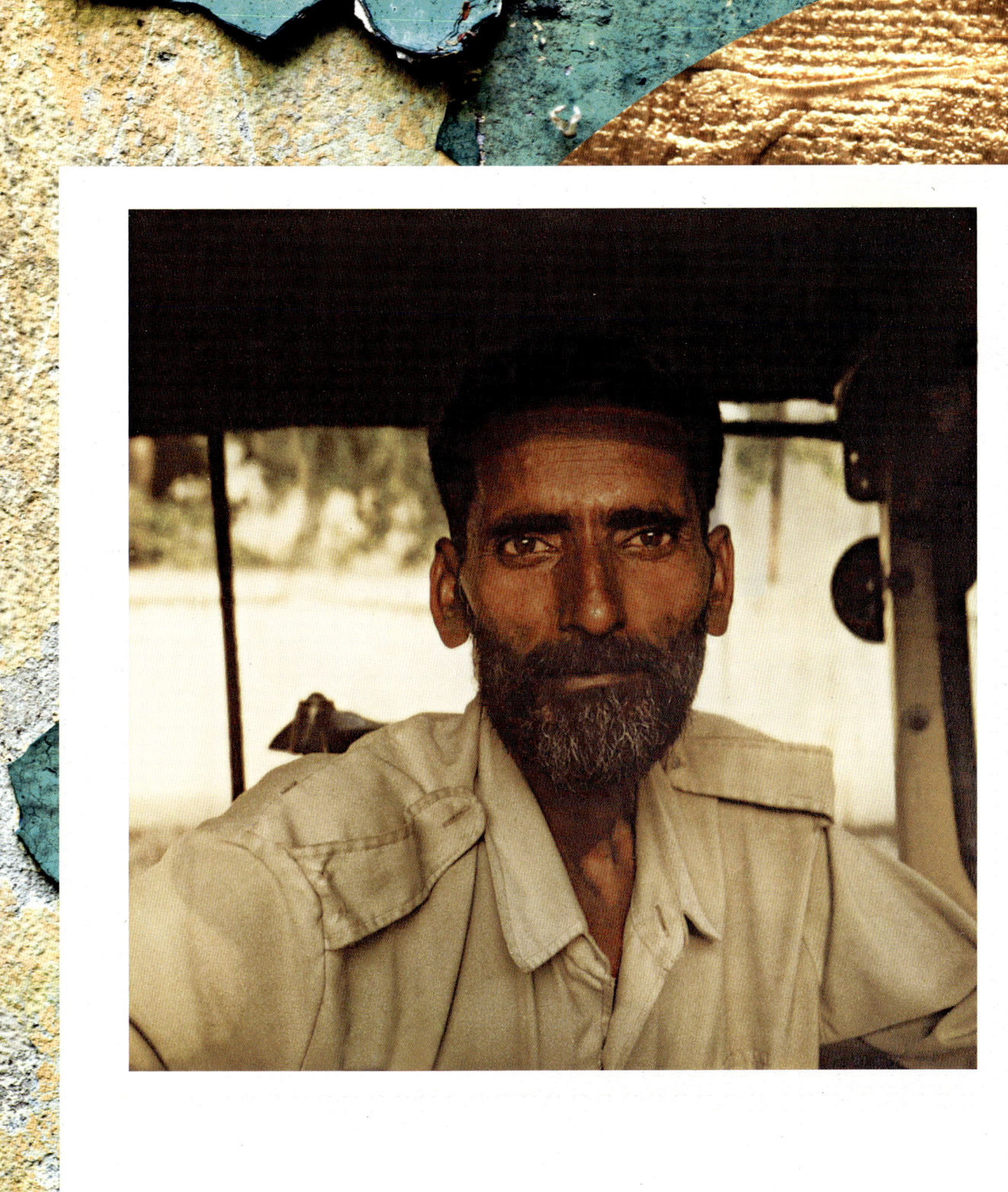

*Above: Abdull. Following page: Horse, Jaipur, 2007.*

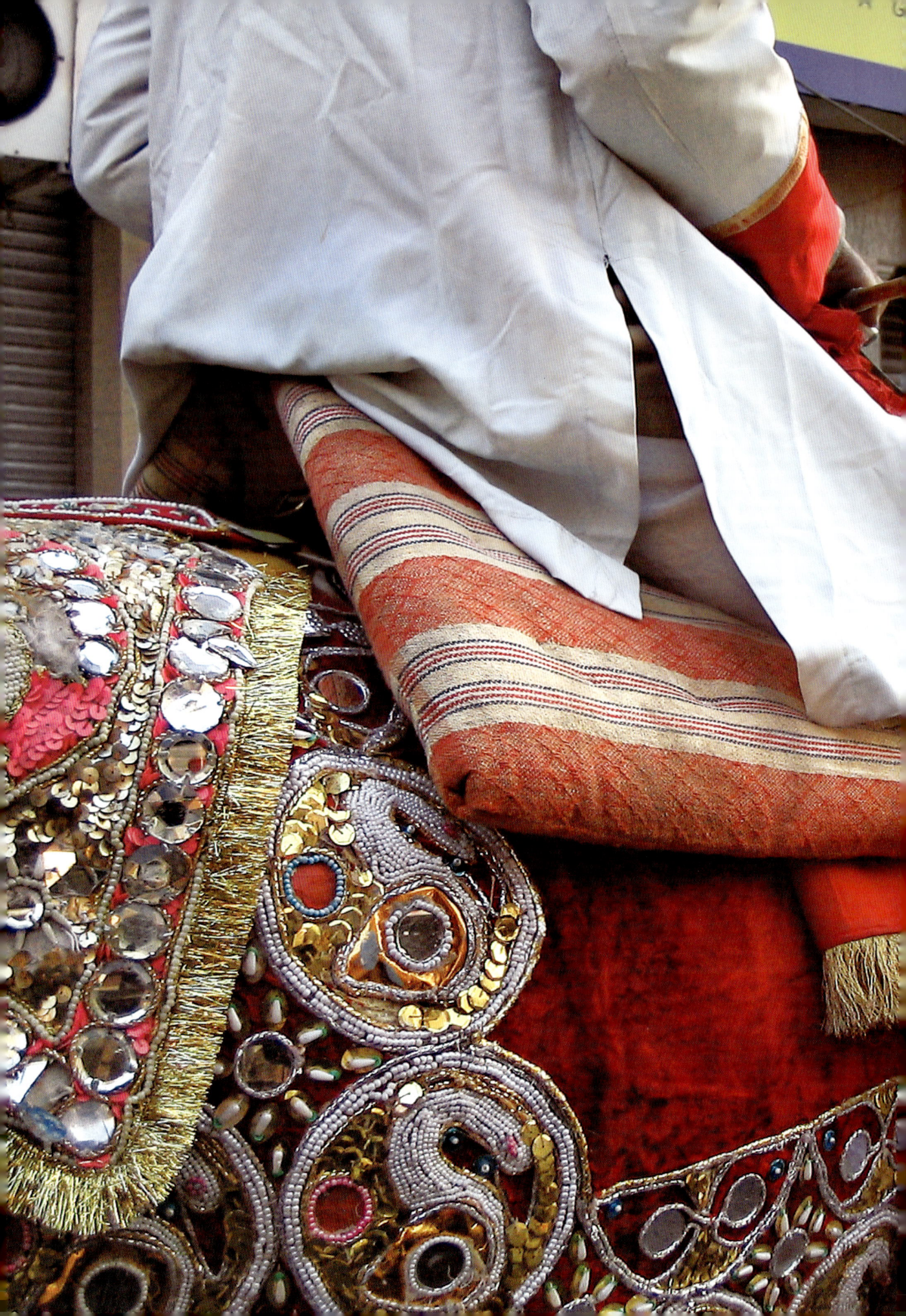

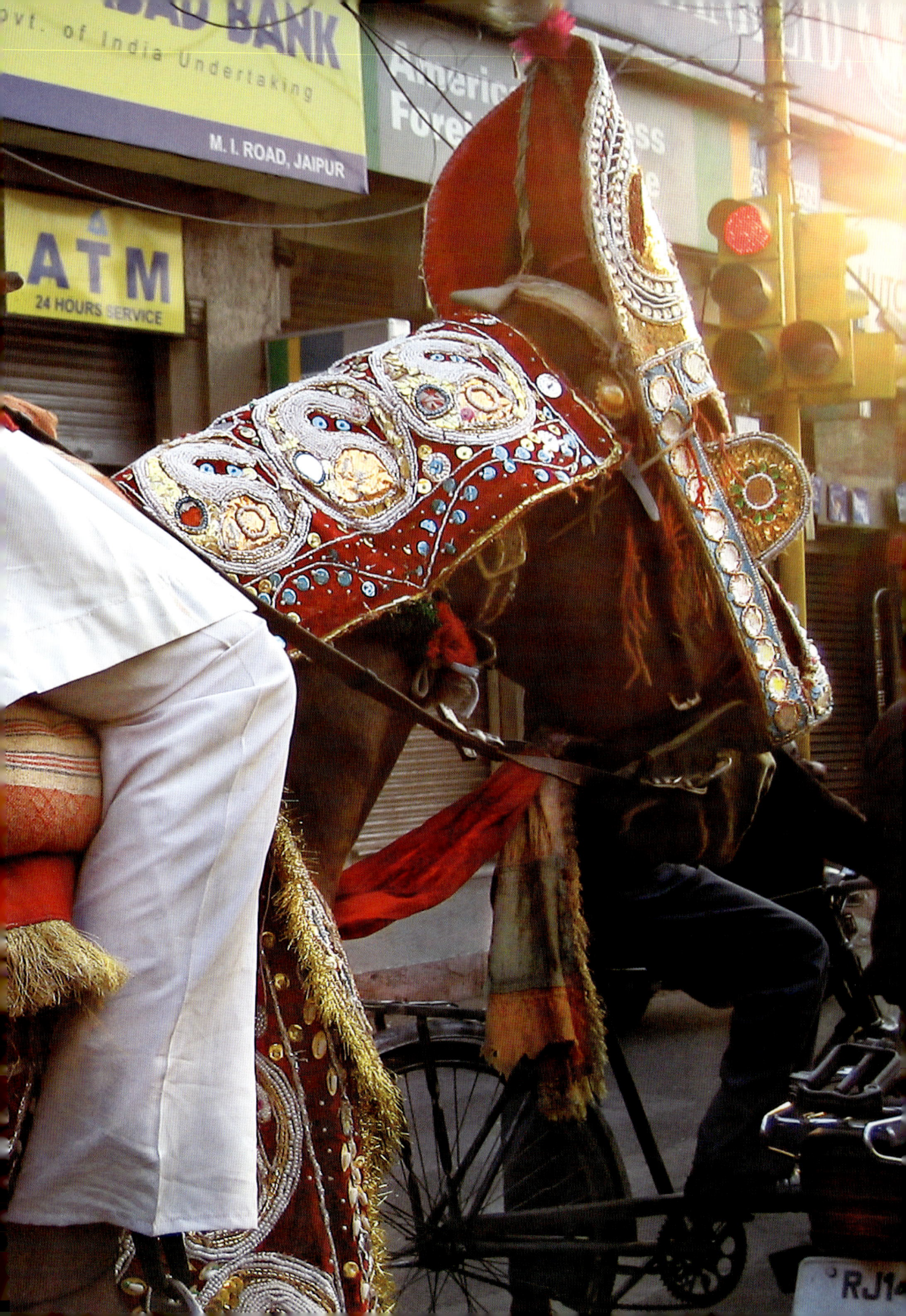

# Wes Anderson
*Film Director*

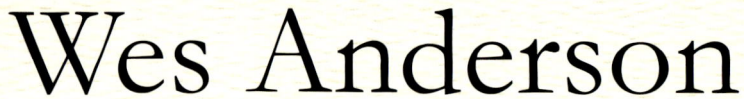

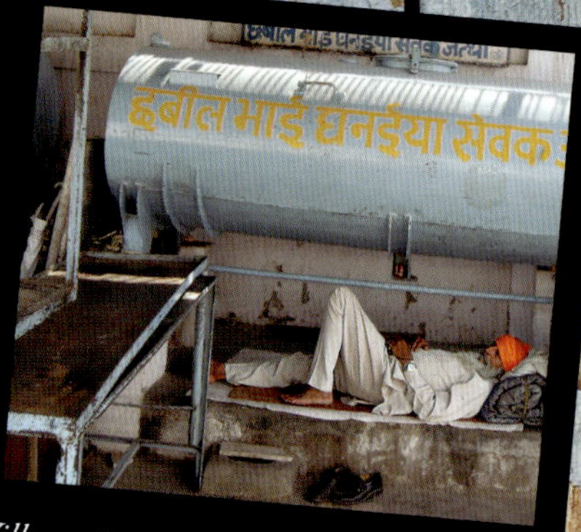

From left: Goatherd with a tall staff, Rohet, Rajasthan, 2006; Resting dog, Dundlee Village, Rajasthan, 2006; Man sleeping beneath a water tank outside a Sikh temple, New Delhi, 2005.

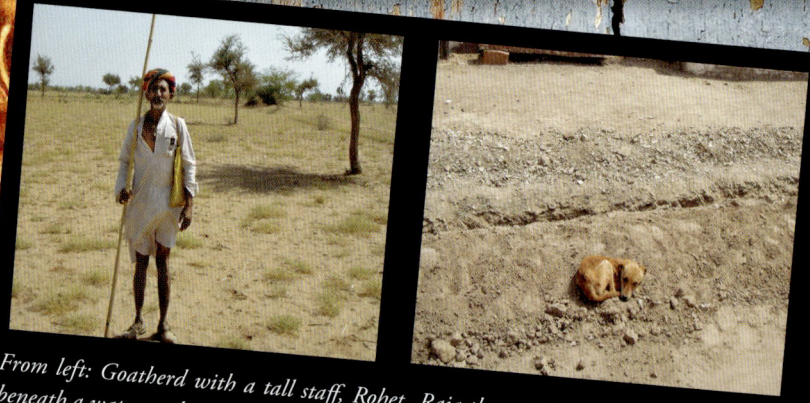

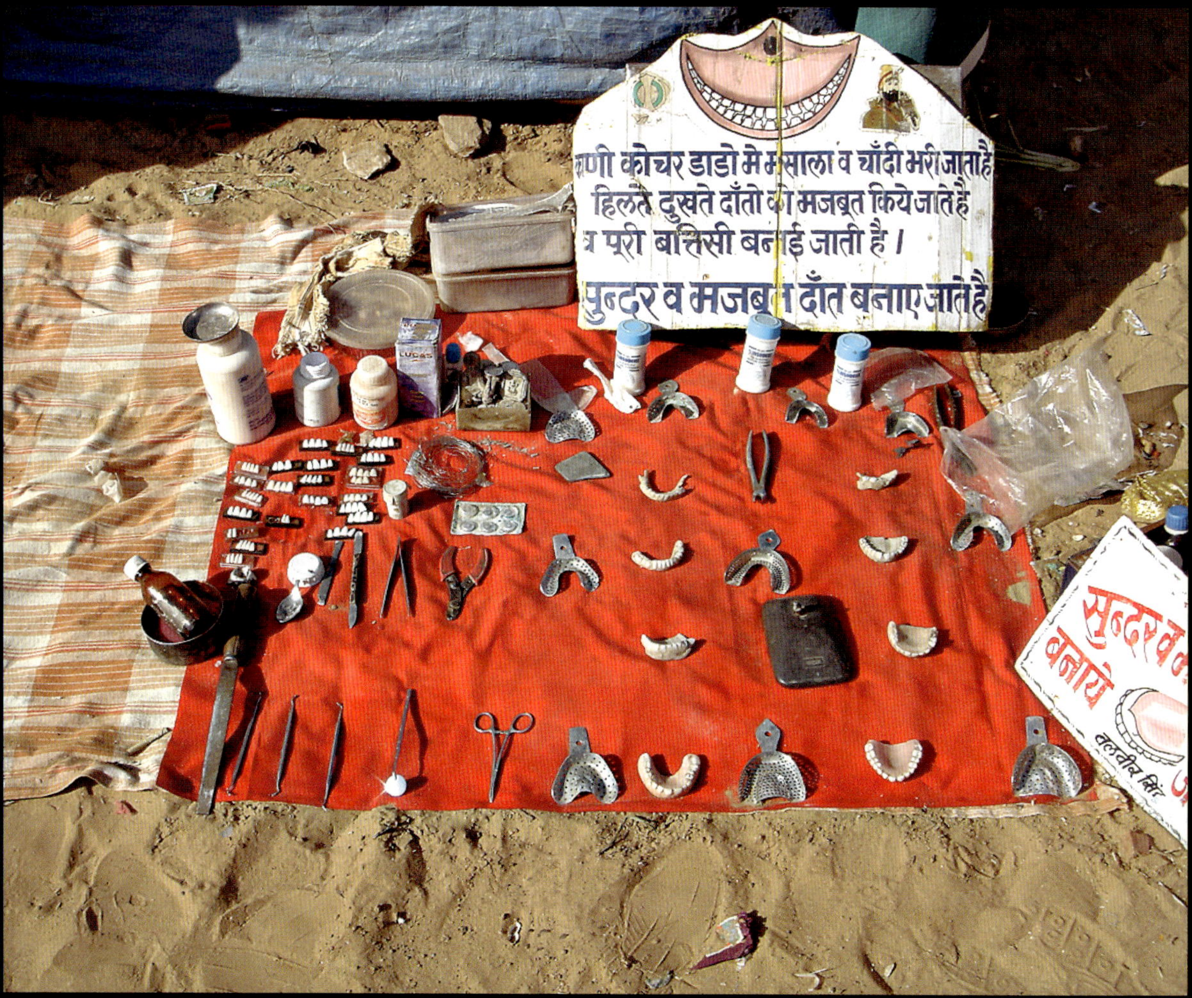

False teeth and various dental instruments for sale, Pushkar, Rajasthan, 2004

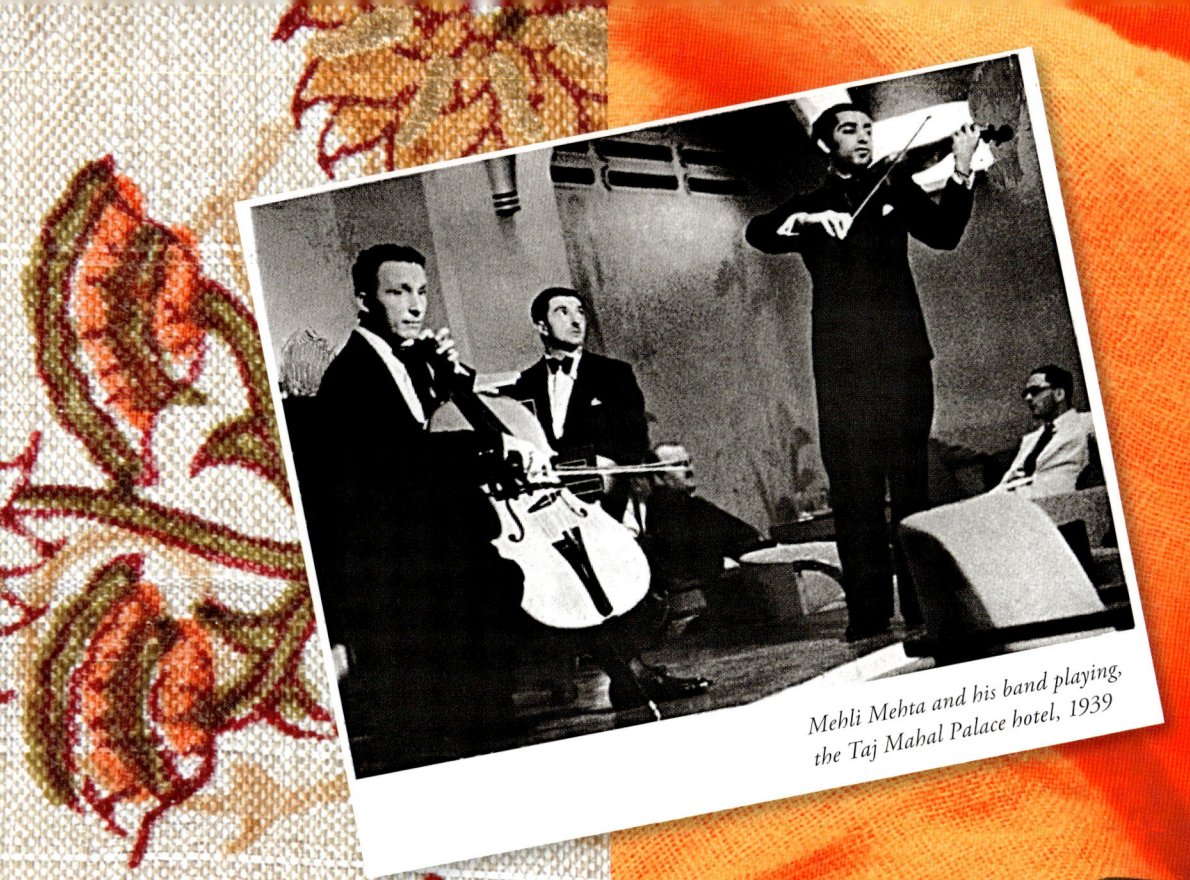

*Mehli Mehta and his band playing, the Taj Mahal Palace hotel, 1939*

# Zubin Mehta
*Music Director, the Israel Philharmonic Orchestra*

The Taj Mahal hotel was a focal point of my youth in Mumbai.

My father, Mehli Mehta, performed there for more than ten years of dinner hours. His trio eventually grew into a sextet.

The Taj was always, then as now, known for the highest quality in both hospitality and cuisine. And it is an architectural wonder: like so many other Mumbai buildings constructed during the British Raj, it is a stylistic mixture of India and Europe that nevertheless stands out as a beautiful monument welcoming all those who approach Mumbai by sea. The proximity to the great Gateway of India only embellishes this majestic part of Mumbai that we all love so much.

The recent tragedy that the hotel, its staff, and its guests have had to endure is something that I condemn vociferously. I hope fervently that such acts of inhumanity are once and for all a thing of the past.

I long to return and occupy once again the Rajput Suite, which my wife and I consider a second home. I was recently at the Taj and stood with tears in my eyes as I read the names of staff members and guests who perished so tragically during those black hours last November. I pray that the Taj Mahal hotel, which is a pride and joy of Mumbai, will open all its doors once again, inviting the world to enjoy Indian hospitality at its best.

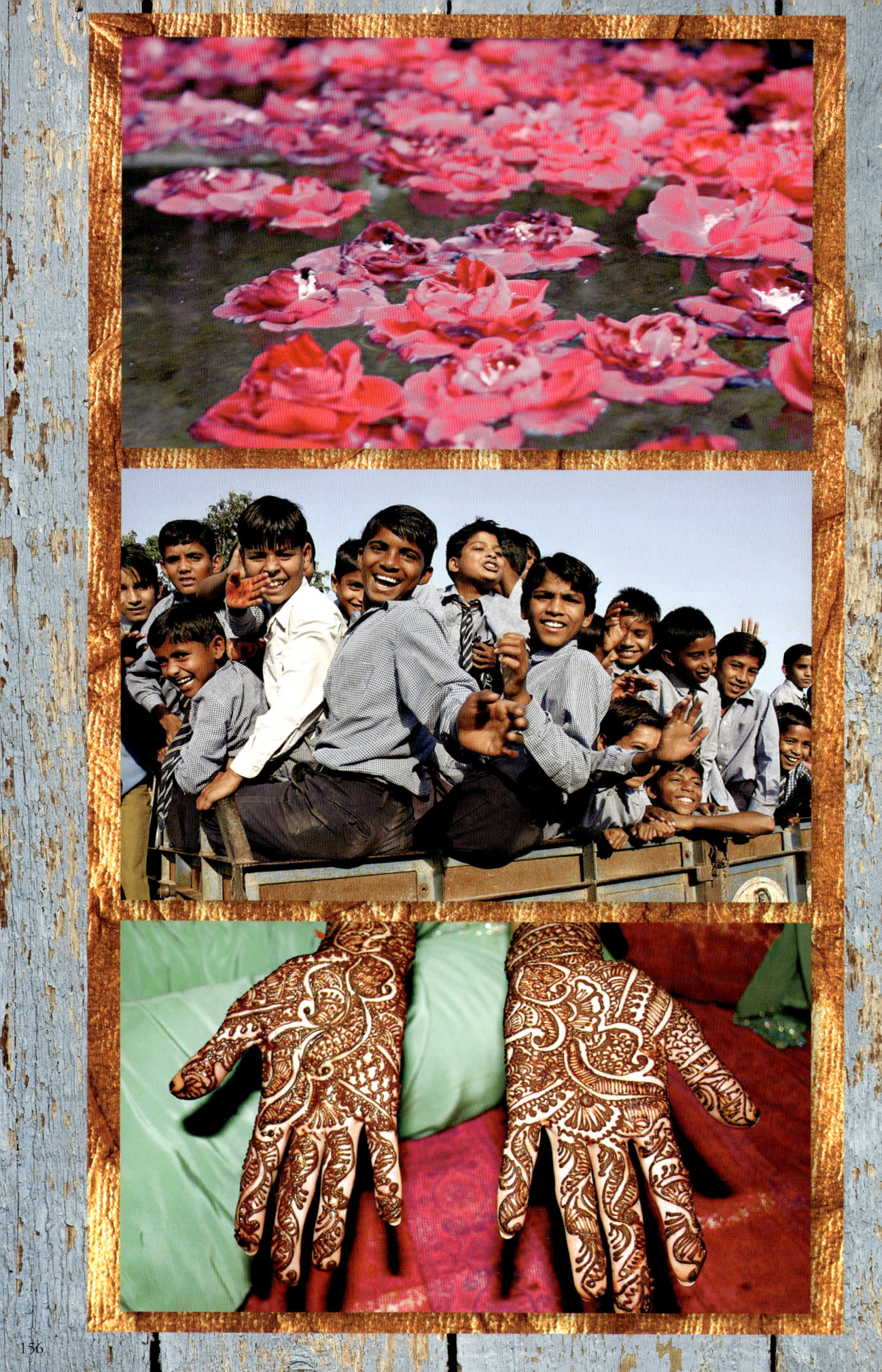

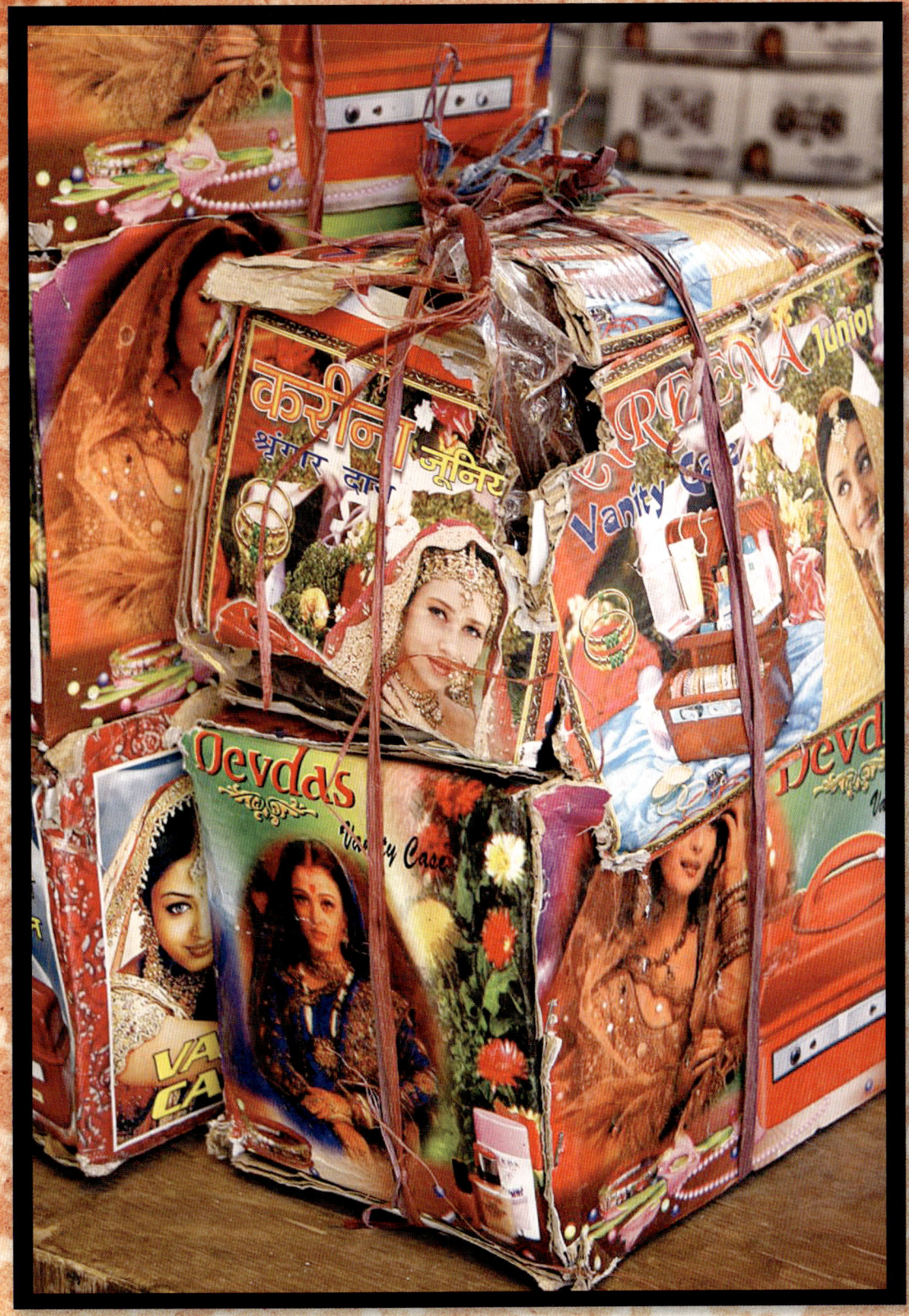

# Yves Carcelle

*Chairman and CEO, Louis Vuitton Malletier*

# Index of Contributors

*This list is alphabetical by first name, as is the book itself, with some variation for design.*

| | | |
|---|---|---|
| Abu Jani | 12 | |
| Adrien Brody | 13 | |
| Aldo Mondino | 16-17 | |
| Alex White | 18-19 | |
| Alice Temperley | 14 | |
| Anand Mahindra | 15 | |
| Andrew Chapman | 38, 82-83, 103, 127 | |
| Anil Kapoor | 20 | |
| Anjelica Huston | 22-25 | |
| Anne Slowey | 26-27 | |
| Anthony Edwards | 28-29 | |
| Antonio Mondino | 16-17 | |
| Anuradha Mahindra | 15 | |
| Bandana Tewari | 30-31 | |
| Billy Farrell | 21 | |
| Bruno Frisoni | 33 | |
| Chandra Bhojwani | 134-135 | |
| Chiara Clemente | 34-35 | |
| Christopher Wray-McCann | 36-37, 52-53 | |
| Cynthia Rowley | 32 | |
| Daniela Federia | 46-47 | |
| Darshan Ahluwalia | 40-41 | |
| David de Rothschild | 39 | |
| Dennis Freedman | 38 | |
| Diane Pernet | 42 | |
| Diane von Furstenberg | 43 | |
| Elizabeth Hurley | 46-47 | |
| Evelyn Lauder | 45 | |
| Fareed Zakaria | 44 | |
| Farzad S. Jehani | 48 | |
| Fern Mallis | 50-51 | |
| Florine Asch | 54-55 | |
| Franca Sozzani | 52-53 | |
| Francesco Clemente | 49 | |
| Fredric Roberts | 4, 10, 58-61 | |
| Giambattista Valli | 62-63 | |
| Graham Nash | 64-65 | |
| Hardeep S. Puri | 6-7 | |
| Harsh Goenka | 56 | |
| Hemant Oberoi | 66 | |
| Hugo Guinness | 57 | |
| Ilse Crawford | 67 | |
| India Hicks | 68 | |
| India Mahdavi | 69 | |
| Ines de la Fressange | 72-73 | |
| Inez van Lamsweerde | 70 | |
| Ira Dubey | 92-93 | |
| Jaclyn Bashoff | 22-25 | |
| James Ivory | 74-75 | |
| Jean François Lesage | 78 | |
| Jean Touitou | 71 | |
| Jeanine Lobell | 76 | |
| Jeffry Aronsson | 77 | |
| Joy Mukhopadhyay | 117 | |
| Jyoti Narula | 130-131 | |
| Karan Johar | 80-81 | |
| Kenneth Cole | 82-83 | |
| Kiki Smith | 84-85 | |
| Kilian Hennessy | 86-87 | |
| Laura Wilson | 88-89, 118-119 | |
| Leetu Shivdasani | 90-91 | |
| Lilette Dubey | 92-93 | |
| M. F. Husain | 94-95 | |
| Maggie Neilson | 142-143 | |
| Mahesh Jethmalani | 97 | |
| Matthew Williamson | 100-101 | |
| Mark Friedberg | 79 | |
| Marvin Traub | 98-99 | |
| Mayank Prajapati | 117 | |
| Melonie Hennessy | 86-87 | |
| Mickey Boardman | 102 | |
| Mickey Drexler | 103 | |
| Milena Canonero | 104-105 | |
| Mitter Bedi | 106-107, 132-133 | |
| Mortimer Singer | 11, 108-111, 159-160 | |
| Mukesh Ambani | 112-113 | |
| Natalie Portman | 114-115 | |
| Naveen Jindal | 116-117 | |
| Owen Wilson | 118-119 | |
| Padma Lakshmi | 120-121 | |
| Pier Luigi Loro Piana | 96 | |
| Preeti Bedi | 106-107 | |
| Puneet Nanda | 130-131 | |
| Rachel Roy | 122-123 | |
| Ratan Tata | 125 | |
| Raymond N. Bickson | 8-9 | |
| Robb Young | 42 | |
| Robert Rabensteiner | 126 | |
| Saif Ali Khan | 127 | |
| Sandeep Khosla | 12 | |
| Sangita Jindal | 124 | |
| Sanjay Kapoor and Genesis | 130-131 | |
| Sebastiano Moschini | 96 | |
| Shallu Jindal | 116-117 | |
| Sheikh Majed Al-Sabah | 129 | |
| Shobhaa De | 132-133 | |
| Silvia Venturini Fendi | 136-137 | |
| Steve McCurry | 138-139, BACK COVER | |
| Stuart Goldfarb | 140 | |
| Tadashi Yanai | 141 | |
| Tarun Tahiliani | 128 | |
| Tina Bhojwani | 11, 134-135, 159-160 | |
| Tory Burch | 142-143 | |
| Valerie Sadoun | 144-145 | |
| Vanessa von Bismarck | 146-147 | |
| Vijay S. Jodha | 117 | |
| Vinoodh Matadin | 70 | |
| Vishakha Desai | 148-149 | |
| Waris Ahluwalia | 11, 150-153, 159-160 | |
| Wes Anderson | 154 | |
| Yves Carcelle | 156-157 | |
| Zubin Mehta | 155 | |

# About the Taj Public Service Welfare Trust

*❝ We are grateful that contributors to* To India With Love *donated their work. Our portion of the proceeds will go directly to the Taj Public Service Welfare Trust. So that you know more about whom you support by buying the book, and so that you may continue to support them, we include this statement of their purpose. ❞*

—Waris Ahluwalia, Tina Bhojwani, and Mortimer Singer

The Taj Public Service Welfare Trust arose from tragedy with the purpose of providing hope and healing to victims of terror, war, natural disasters, and other events that disrupt life.

The recent events in Mumbai have left many in need. We cannot replace that which is lost, but we can help heal.

In the aftermath of the unprecedented attack, we have witnessed an outpouring of support from well-wishers in India and across the globe. In response, we have set up the Taj Public Service Welfare Trust to provide immediate relief to individuals and families affected by the recent terror attacks in Mumbai: the general public, police, firemen, and security forces, and employees of the Taj and other establishments.

The trust will henceforth come to the aid of victims of terror, natural calamities, and other tragic events that inflict damage on life and property.

Now is the time for us to conquer despair with compassion. And keep the light of humanity burning bright.

Individuals or companies wishing to donate, as well as intended beneficiaries, can contact us at:

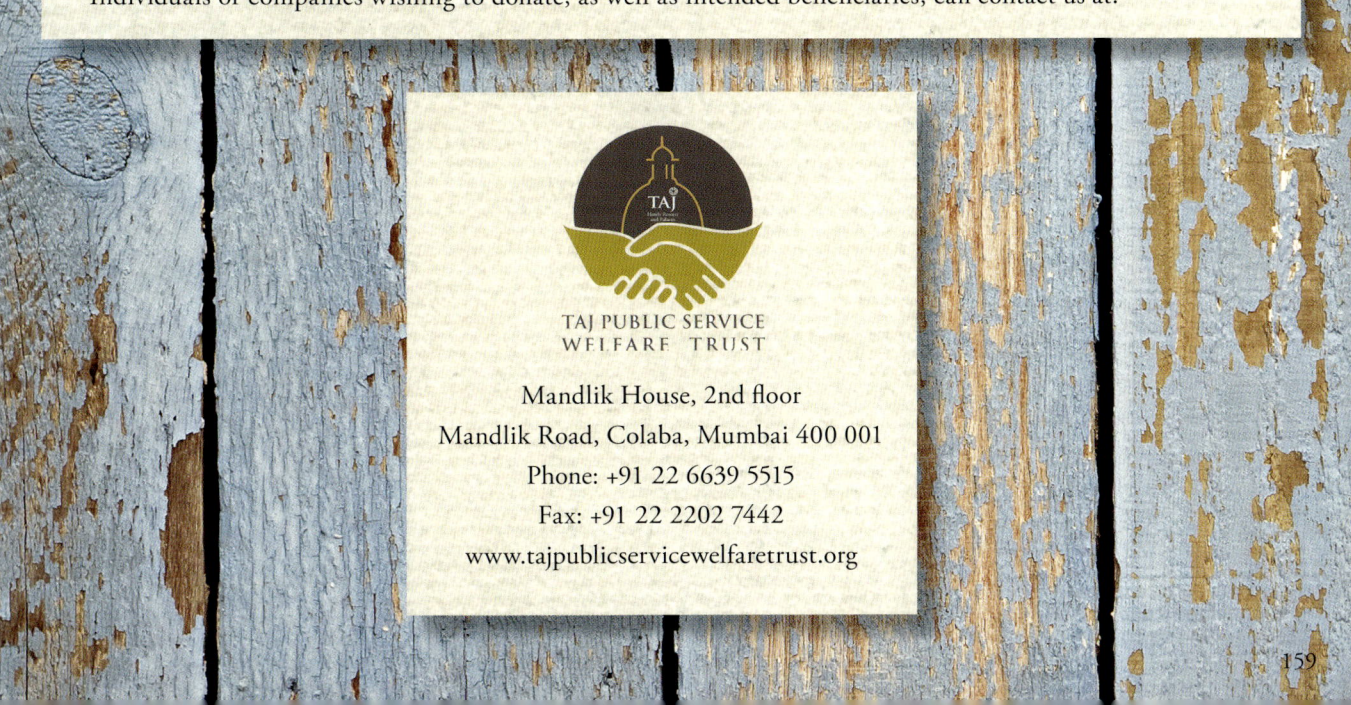

**TAJ PUBLIC SERVICE WELFARE TRUST**

Mandlik House, 2nd floor
Mandlik Road, Colaba, Mumbai 400 001
Phone: +91 22 6639 5515
Fax: +91 22 2202 7442
www.tajpublicservicewelfaretrust.org

# About the Editors

We founded Mumbai: We Got Your Back to raise spirits, awareness, and funds by leveraging the creative arts to draw attention and travelers to Mumbai and India. For more information, look us up at www.mumbaiwegotyourback.com.

**Waris Ahluwalia** creates objects of beauty for the House of Waris, acts in movies, and is an aspiring activist. Born in India and raised in New York, he hopes to share with the world the impact India has on his heart and soul.

**Tina Bhojwani** is a New York-based fashion executive specializing in international business development. She currently is Senior Vice President at Link Theory Holdings (US) Inc., overseeing the globalization of the Theory and Helmut Lang brands. With deep family roots in Mumbai, Tina has spent considerable time there over the years and has a profound and passionate connection with this vital city.

**Mortimer Singer** is senior vice president of Marvin Traub Associates, a New York-based management consulting firm focused on advising retail and consumer goods companies on their strategy and business development needs. Morty is also a founding partner of TSM Capital. Among other projects around the world, he has advised Indian retailers on bringing Western brands to India. Morty and his wife, Amy, adore India and their Indian friends, and keenly await the day when they can bring their newborn daughter, Daisy, to visit both.

# Acknowledgments

This book would never have come together without the help of hundreds of friends across the globe. You know who you are—thank you so much. We are extra grateful to Nathan Kilcer for designing our logo and to Sima Patel for our web site. Thanks also to Prosper and Martine Assouline and their team, including Garance Boulet, Perrine Scherrer, Sophie Fels, and Miriam Hiersteiner, as to Andrew Chapman, Madeline Gray, and Andrew Thomas.

**Waris Ahluwalia** would like to thank all the contributors in the book for sharing their memories: I am forever grateful to you. In addition, thank you to the following people for their involvement and for making this book a reality—including my late father, Paramjit S. Ahluwalia, for showing me strength and courage by living it—Darshan Ahluwalia, Jaclyn Bashoff, Melissa Chung, Chiara Clemente, Iana dos Reis Nunes, Steve Eckelman, Nathan Kilcer, Shaheen Knox, Alessia Margiotta Broglio, Caleb Lanier, Linda Lynch, Meghan McElheny, Will Nash, Ricardo Ortiz Kugelmas, Bandana Tewari, Kathryn Typaldos, and Laura Wilson.

**Tina Bhojwani** would like to express sincere gratitude to all of the family and friends who supported this special project: I would like to especially thank Andrew Rosen, my boss and mentor for the past eight years. Much appreciation goes to Marie Moatti, whose efforts led to many contributions from her friends in Paris, who are so passionate about India. Also, many thanks to Sheikh Majed for encouraging this project in its early stages and for continuing to be involved with Mumbai: We Got Your Back. Last, but certainly not least, thanks are due to Leetu Shivdasani, whose dedication greatly enhanced the book's profile in the city that inspired it.

**Mortimer Singer** would like to extend an especially warm thank-you to the iconic retailer and Indiaphile Marvin Traub, whose great passion for India he has inherited, and without whom he would yet to have visited the subcontinent. He would also like to thank Amy Hafkin, whose tenacity and enthusiasm were instrumental in helping secure some of this book's major contributors, and Rohan Gopaldas at the Indian Hotels Group, our eyes and ears on the ground in India.